Endorsements for *The Third Choice*

Mark Durie has written a wise and remarkably compendious study inspired by the urgent question W. Montgomery Watt posed in 1993: "...does the *Sharia* (Islamic Law) allow Muslims to live peaceably with non-Muslims in the one world?" *The Third Choice* challenges non-Muslims and Muslims alike to lift the shroud of silence and reject the steady revival of Islam's ancient, discriminatory system of dhimmitude. Although Durie demonstrates unabashedly how Islam's doctrines have led too many Muslims to impose intimidation and self-rejection upon others, his ultimate message is one of hope: that truth, applied with love will release a deep-seated compassion and healing between peoples.
ANDREW BOSTOM, author of *The Legacy of Jihad* and *The Legacy of Islamic Antisemitism.*

Those who want help discerning the truth amidst the myriad of contradictory reports about Muslim-Christian relations, should read this book. Those who want to understand why Christians in Islamic states frequently present as energetic propagandists for those who repress and persecute them, should read this book. *Dhimmis* and former dhimmis who want deliverance from the deep and captivating, psychologically and spiritually crippling spirit of dhimmitude – a spirit that remains even if the threat is removed – should read this book. The insights in *The Third Choice* will equip many with the understanding they require if they are going to face the world's information deluge with discernment; and enable many who are crippled by fear, hate or remorse to find freedom, healing and restoration. Mark Durie's book is a book for our times.
ELIZABETH KENDAL, religious liberty researcher, analyst and writer

This extraordinary book shows how the behavior of violent Islamic groups, and even of many "moderate" non-Muslim spokesmen in the West, follows a discernible and consistent pattern deriving from the directives of Islamic law for the treatment of non-Muslims. What makes it all the more remarkable is how willing and even eager non-Muslim leaders can be to comply with the *Sharia*'s supremacist demands. *The Third Choice* shows clearly that the strictures of dhimmitude are oppressive, that they are by no means antiquated relics of the past, and that non-Muslims are in peril globally from Muslims laboring to implement them anew. As such it stands as a vital wake-up call for an increasingly drowsy Free World.
ROBERT SPENCER, author of the New York Times best-sellers *The Politically Incorrect Guide to Islam (and the Crusades)* and *The Truth About Muhammad.*

Mark Durie's new book, *The Third Choice: Islam, Dhimmitude and Freedom*, is highly recommended reading. It insightfully throws light on Islam and its theological, political and legal ideology towards non-Muslims, especially Christians and Jews. The concept of dhimmitude, with its humiliation and subjugation of "non-believers", needs to be understood if we want to uphold universal human rights and religious liberty in our day and age. Not politically correct appeasement policies, but truthful and above-board information, along with critical analysis of historical and current realities concerning Islam, will help us to face the challenge of this ideology with its consequences for church and society. This book encourages us to face this challenge squarely and choose the truth in freedom and dignity.

ALBRECHT HAUSER, Canon of the Evangelical-Lutheran Church in Württemberg and a Trustee of the Barnabas Fund

Islamic revival is the greatest challenge to Christianity this century. It is fuelling an upsurge of violence against non-Muslims throughout the world as Islamists, emboldened by a righteous sense of entitlement, aspire to institute *Sharia* worldwide. Mark Durie astutely observes that institutions such as *jihad* and dhimmitude, arising from this Islamization movement, threaten spiritual freedom: unless Christians resist the hatred and discrimination of dhimmitude, they too will become its victims. Exposing the oppressive nature of the *dhimma* system, Durie offers the reader tools to confront this challenge. *The Third Choice* is an important reference to help Christians and others overcome the fear and violence that defines the legacy of dhimmitude.

KEITH RODERICK, Secretary General, Coalition for the Defense of Human Rights; Canon for Persecuted Christians, Diocese of Quincy; and, Washington Representative, Christian Solidarity International.

With *The Third Choice*, Mark Durie has introduced real Islam in a scholarly manner, from its foundational doctrines to its political, social and moral philosophies – from its root to its branches. He aims to inform people that Islamists will not only be unable to tolerate freedom themselves; they will follow the model of their prophet to put an end to the freedom of others. *The Third Choice* emphatically calls on all to study Islam personally and understand its quest for dominance.

DANIEL SHAYESTEH, former Iranian Republican Guard, co-founder of Hezbollah and author of *Escape from Darkness*.

Ideas have consequences. Some powerful ideas and views of the world have been in circulation for centuries, yet they have been hidden from sight, their true implications concealed. Mark Durie's excellent book not only unveils the history of an influential set of ideas; it shows their application and outworking both in the past and for the present. *The Third Choice* is a must read for anyone interested in Islam and for all concerned with human flourishing. This book will disturb, inform, educate and challenge. I hope you will read it, reflect on it, and pass it on to others.

STUART MCALLISTER, Vice-President of Training and Special Projects, Ravi Zacharias International Ministries.

THE THIRD CHOICE

To Manly Cohen

Mark Durie

21 September 2010

About the author

Mark Durie is a theologian, human rights activist and pastor of an Anglican church. He has published many articles and books on the language and culture of the Acehnese, Christian-Muslim relations, and religious freedom. He is a graduate of the Australian National University (BA Hons, PhD) and the Australian College of Theology (DipTh, BTh Hons). After holding visiting appointments at the University of Leiden, Massachusetts Institute of Technology, Stanford University, and the University of California at Los Angeles and Santa Cruz, he became Head of the Department of Linguistics and Language Studies at the University of Melbourne, was elected a Fellow of the Australian Academy of the Humanities in 1992, and awarded an Australian Bicentennial Medal in 2001 for contributions to research.

By the same author

Revelation: Do we Worship the Same God?
CityHarvest 2006

For more information on Mark Durie's books

www.markdurie.com

THE THIRD
CHOICE

Islam, Dhimmitude and Freedom

MARK DURIE

Foreword by Bat Ye'or

db

DEROR BOOKS

Scripture taken from the Holy Bible,
New International Version.
Copyright © 1973, 1978, 1984 Biblica.
Used by permission of Zondervan Bible Publishers.

Printed in the United States of America
and the United Kingdom.

ISBN: 978-0-9807223-0-7

[Hardcover imprint:
ISBN: 978-0-9807223-1-4]

Deror publications are distributed in the USA
and the UK by Ingram Book Group:
orders@ingrambook.com

Orders for Australia and New Zealand:
inquiries@derorbooks.com

The Library of Congress has catalogued
the first paperback edition as follows:

The third choice : Islam, dhimmitude and freedom / Mark
Durie ; foreword by Bat Ye'or.
p. ; cm.

Includes bibliographical references (p. 239-250) and indexes.

ISBN: 9780980722307 (Australian ed.)
        9781926800004

1. Islam—Relations. 2. Jihad. 3. Islam—Relations—
Christianity.
4. Freedom of religion—Islamic countries.

Durie, Mark, 1958–

BP170 .D87 2010

CONTENTS

Acknowledgements

This project would have been impossible to undertake without the path-breaking work of Bat Ye'or, who for more than thirty years pioneered and established the study of dhimmitude. I first encountered Bat Ye'or's writings in the mid-1990's, and the influence of her careful scholarship, original ideas, and profound analyses, developed in articles and books from the 1970's on, can be found all throughout this book. She was the scholar who first demonstrated the causal link between Islamic legislation and theology on the one hand, and the psychosocial condition of *dhimmis* on the other, a link which transcends time, geography and ethnicity. She made available a wide variety of painstakingly gathered primary source materials on the *dhimma* and *dhimmi* peoples at a time when this subject was shrouded in silence and denial.

I also gratefully acknowledge my indebtedness to the compilation of sources in Andrew Bostom's two edited collections on *jihad* and Islamic antisemitism, and also to the Royal Aal al-Bayt Institute for Islamic Thought for the collection of commentaries made available through altafsir.com.

I am thankful for the support of so many individuals, whose feedback, advice and encouragement have contributed much to the genesis of this book. Without their help, this book could never have been written.

I particularly wish to thank Esther Abihail for her invaluable assistance in translating classical Arabic sources.

ooooo

FRONT COVER: A depiction of the annual collection – known as *devshirme* – of Christian children. In a system of human tribute, boys were enslaved from the *dhimmi* communities of the Ottoman Empire, and either sold or converted to Islam and trained to serve as janissaries in the sultan's army. A minority also became administrators.

In this scene, set somewhere in the Balkans, selected Christian boys, clothed in their new uniforms, stand ready for travel under the watchful eye of a guard, as functionaries count funds and write up lists of names. To one side, a mother and her priest remonstrate with a janissary officer, once a *devshirme* boy himself; at the back a distressed woman stands with arms wide as a girl clings to her dress; and at the lower right a father stands ready to hand over his son, as an older man looks on with compassion. (From the *Süleymanname*, a sixteenth century illustrated history of Süleyman the Magnificent, preserved in the Topkapi Palace Museum, Istanbul.)

Foreword by Bat Ye'or

Since 9/11 the concept of dhimmitude – first elaborated in the 1970's and initially known only to a handful of specialists – has become widely recognized as its complexities and implications have been investigated and popularized. The first path breaking, iconoclastic presentations of dhimmitude as an aspect of history are being transformed into rich and diverse analyses of modern history and sociology. Mark Durie's book belongs to this new trend, but has the added distinctive that it seeks the healing of those affected by dhimmitude.

Although conceived and written with a profound Christian sensitivity, Durie's book can be read with the greatest profit by people from all persuasions, including atheists. In *The Third Choice*, the author examines the most crucial challenges of this new century. Today, whoever does not have a clear understanding of the complexities of the word *dhimmitude* can be considered an illiterate in matters of modern international policy, and blind to present and future realities.

Durie exposes in clear language the multidimensional aspects of dhimmitude, a concept that pertains to a fourteen-centuries-old civilization, birthed through *jihad*, and structured in accordance with the strict requirements of the *Sharia*. Dhimmitude has produced endless wars and suffering, and left its mark on countless historical and literary documents. Dhimmitude is the captive history of captive non-Muslim peoples, conquered by *jihad* and distributed across Africa, Asia and Europe. The author examines with rigorous precision the basic foundations of Islam – the Quran, *hadiths*, *sira* and *Sharia* – and exposes their inner connections with the political, economic and social system of dhimmitude for which they are the basis, and over which they exercise religious guardianship.

The strict scholarly rationalism of the author is particularly evident in the chapter on the theological significance of *jizya*, the head tax paid by non-Muslims under Islamic rule. Here Durie brings numerous and irrefutable sources illustrating the meaning, implications and religious justification of the *jizya*, which is the cost paid by non-Muslims for the right to live, albeit in humiliation. The *jizya* ritual, writes Durie, forces the *dhimmi* subject – through his participation in it – 'to forfeit his very head if he violates any of the terms of the *dhimma* covenant, which has spared his life'. The author sheds new light on the *jizya* ritual, which he calls an 'enactment of one's own decapitation'. His discussion of this virtual beheading brings new depth to the Muslim-non-Muslim relationship. Still today – in the *jihad* wars throughout the world, or the jihadists' threats against the West – the *jizya*'s symbolism expresses a fundamental dimension of the theological and political relationship between Muslims and non-Muslims.

Too few Westerners grasp that the concept of dhimmitude is crucial to understanding the relationship between Islam and non-Islam. As Durie argues, through a conspiracy of silence, the heads of state, church and community leaders, universities, and media smother its reality under a blanket of ignorance. With numerous examples, the author denounces this intimidated concealment, which, he affirms, is undermining Western Judeo-Christian civilization and is contrary to human freedom and dignity.

While the author's study encompasses a wide register of political and legal areas, he does not neglect the human impact of dhimmitude, with its painful manifestations of moral abjection, self-destruction, fear, denial and loss of dignity. Durie reminds us, with compassion and empathy, that scholarly studies on dhimmitude should not mask the physical and moral sufferings of populations living in perpetual denial of their most basic rights and personhood. The dimension of this human tragedy, perpetuated through generations, is a predominant concern of his mission, since he dedicates his book 'to the healing and freedom of all those who have fallen within the reach of dhimmitude, whatever their religious convictions, non-Muslim and Muslim alike.' His purpose is 'to offer resources for understanding these subjects and the links between them. The ultimate purpose of the book, to which the chapters take the reader in stages, is to offer resources for securing freedom from the legacy of dhimmitude.'

If Durie goes so deeply and consistently to confront dhimmitude, it is because this specific type of evil is not something of the past, something that its promoters have renounced or agreed to relinquish; rather, this violation of human psychological and physical rights continues to develop freely in local and international politics, whether by violent jihadist threats and terrorism, or through entrenched and chronic religious discrimination.

For Durie, liberation from dhimmitude requires the rejection of the gratitude and admiration of victims toward their oppressors. Consequently, the author considers it imperative that non-Muslims know Islam. In clear language, free from political correctness, and backed by an impressive scholarly knowledge, he unfolds step-by-step the basic foundations of Islam and exposes their inner correlations with *jihad* and dhimmitude, two theological and legal Islamic institutions that shape traditional Muslim behavior toward non-Muslims. Moreover, the concealment of dhimmitude confronts us with the moral and political consequences of denying evil. There is a danger, Durie points out, that undiscerning acceptance of a narrative of Muslim victimhood, brought into focus by a doctrinal necessity of Islam, is used as the moral validation of *jihad*. The appeal to Muslim victimhood as incitement to *jihad* and dhimmitude against non-Muslims needs to be unmasked, as a step toward world peace.

In wondering how to dismantle dhimmitude, the author provides a discussion of its ideologues and its deniers, and a detailed classification of its diverse manifestations in Muslim countries today, by examining it at different levels. Being a pastor, he is concerned with healing the souls and bodies of numerous present-day victims of *jihad*; but the more complex wounds also worry him, those that internalize resignation and engender self-debasement.

This book by an Anglican minister brings many innovative views. Durie takes his place among the handful of Christians who have not hidden the common bondage of Jews and Christians in dhimmitude – he even underscores the central significance of Muhammad's wars against the Jews of Arabia for the development of the *jihad*-dhimmitude strategy, which was later to be directed against Christians and others. Durie's book is a milestone in overcoming a long overdue lack of awareness of Christian martyrdom under Islam, as linked to and mirrored in a twin Jewish ordeal still denied by many Christians.

Durie not only provides a strong denunciation of dhimmitude and, thereby a forceful confrontation with its reality, he also offers a path to escape from the tyranny of evil and recover one's freedom. Throughout this reflection on dhimmitude, the reader is confronted with the question of how to recognize evil, how to live with it while preserving one's own moral probity, and how to overcome it by developing inner spiritual forces. And while drawing nearer to the oppressed, one also draws nearer to the oppressor and may ask: can victims be healed if they do not go toward their oppressors and try to heal them also? Is this not the existential meaning of suffering, to bring about the healing of the world?

Preface

*See to it that ... no bitter root grows up
to cause trouble and defile many.*
Letter to the Hebrews 12:15

Rejection is one of the most disturbing and destructive of human experiences. It forms the bitter root of many ills, defiling its victims with anger, hatred of others, self-hatred, a wounded spirit, and despair. Rejection is a tear in the fundamental fabric of human identity, a gouge in the divine image. Overcoming rejection is the core of spiritual healing, leading to restoration, freedom, new hope, and a reclaimed destiny.

Rejection can be manifested in individual lives. It can also be expressed in the collective historical consciousness of communities and societies, where one group has been demeaned by another.

One of the most profound and least-understood manifestations of rejection in human history is the Islamic institution of the *dhimma*, the theologically-driven political, social, and legal system, imposed by Islamic law upon non-Muslims as an alternative to Islam (i.e. conversion) or the sword (i.e. death or captivity). The *dhimma* is the 'third choice' offered to non-Muslims under *jihad* conditions, and those who have accepted it are known as *dhimmis*. Their condition, *dhimmitude*, forms the subject of this book, which describes the challenge posed by Islam's treatment of non-Muslims, exposes the spiritual roots of this challenge, and offers a solution.

Whereas rejection is an expression of the power of evil to damage, overwhelm and ultimately destroy human beings, the triumph of grace is the defeat of rejection, ushering in love and reconciliation where once there had been bitter despair. An invitation is issued here for the reader – whatever his or her faith background – to walk along a road through understanding, and ultimately to freedom from dhimmitude and its demeaning spiritual effects.

The resources offered here include a truth encounter with the Islamic doctrines of *jihad* and dhimmitude, informed by the life and example of Muhammad. Together these have imposed rejection upon non-Muslims under the *Sharia* down through history to the present day.

Renouncing enmity

In the current atmosphere of fear and uncertainty concerning religious differences, there is a tendency to divide the world into two camps of 'enemies' vs. 'friends'. Tolerance, we find, has its limits, and it comforts us to think that we are of the 'right' party.

We must steadfastly seek to resist such a divisive understanding of people. Although there are some who might call people of one faith or another their 'enemies', Jesus' instructions are pertinent: 'Love your enemies'.[1] We can also be mindful of the wise counsel Abigail gave to David, when he was on his way to wreak vengeance on her husband Nabal, not to 'have on his conscience the staggering burden of needless bloodshed or of having avenged himself'.[2]

In this context, recourse to the language of marginalization or retribution is a needless spiritual defeat. We must be prepared to call bad ideas evil if that is what they are. Yet, in doing this, it is not up to us to condemn people as evil, let alone to issue declarations of hatred and enmity against them.

When Jesus was advising his followers of the inevitability of their future suffering, he warned them against allowing bitter experiences of rejection to fuel enmity in their hearts. Instead, looking upon persecution as a blessing, they should aim to do good to their persecutors, blessing them and interceding on their behalf.[3]

In this struggle, the dividing line between good and evil is not something that separates one person from another. As Aleksandr Solzhenitsyn learned in the Soviet gulags, it runs through each and every human heart:

> In the intoxication of youthful successes I had felt myself to be infallible, and I was therefore cruel. In the surfeit of power I was a murderer, and an oppressor. In my most evil moments I was convinced that I was doing good, and I was well supplied with systematic arguments. And it was only when I lay there on rotting prison straw that I sensed within myself the first stirrings of good. Gradually it was disclosed to me that **the line separating good and evil passes not through states, nor between classes, nor between political parties either – but right through every human heart** – and through all human hearts.[4]

---

1 Matthew 5:43.
2 1 Samuel 25:31.
3 Luke 6:20-23, 27-28.
4 The *Gulag Archipelago*, p.25.

Statement of purpose, and a dedication

The Third Choice has been written to meet three main purposes:

- To explain the nature of the *dhimma* pact;
- To enable non-Muslims to withstand the *dhimma* and find freedom from it;
- To help people understand the nature and impact of Islamic politics in the world, both today and in the past, and especially its impact upon the human rights of non-Muslims.

People of many faiths and none need to find freedom from the age-old legacy of the *dhimma*, and Muslims too, for dhimmitude degrades oppressors and oppressed alike. This book is therefore dedicated to the healing and freedom of all those who have fallen within the reach of dhimmitude, whatever their religious convictions, non-Muslim and Muslim alike.

For millions today, dhimmitude is not only an all-too-familiar lived daily reality; it is also a personal inheritance, extending back in the generational line beyond memory. Whether dhimmitude is a part of the reader's personal history or not, my desire is that this book will help equip him or her to live as a free person, able to renounce and reject the *dhimma*'s false and demeaning claims.

CHAPTER I

Worldviews and Truth

Speak the truth to each other ... love truth and peace.
Zechariah 8:19

Pastor Rinaldy Damanik on truth

Until recently Poso was a little-known community in the eastern islands of Indonesia. The name Poso began to be mentioned in world news reports when conflict broke out there at the end of the 1990's. There were a series of attacks against local Christians, and also attacks on Muslims. Over time the fighting came to be driven by the presence in the area of an al-Qaida-linked training camp run by a militant organization known as the *Laskar Jihad*. The trainee *jihad* fighters would spread out from this base to practice their combat skills on the local non-Muslim communities, which included Christians and Hindus. After attacks, they would boast about their exploits on their website. This violence frustrated attempts of local residents to achieve reconciliation and peace.

Officials turned a blind eye to these jihadists, and even supported them. The future president of Indonesia, Susilo Bambang Yudhoyono, was Indonesia's top political and security minister when he said of the Laskar Jihad militants:

> They ... play a role in defending truth and justice that is expected by Muslims in Indonesia. For me, as far as what they are doing is legal and not violating the law, then this is OK.[1]

A local pastor, Rinaldy Damanik, began to lobby for the conflict in the Poso region to be resolved.[2] When the National Chief of Police, Da'i Bachtiar and the future Vice President Jusuf Kalla visited Poso in 2002,

---

1 Yudhoyono's statement predates the Bali bombing of October 2002, but was included in a video clip on the Australian SBS television program Dateline 'Inside Indonesia's War on Terror' on October 12, 2005, viewed 10 January 2008, <http://clearinghouse.infovlad.net/archive/index. php?t-4199.html>.

2 This account is largely based upon a report from Ibrahim Buaya, 'Three Teenage Girls Beheaded in Terror Campaign Against Central Sulawesi Christians'. IndonesiaWatch. October 29, 2005, viewed 8 May 2009, <http://www.geocities.com/haroekoe/jubileecampaignusa011105. htm#ibrahim>.

they told local people that they must be thankful for the protection the government was providing, and the safety they were enjoying. However, just that week five Christian villages had been attacked and looted by jihadists, and among the crowd were people who had lost homes and loved ones. When the crowd booed the speakers, Pastor Damanik stepped forward and challenged the visiting dignitaries to be realistic. Arrest the perpetrators, he said, and the local people could begin to believe the rhetoric.

A few days later, another Christian village was being attacked. Pastor Damanik was helping the refugees when he was arrested by the authorities on the false charge of possessing weapons. After a disgraceful trial, during which prosecution witnesses confessed to being coerced by the police, Damanik was sentenced to three years in prison. (He was released in November 2004.)

During his time in prison, Pastor Damanik had a vision or dream, during the course of which he wrote these words:

> ... although truth is difficult and very expensive we don't have any choice. We have to be willing to pay the expensive price. The alternative is to say goodbye to the truth. The truth lover has to fight extra hard to be someone with an iron will and at the same time be a person with a pure and transparent heart (like glass). The iron will is strong; it cannot be bent. It is unswerving in its commitment to truth ... The glass heart is one that is clean from one's own hidden interests and personal agenda. As with glass, the truth lover is sensitive and easily broken over the injustice and falsehood in the world. This broken-heartedness is not a sign of weakness, but it is a sign of strength and power. He is strong willed and his sharp mouth is able to speak out in the face of untruth and the falsehood of his surroundings. His heart cannot be still or quiet. His heart is always full of fight against injustice.[1]

We live in an era when in-trays and in-boxes are stuffed full of information. Among all the noise and mounting piles of words, truth can be hard to come by, even harder to recognize when it does come our way, and costly to take seriously when it is recognized. Indeed, accepting the truth can be the most painful option, as lies or half-truths are often more comforting, and make fewer demands upon us than the plain, unadorned truth. Yet, as Pastor Damanik has said, the truth is

---

1 Mona Saroinsong and Ian Freestone. Undated. 'Working for peace despite persecution,' viewed 19 February 2009, <http://www.cca.org.hk/resources/archive/assembly/12ga/theme/booklet/03a-stories.htm>.

immensely precious, something to be loved and sought after. It is well worth the great price it exacts of us.

Competing worldviews

This book engages with two reactive subjects, which take courage to consider realistically:

- The example and teaching of Muhammad, and his impact upon the faith known as Islam; and
- The treatment of non-Muslims by Islam, specifically the condition known as dhimmitude.

My desire is to offer resources for understanding these subjects and the links between them. The ultimate purpose of the book, to which the chapters take the reader in stages, is to offer resources for securing freedom from the legacy of dhimmitude.

The use which you, the reader, will be able to make of this material will be significantly influenced by your worldview. Everyone must make sense of the world as best they can. Worldviews are cognitive frameworks which provide a grid for finding truth in the world around us. They depend upon powerful assumptions, which often remain hidden from sight, beyond question. It can be unsettling to encounter information or perspectives which undermine or contradict our worldview and which subject its assumptions to scrutiny. Our minds may refuse to accept the implications of what our eyes and ears are receiving. We can even struggle against or try to suppress the truth, just in order to protect a faltering and failing worldview, together with its false assumptions.

A conflict of worldviews could be observed in responses to the campaign of Lina Joy, a Malay woman, to have her conversion to Christianity recognized by the Malaysian courts. The problem for her was Islam's apostasy law, which disallows conversion from Islam, and stipulates that those who leave Islam should be put to death.

On the one hand, the apostasy law can be regarded as a sign that Islam is weak. Al-Jazeera suggested, in discussing Lina Joy's case, that if Malaysia allows conversions to Christianity this could trigger off 'mass conversions' from Islam.[1] As Bandow pointed out, this viewpoint

---

1 'Tougher law for Malaysia converts.' AlJazeera.net. 27 June 2007, viewed 30 June 2007, <http://english.aljazeera.net/NR/exeres/BC3FDD7B-66C9-467D-AD7D-F77EAB74B27D.htm>.

'suggests that even Islam's strongest adherents have serious doubts about the credibility and appeal of their religion'.[1]

On the other hand, Muslim authorities assert that the apostasy law demonstrates Islam's completeness, truth and perfection:

> Complained Wan Azhar Wan Ahmad, senior fellow at the Institute of Islamic Understanding: 'If Islam were to grant permission for Muslims to change religion at will, it would imply it has no dignity, no self-esteem. And people may then question its completeness, truthfulness and perfection.'[2]

Does the Islamic apostasy law demonstrate Islam's weakness or strength? It all depends upon your worldview.

Sometimes a worldview may cost little for us to give up. When conducting linguistic fieldwork in a remote Indonesian village, I was once asked by a woman whether it was true that earthquakes were caused by a pair of giant buffaloes fighting under the earth. She readily accepted my explanation that the tremors were caused by geothermal processes deep within the earth: seemingly it cost her little to do so.

Another time, another village woman asked me how the Apollo astronauts, whom they had watched on television, had managed to reach the moon, because to do so they would have needed to pass through the seven heavens, and the portals to each of the heavens is known to be guarded by a different Muslim angel. Why had the astronauts not reported meeting these angels?

The worldview stakes were higher here. The evidence of her eyes – seeing a television image of an American astronaut walking on the moon – was up against religious cosmology. How was she to back away from beliefs she had been taught as an integral part of her faith? I answered her as best I could, but she was skeptical, for she potentially had much to lose.

Some Muslims are seeking to impose an Islamic worldview today upon Muslims and non-Muslims alike, all around the world. The evidence of at least the partial success of this effort can be observed in newspapers, school textbooks, the writings of scholars, and the pronouncements of politicians. There has been a widespread reshaping of worldviews to embrace Islamic perspectives.

---

1 Bandow, Doug. 2007. 'The Right Not to be a Muslim: in Malaysia, don't try to convert if you're a Muslim.' *National Review Online.* 8 June 2007, viewed 8 May 2009, <http://article. nationalreview.com/?q=Y2IyZmU2NDljNmEwMjIxNGNmMzI4NzFjZmNiMTQ5YjI>.
2 Ibid.

Let me offer just a few examples from the Australian press. These examples could be replaced by similar examples from just about anywhere in the world.

Interfaith Marriage: Sydney and Malaysia

In January 2002 the *Sydney Morning Herald* ran a story about marriages between people of different faiths. Featured was the case of an Australian man who had married a Malaysian woman. She was a Muslim, but he had not been one. What was described as their 'multifaith' marriage was held up by the reporter as an example of tolerance and harmony – a positive message for the public after the 9/11 horrors. Yet the man had been required to convert to Islam before he could be united with his bride. Islamic law allows non-Muslim women to marry Muslim men, creating an Islamic household, but the reverse is forbidden: a Muslim woman must never marry a non-Muslim man. This marriage was no 'multifaith' marriage at all, as the newspaper claimed, but a purely Islamic one, between a Muslim woman and a Muslim man.

The story of this marriage came back to me as I was reflecting five years later on the rejection, in May 2007, by Malaysia's Federal Court of Lina Joy's request to be registered as a Christian. A believing Christian for years, Lina had asked the state of Malaysia to recognize her chosen faith, so that she could lawfully marry a Christian man. However this request was rejected, on the grounds that Lina was a Muslim (she had been born one). As in Malaysia it is illegal for a Muslim woman to marry a Christian man, Lina's request to be allowed to marry her fiancé was blocked. The Chief Justice said 'No one is stopping her from marrying. She is merely required to fulfill certain obligations, for the Islamic authorities to confirm her apostasy, before she embraces Christianity.' In other words, she is a Muslim and unable to marry a Christian until an Islamic *Sharia* court allows her to leave Islam.

The key point about the stories of these two couples, is that the *Sydney Morning Herald*, when reporting a marriage which revealed Islam's intolerance of other faiths, instead counted it a sign of tolerance that a 'Christian' man had married a Muslim woman. On the other hand, the Malaysian Chief Justice, in defending the court's ruling for Lina Joy, claimed that she was not being prevented from marrying. These skewed reports, describing intolerance as tolerance, submit to an ideological requirement of the worldview of dhimmitude, that Islam's impositions upon non-Muslims are to be regarded as generous and tolerant.

That this worldview lacks any semblance of reciprocity was brought out by David Hodgson, Judge of the Supreme Court of New South Wales, commenting on the Lina Joy case:

> Suppose there was a law enforced in Australia, which made conversion from Christianity a criminal offence, punishable by order of Christian tribunals. Suppose that there was also a law that prevented a woman who had converted from Christianity to Islam from marrying a Muslim man, unless she obtained a certificate from a Christian tribunal that she was no longer a Christian, and that these certificates were difficult to obtain. I'm sure Muslims in Australia would find this utterly repugnant, and rightly so.[1]

'Arts of Islam'

Our second example comes from the *Weekend Australian* newspaper of June 23-24, 2007, which included a multi-page spread 'The Arts of Islam'[2] to promote an exhibition of the magnificent collection of Nasser David Khalili, a Jew of Iranian extraction. Previously this collection had been widely exhibited throughout the United States.[3]

Khalili said of his collection: 'We are trying to give the public a visual interpretation of Islam.' The lead article, by Penny McLeod, stated, 'It is hoped that highlighting collections and exhibitions of Islamic art will help bridge the cultural gap between the Judeo-Christian and Muslim worlds and promote understanding.'

The Muslim Arab tribespeople who spread out from Arabia to conquer the Middle East did not bring significant visual artistic traditions with them. However, they did conquer brilliant civilizations, which had highly developed arts and crafts, including Persians, Egyptians (Copts), Greeks, Armenians, and Hindus. After Islamic conquest, vast non-Muslim populations, initially majorities in their ancestral lands and enduring harsh conditions of military occupation, continued to produce art. At what point did their artistic creations become 'Islamic'?

Remarkably, the articles in the *Weekend Australian* give the impression that, not only was the artistic production of the *dhimmi* (non-Muslim) populations 'Islamic Art', but it owed a crucial debt to the Muslim conquerors:

---

1 David Hodgson, 'Malaysia's Shackles on Religious Freedom.' *The Sydney Morning Herald*, June 22, 2007, viewed 8 May 2009, <http://www.smh.com.au/news/opinion/malaysias-shackles-on-religious-freedom/2007/06/21/1182019279687.html?page=fullpage>.

2 'The Arts of Islam', a special advertizing report. *The Weekend Australian*, June 23-24, 2007.

3 See <http://www.khalili.org/exhibitions.html#islamic>, viewed 2 August 2009.

The co-ordinating curator of the Arts of Islam, Charlotte Schriwer, said that as Islam spread, Islamic art in some places, such as Armenia, South China and to some extent India, became the art of non-Muslim and minority populations. 'Quite often Islamic art is produced by other ethnic or religious groups', Ms Schriwer said. 'The Armenian Christians produced art for the Muslims ... tolerance was much higher than it is now.'

Note the wording: it is suggested that Islamic art 'became the art of the non-Muslims'. In fact the opposite was true: the art of the conquered non-Muslims came to be known as 'Islamic Art'. Note also the suggestion that non-Muslims were the 'minority': in fact for at least the first four centuries of Islamic rule, non-Muslims were the majority throughout the Muslim world.[1]

Imagine if, centuries from now, a curator of a museum were to write the following words in the catalogue for an exhibition of North American Indian indigenous art: 'As European Christianity spread, Christian art became the art of the indigenous Americans. Quite often Christian art was produced by other ethnic groups, like the American Indians. These indigenous peoples produced art for the Christians ... tolerance was much higher than it is now.' Such a report, referring to the work of twentieth century American Indian artists, should rightly be deemed offensive and even ludicrous.

Indeed the comparison is still not adequate, because for centuries the Muslims were the minority, and the occupied peoples the majority, so a closer analogy would be to call the creations of Hindu artists from the time of the British Raj 'Christian, English Art'.

Why is it permitted to speak in such a derogatory way about non-Muslims living under Islamic rule, without the offense being immediately apparent, yet it would be unthinkable in this day and age to make such statements about Hindus or American Indians living under European domination?

The key to answering this question lies in very specific ideological requirements imposed by the system of Islamic dhimmitude. These include:

- Conquered populations are regarded as indebted and obligated to Islam – hence the suggestion that Islam brought them their art.
- After conquest, non-Muslims do not have their own distinct identity or history, because the land has become Islamic territory

---

1 See Griffith, *The Church in the Shadow of the Mosque*, p.11.

– hence the art produced by the Christian Armenians is 'Art of Islam', not 'Christian Art' or 'Armenian Art'.
  ▪ Non-Muslims should be grateful for Islamic conquest – hence the observation that it was a sign of Islamic 'tolerance' that Muslims used Armenian art.

Seeking a better way

This book is dedicated to challenging the worldview of dhimmitude. False and fantastic worldviews must give way to truth and reason.

I am sure that the authors of the newspaper articles from 2002 and 2007 did not understand that they were laboring under age-old ideological constraints of dhimmitude, imposed by Islam.

Khalili appeared to be unaware of his spiritual inheritance as an Iranian Jew in this respect. The power of a false worldview relies upon its inherent contradictions and falsehoods being concealed from those who subscribe to it.

Some might argue, in post-modern fashion, that worldviews are neither true nor false, but simply constructs, and each one is as valid as the next. Yet the worldview is indeed false which has buffaloes banging their heads under the earth every time there is an earthquake. The idea that Muslim angels guard the portals of the seven heavens, and American astronauts would need their permission to pass through the heavens – this too is a fiction. Worldviews can be interesting, appealing, and even entertaining, yet still irredeemably untrue.

We will be examining the worldview of dhimmitude in greater detail in the chapters to follow, and providing resources for understanding and exposing it.

Overview of this book

The process of the explanation offered here commences with an explanation of how Islam works (Chapters 2-4) leading into a discussion of Muhammad's dealings with unbelievers (Chapter 5). This lays the ground for the exposure of dhimmitude and its effects (Chapters 6-8), and a brief conclusion (Chapter 9).

CHAPTER 2

Setting the Stage

All those believers who do not follow Islam are losers.
Muammar Gaddafi[1]

The need for understanding

A good deal of confusion surrounds the subject of Islam. All people
– not only Muslims – have a right to study and learn about Islam for
themselves, yet there are many conflicting voices in the marketplace of
ideas, both Muslim and non-Muslim, which compete for authority to
influence our minds and shape our worldviews about this significant
faith.

Some of these voices are advocates for multicultural harmony, urging
tolerance and respect. Other voices are those of the preachers, calling
people to follow Islam as the one true religion. Other voices are more
militant, announcing that their faith will conquer the world. Some seem
intent on demonizing Islam and its adherents. Still other voices are
conciliatory, offering comfort and reassurance.

What should we make of this confusion? How can we respond to
competing claims about what Islam is, or is not, and discern the truth
among them?

The first step is to consider what Islam is, and how it works, and to do
this we need to consider the foundations of the faith.

Turtles all the way down?

An apocryphal story is told about the philosopher William James.[2]
After addressing a meeting James was approached by an old lady, who
said she wanted to ask him a question: 'Young man,' she said, 'What
does the earth rest upon?'

The philosopher answered that the world spins around the sun.

---

1 'Africa: Anti-Christian Gaddafi Takes Over as AU Chair.' Catholic Information Service for
   Africa (Nairobi), February 3, 2009, viewed 8 May 2009, <http://allafrica.com/stories/20090
   2030686.html>.
2 Some versions substitute Bertrand Russell for James.

The woman was shocked: 'Do you seriously expect me to believe that you and I, whose feet are so firmly planted on the floor of this room, are in fact spinning through space at breakneck speed? That is the most ridiculous thing I have ever heard!'

So the philosopher asked the woman, 'Well, what do you believe the world is resting on?'

The quick reply came back: 'A turtle'.

'It must be a large one. And what would this turtle be resting upon?'

'Another turtle'.

A smile began to play on the great philosopher's face, but just as he was about to pose another question, the old lady interrupted: 'Don't you worry, young man. It's turtles all the way down!'

Islam is not 'turtles all the way down'. It has a foundation. To understand Islam, you need to know that it is built upon Muhammad. His person and life is the basis upon which the whole religion rests. In a Christian Sunday School, it is something of a cliché that the answer to every question is 'Jesus'. In Islam, the key to understanding faith, and the answer to a great many questions, is 'Muhammad'.

Why is this so?

Islam is based upon the belief that messages from Allah were sent down to the man known as Muhammad ibn 'Abdullah 1400 years ago, and that he lived out these messages in an exemplary way. Muhammad passed on the guidance he had received to others, and called all humanity to follow him as well. Building upon the base of Muhammad's life and teaching, interpretive systems were developed by his disciples, giving rules for living, which humanity was supposed to follow from then on.

This chapter and the two which follow it set out these foundations of Islamic belief and religious practice. The focus is on core teachings and characteristics of Islam, including its laws and authorities, as well as on factors which can make it difficult to know the truth about Islam. There is also discussion of the very complex issue of how Muhammad's example and message influence the everyday lives of Muslims.

My purpose here is truth-empowerment: to place in the hands of the reader tools which they can use to understand and critique aspects of Islam for themselves, using Islam's own authoritative texts. For this reason, I will mainly refer to readily available primary sources. These resources can provide reference points for readers to help make sense of the many claims about Islam which crowd in upon us from the marketplace of ideas.

The compass of faith

Religious communities and their faith can be compared to a ship and its compass. The ship may tack back and forth in the wind, or go on detours, but in the end, the compass has the potential to redirect the ship towards an intended destination. Even if a ship is blown way off course, a navigator can remember to consult the compass and reset the sails and rudder, pointing the ship in the right direction.

When we talk about religion, it is clear that we are engaging with beliefs, with behavior, and with the relationship between the two. Just as the captain's orders and the actual course followed need not be the same thing, what people believe need not be the same as what they do.

It is not difficult to find examples of religious principles that people do not follow. Jesus banned divorce, but Christians in many cultures practice it today. Islam allows polygamy, yet this institution was banned in Turkey after the reforms of Ataturk.[1]

As another example, consider the core Christian doctrine that Jesus Christ will come again. This was taught by Jesus himself, and reaffirmed in the Creeds of the church.[2] The Second Coming is one of the core beliefs of Christianity, but Christians do not always live as if Christ might return tomorrow: for many, this doctrine has little or no impact on daily living.

The link between belief and action need be neither automatic nor straightforward, but it is nonetheless very real. The influence of belief upon action can be very subtle, and be mediated over long time periods.

In the long term the connection between belief and action can be extremely influential and powerful. Religious teachings can and do shape and change whole societies, transforming the way people live their daily lives.

---

1 Nevertheless, according to a 2004 poll, a majority of Turks would see nothing wrong with polygamy. Matthew Campbell, 'One wife or two? A new Turkish divide.' *The Sunday Times*, October 3, 2004, viewed 8 May 2009, <http://www.timesonline.co.uk/tol/news/world/article 489773.ece>.

2 E.g. Matthew 24:44 'the Son of Man will come at an hour when you do not expect him', and in the words of the Nicene Creed: 'He (Christ) will come again in glory to judge the living and the dead'.

Polygamy or monogamy: Islam or Christianity

A clear example of the link between belief and behavior is found in marriage laws. It is due to the influence of the Christian religion that monogamy is the law across Europe today, and due to Islam that polygamy is practiced in the Islamic Middle East. However much individuals may diverge from the standard of monogamy in their private lives, Western legal systems, influenced over centuries by Biblical ethics, still reflect the view that a husband and wife are bound exclusively to each other in a life-long covenant of marriage. It is for this reason that European secular states still do not make allowances for polygamous marriages, such as are found in Islam, where one man can be lawfully married to up to four women, although they are under increasing pressure to do so. The United States was founded with a secular constitution, but monogamy was such a non-negotiable part of American ethical thinking – due to Christian influence – that the territory of Utah was required to outlaw the Mormon practice of polygamy before it could be granted statehood.

In the domain of marriage laws, the Christian faith continues to influence what were once Christian societies, not because all or most individuals now want to follow Christ, but because the whole of culture has been shaped over centuries by the norms of the Christian religion.

Temporary marriage within Islam: Shi'a vs. Sunni

Another marriage-related example is the Shi'a institution of *mut'a* or 'temporary marriage'. This is lawful in Iran, but not, for example, in Indonesia. Why is this so? The difference is that Iran follows Shi'a Islam, while Indonesia follows Sunni Islam.

In the Islamic institution of *mut'a*, a man makes a payment to a woman for a temporary liaison, for some hours, a few days, or perhaps for as long as several years. According to *hadiths* (traditions of Muhammad), this practice was instituted during Muhammad's life-time as a concession to men who were away from their homes on military expeditions:

> 'Abdullah (b. Mas'ud) reported:
>
> We were on an expedition with Allah's Messenger and we had no women with us. We said: 'Should we not have ourselves castrated?' He [Muhammad] forbade us to do so. He then granted us permission that we should contract temporary marriage for a stipulated period giving her a garment [in payment] ...[1]

---

1 *Sahih Muslim.* The Book of Marriage (*Kitab al-Nikah*). 2:8:3243.

Although both Sunnis and Shi'ites accept that Muhammad approved the practice of temporary marriage, not all Muslims allow it today. According to Sunni Muslims, the practice was later abrogated, so it is not recognized in contemporary Sunni Indonesia. However Shi'ites have retained the practice, basing it upon their reading of Q4:24 in the Quran.[1] Consequently, *mut'a* is legal today in Shi'ite Iran.

This difference between Sunni and Shi'ite religious beliefs and practices has a great impact on people's lives. Many Iranian women today make a living out of the 'dowries' they receive from these lawful, religiously sanctioned, yet temporary sexual relationships, which may last no more than a few hours.

Female Circumcision and Shafi'i law

Female circumcision is widely practiced in the Islamic world, but not equally in all regions. It is practiced, for example, in Egypt, southern Arabia, Bahrain, Kurdistan (but not among Iraqi Arabs), Somalia, northern Sudan, Brunei, Malaysia and Indonesia. It is not widely practiced in many other Muslim regions, including Bangladesh, Pakistan, Iran, northern Arabia, Algeria or Turkey, but of the 32 countries where it is commonly practiced, 29 are member states of the Organization of the Islamic Conference.[2]

The modern distribution of female circumcision among Muslims cannot be explained in terms of geography, nor in terms of pre-existing cultures before the arrival of Islam. The Acehnese in Indonesia were Hindus before converting to Islam, yet they practice female circumcision, while Indian Muslims, who also converted out of Hinduism, do not generally follow the practice.

The simple explanation for the distribution of female circumcision among Muslims in the world today is that, while all four schools of Sunni Islam allow the practice, it is only the Shafi'i school which makes it mandatory. Wherever female circumcision is widely practiced among Muslims, this is a region where the Shafi'i version of *Sharia* law prevails. In this case it is belief which determines behavior, not perfectly, but to a very significant degree.

---

1 For a detailed discussion of this Sunni-Shi'ite dispute, see Sachiko Murata, *Temporary Marriage in Islamic law*.

2 'Specific Human Rights Issues: Women and Human Rights.' NGO written statement by the Association for World Education to the Sub-Commission on the promotion and protection of Human Rights, United Nations Human Rights Commission, 57th session, 2005 (E/CN.4/Sub.2/2005/27).

Stereotyping: two opposite errors

A real danger when thinking about religion is to resort to stereotypes. False stereotypes may be negative, e.g. 'dogs are dangerous', but they can equally be positive, e.g. 'dogs are friendly'.

Our view of Islam – or indeed of any faith – can be distorted in two opposite ways: we can use an interpretive grid of suspicion, so that we are all too willing to believe the worst of Islam. Or we can distort Islam by using a grid of obligatory respect, being determined to think the best, whatever the evidence. Both attitudes are widely held in the present time, and each brings its own risks.

These two different kinds of stereotyping can be related to faulty thinking about the relationship between belief and behavior.

Some are only too ready to stereotype adherents of a religion based on the existence of a few verses in their scriptures. This can reflect a tendency to overestimate the authority of belief, or to underestimate the contribution of interpretation in shaping belief. It is not the case that just because something is written in a 'holy book', believers will always follow it to the letter. Jesus said that if your right hand causes you to sin, cut it off,[1] but if we don't see many Christians walking around missing their right hands, this is not because they think they are sinless!

On the other hand, some make the equally mistaken assumption that sacred writ is irrelevant and can be made to mean whatever anyone wants it to, in accordance with the mantra that 'all religions are the same'. This extreme relativist position is accepted unthinkingly by many living in the West today, either to condemn religion out of hand, or to excuse it from critical evaluation.

The assumption that all religions say the same things is sometimes used as an argument that there is no need to look for a theological explanation for *jihad* terrorism. After all – so the story goes – aren't all religions the same, and don't people do terrorism in the name of Buddhism or Christianity, as well as Islam? Don't all religions have their extremists?!

A common response among Western secularists to complaints about passages in the Quran is to assert that people can just as easily promote evil from the Bible. The former Australian Attorney General, Philip

---

1 Matthew 5:30.

Ruddock, had the habit when making public speeches of citing a verse from 1 Peter, to suggest that the Bible can be used to justify slavery:

> Slaves, submit yourselves to your masters with all respect, not only to those who are good and considerate, but also to those who are harsh.[1]

Ruddock used this example many times in public to minimize concerns about Islamic doctrine as a social force in Australian society. His argument was that the Bible would appear to endorse slavery, but modern Christians do not endorse it, so it is wrong to assume that just because some of the verses of the Quran advocate bad things, Muslims will necessarily seek to do these things.

It is an irony that the example of slavery in fact demonstrates the power of religious scriptures to influence behavior, and the contrast between the Bible and the Quran. It was Christian reformers, such as the Quakers and William Wilberforce, who led the movement for the worldwide abolition of slavery, and they did this on the basis of a **theological** conviction, derived from scripture, that all people are created equal, and slavery was a moral evil in God's sight. Under the influence of this Christian perspective, abolition was imposed upon the Islamic world by the European powers: indeed Saudi Arabia, the homeland of Islam, only abolished slavery in 1962, after more than a century of political pressure from the West.[2]

Certainly the New Testament does acknowledge the existence of slavery and gives advice to slaves as well as to slave-owners on how to live Christian lives.[3] Nevertheless, slave-traders are referred to, along with murders, adulterers, perjurers, perverts and liars, as 'lawbreakers and rebels, the ungodly and sinful, the unholy and irreligious', whose manner of life is 'contrary to the sound doctrine that conforms to the glorious gospel'.[4] More than this, the principles of freedom and redemption which inspired the modern abolition movement were based upon the Bible, being rooted in the story of the Exodus, in which Hebrew slaves were liberated from Egypt. In reality, Biblical theology has made a profound contribution to the eradication of slavery, and the history of the abolition movement proves the power of religion to influence people's actions. Philip Ruddock's example was ill chosen.

---

1 1 Peter 2:18.

2 Bernard Lewis, *What Went Wrong?* p.89.

3 1 Corinthians 7:20-24; Ephesians 6:5-9; Titus 2:9-10; 1 Peter 2:18-21.

4 1 Timothy 1:9-11.

The evidence against the extreme relativist position is overwhelming. Just as different political ideologies produce radically different societies – contrast communist North with capitalist South Korea – it is also the case that different religions exert powerfully distinct influences. The Quran does not produce the same kinds of societies as the Bible, and Marxist atheism produces different results again. Many highly significant political and social differences between Europe and the Middle East correlate with their distinct religious heritages.[1]

Although people today differ greatly in the weight they are willing to give to religion as a significant influence on human behavior, nevertheless, as the twenty first century unfolds, there will need to be a growing appreciation of the profound role of religion in shaping behavior. Religion is not going to fade away: it will endure as one of the great determinative influences on world affairs.

What is the human problem?

Before we describe the foundational beliefs of Islam, it is necessary to consider what Islam regards to be the greatest problem facing humanity.

Secular humanists might say that the greatest human problem is the perpetuation of limiting social and economic conditions, which reduce individual persons' capacity to realize their full potential.

A Marxist might say the human problem is the perpetuation of class distinctions and unequal control of the means of production.

If you were to ask almost any Christian congregation in the world what is the primary human problem, their answer would be 'sin'.

So what is the human problem according to Islam?

The human problem according to Islam

According to Islam, the human problem is **ignorance** (*jahiliyyah*).

Imagine being brought as a slave into your master's house, but you do not know what you are supposed to do to please your master. You may sense that you have a job to do and the house even appears to have rules for those who live in it. Yet no one has given you a job description, or explained how the house is supposed to be run. So you wander around the corridors, getting in the way, and making all sorts of trouble,

---

1 For extensive discussions of this issue, see Alvin J. Schmidt, *The Great Divide*, and Ibn Warraq, *Defending the West*.

constantly at risk of incurring the master's displeasure, because you do not know what your job is or how you should do it.

The solution to your problem is **guidance** (*huda*), one of the central concepts of Islam. The master of the house, as an act of kindness, has pity on you, and gives you a book of guidance. Furthermore, because your master is merciful, he also points out someone to you as an example to follow in his service. These two invaluable aids for Allah's slaves are the book (the Quran) and the example (Muhammad).

According to Islam, Muhammad was not the first prophet. All down the ages Allah had provided messengers, or prophets, beginning from Adam. These repeatedly gave humanity guidance from Allah about how to live according to his laws. In this Allah has been merciful since the beginning of creation. Although the guidance of earlier prophets was diluted or lost, in the fullness of time Muhammad was sent as the final and eternally secure guidance for all humanity.

What then does Islam conceive to be the result of right guidance? What happens for those who submit to it?

For those who submit to Allah and accept his guidance, the intended result is **success** *(falah)* in this life and the next. The call of Islam is a call to success.

This call to success is proclaimed in the *adhan*, or call to worship *(salat)*, which sounds forth to Muslims five times a day:

> Allah is Greater! Allah is Greater!
> Allah is Greater! Allah is Greater!
> I witness that there is no god but Allah.
> I witness that there is no god but Allah.
> I witness that Muhammad is the messenger of Allah.
> I witness that Muhammad is the messenger of Allah.
> Come to worship. Come to worship.
> **Come to success. Come to success.**
> Allah is Greater! Allah is Greater!
> Allah is Greater! Allah is Greater!
> There is no god but Allah.

The Quran emphasizes the importance of success a great deal. It teaches that those who submit to Allah will find success in this life and the next. The Quran divides humanity into winners and the rest. Those who do not accept Allah's guidance are repeatedly called 'the losers' (*al-khasirin*):

Whoso desires another religion than Islam,
it shall not be accepted of him;
in the next world he shall be among **the losers**. (Q3:85)

If thou associatest other gods with Allah,
Thy work shall surely fail and thou wilt be among **the losers**. (Q39:65)

In summary, Islam sees ignorance as the problem, guidance as its solution, and success as the result of guidance. If you keep in mind the following key, you will understand the heart of Islam.

Islam: ignorance ➤ guidance ➤ success

The human problem according to the Bible

In the Bible there is mention of ignorance, of guidance, and of success, but these are not the central themes that they are in the Quran, because the Bible's message is based on a completely different understanding of the human predicament. Indeed the Islamic emphasis on success can seem surprising to people whose religious worldview has been shaped by the life of Christ. The climax of the story of the whole Bible, for Christians, is the apparent 'failure' – what Paul calls the 'folly'[1] – of the crucifixion of Christ, and God's faithfulness to his constantly failing people.

The human problem, according to the Bible, is not ignorance, but **sin**, which is the opposite of holiness and righteousness. Sin is a breach of relationship through disobedience. It is wrongdoing and rebellion which separates human beings from God, making it impossible for them to be in his holy presence or enjoy right relationship with him. From the point of view of the Bible, while ignorance can contribute to the problem of sin, it is not the root cause of it.

Adam and Eve, when they sinned in the Garden of Eden, did not fall because of ignorance – quite the contrary: the instruction not to eat the fruit had been made abundantly clear to them. Likewise, the people of Israel did not fall under God's judgment before their exile because of ignorance – they already had the laws of Moses – but because they rebelled against God in full knowledge of the guidance he had given them. Indeed before the people enter the promised land, Moses testifies against them that, although informed by God's laws, they will surely fall into sin.[2]

---

1 1 Corinthians 1:18ff.
2 Deuteronomy 31:15-21.

Paul writes in his letter to the Romans of the paradox that the more 'guidance' people receive through the law, the more their sins bring them under judgment.[1] Everyone, he writes, comes under this judgment, even those without the benefit of a revealed divine law code, because God's nature has been revealed even in creation, so that all people are 'without excuse'.[2]

What then saves us from the problem of sin? The solution, according to the Christian reading of the Bible, is God's **forgiveness**, promised in the covenant and secured by the sacrifices of temple worship in the Hebrew Scriptures. In Christian belief, forgiveness is ultimately provided through the sacrificial offering by Christ of his own life on the cross. This brings rescue from the curse of sin, and victory over the power of evil. The traditional term for this rescue is **salvation** (Hebrew *yeshu'ah*, Greek *soteria*).

Whereas in Islam guidance is meant to bring success – in this life and the next – the result of forgiveness in the Bible is salvation – in this life and the next. The Biblical emphasis is not on any superiority of the person – as the word *success* could imply – but on the gracious action of God in effecting the rescue.

Whereas Islam sees the world as divided into winners (the rightly guided) and losers (the ignorant) in Christianity the world is divided into the lost (the unsaved) and the found (the saved):

Christianity: sin ➤ forgiveness ➤ salvation

A rescued person is not the same as a successful person. A rescued person is humbled by their experience, but a successful person will tend to feel superior and proud of their success. From the perspective of Islam, the losers are the humiliated ones, but from the perspective of Christianity, the saved are the humbled ones.

These deep differences in understandings about the human problem and its solution mean that Islam and Christianity produce quite different values. For example, in Islamic cultures, which have been shaped by a success-oriented theology, there is a greater emphasis on honor and shame, and this has a considerable influence on how the Islamic *Sharia* treats non-Muslims, as we shall see.

---

1 Romans 7:10.
2 Romans 1:18-20.

Success or salvation

It is commonplace for those who make comparisons between faiths to mix up concepts from different religions. A Christian might ask about the Islamic view of salvation, or a Muslim might ask how Christians understand success. Yet such questions cause confusion, because the fundamental outlook in the two faiths is so different. Yes, Islam has an understanding of salvation, just as the Bible has an understanding of success. But the basic outlook in Islam is not oriented to salvation, nor is Biblical faith based upon success.

This contrast has been made clear by the Muslim writer al-Faruqi:

> Islam holds man to be not in need of any salvation. Instead of assuming him to be religiously and ethically fallen, Islamic *da'wah* [proclamation] acclaims him as the *khalifah* [representative] of Allah, perfect in form, and endowed with all that is necessary to fulfil the divine will indeed, even loaded with the grace of revelation! 'Salvation' is hence not in the vocabulary of Islam. *Falah* [success], or the positive achievement in space and time of the divine will, is the Islamic counterpart of Christian 'deliverance' and 'redemption'.[1]

Success in Islam is not simply a spiritual concept. Muslims down the ages have regarded Islam's military victories as proof and vindication of Muhammad's prophetic office, as 'Ali Tabari stated in his semi-official defense of Islam in the 9th century:

> ... his [Muhammad's] victory over the nations is also by necessity and by undeniable arguments a manifest sign of prophetic office.[2]

As we shall see, one of the manifestations of this ideology of success is the system of the *dhimma*.

---

1 Isma'il R. al-Faruqi, 'On the nature of Islamic Da'wah', p.41.
2 A. Mingana, trans. 1922. *The Book of Religion and Empire*, p.14. See also Browne, *The Eclipse of Christianity in Asia*, pp.14, 90.

CHAPTER 3

The Basics

The Prophet is the greatest man that ever lived.
Muslim protestor in Los Angeles

Those who read the Quran and Sunnah can understand the facts.
Sheikh 'Abdul Aziz al-Sheikh, Grand Mufti of Saudi Arabia[1]

We will now consider the fundamentals of Islam.

The word *Islam* is Arabic, meaning 'submission'. The word *Muslim* is derived from the same root, and means a 'submitter', someone who surrenders to Allah.[2]

What does this submission mean? The dominant picture of Allah in the Quran is the sovereign master, who has absolute authority over all things. The correct attitude to take towards this master is that of an obedient slave. This identity of a Muslim is summed up in the common Islamic name *'Abdullah*, which means 'slave (or servant) of Allah'.

Allah demands submission from all humankind, for his household includes the whole world. Those who do not submit to him are seen as being in a state of rebellion and risk his judgment, which is a very serious matter, for in the Quran Allah is said to be severe with wrong doers.

How then can people submit to Allah? A good place to start to answer this question is by considering what it means to become a Muslim.

How to Become a Muslim

Entering Islam is simple. It is just a matter of saying and adhering to the following statement, the Islamic creed:

Ashhadu an la ilaha illa Allah,
wa ashhadu anna Muhammadun Rasulu Allah

---

1 P.K. Abdul Ghafour, 'Learn about Islam, Mufti tells Benedict'. *Arab News*, September 18, 2006, viewed 8 May 2009, <http://www.arabnews.com/services/print/print.asp?artid=86719&d=18& m=9&y=2006&hl=Learn%20About%20Islam,%20Mufti%20Tells%20Benedict>.

2 The word *Islam* 'submission' is derived from the tri-consonantal Arabic root *s-l-m* 'to be safe'. This same root can also be used to form the word *salam* 'peace'.

'I confess that there is no god but Allah,
and I confess that Muhammad is Allah's Messenger.'

If you understand this statement, you understand Islam. If you give it your assent, and recite it for yourself, you have become a Muslim.

The crucial question of **how** to be a 'submitter' to Allah finds its answer in the statement 'Muhammad is Allah's Messenger.' Being a Muslim – a 'submitter' – means accepting the guidance of Muhammad. True submission to Allah means following Muhammad, who is regarded as the unique, final messenger of Allah. Through the revelation to him of the Quran, and also through his lived example and teaching, Muslims receive guidance from Allah about their total way of life, showing them how to submit to Allah in the way Allah himself desires of humanity.

For those who choose to follow Muhammad's guidance, how then can they learn of it? The guidance of Muhammad is found in two sources, which together comprise the Islamic canon:

- The *Quran* is a book of revelations given to Muhammad from Allah.

- The *Sunna* is the example of Muhammad, which includes:

  Teachings: the things Muhammad taught people to do.

  Actions: the things Muhammad did (and sometimes what his companions (*sahabah*) did).

Obedience to Muhammad's *Sunna*, and a commitment to follow it, are absolutely fundamental in Islam. It is therefore of vital importance to observant Muslims to know how Muhammad lived, what he said and did.

The *Sunna* of Muhammad

Before considering the question of how to access information about the *Sunna* of Muhammad, we need to establish that the authority of Muhammad's *Sunna* is regarded as a foundational, basic principle of Islam.

The Quran repeatedly and in many ways states that Muhammad's commands are to be obeyed as true guidance, without regard to personal opinions. This means that it is not open to interpreters to ignore

Muhammad's example, nor just to rely on the Quran: if one takes these verses seriously, there can be no such thing as a Quran-only Islam.[1]

Muhammad's instructions are Allah's guidance for the faithful:

> O believers, obey Allah, and obey the Messenger ... (Q4:59)

> Whosoever obeys the Messenger, thereby obeys Allah ... (Q4:80)

> Allah guides whomsoever he will to a straight path.
> They say, 'We believe in Allah and the Messenger, and we obey.'
> (Q24:46-47)

> Say: 'Obey Allah and obey the messenger.' ... If you obey him, you will be guided. (Q24:54)

> It is not for any believer, man or woman, when Allah and His Messenger have decreed a matter, to have the choice in the affair. Whosoever disobeys Allah and His Messenger has gone astray into manifest error. (Q33:36)

No one is a believer until they willingly submit to Muhammad's guidance:

> ... they will not believe till they make thee [Muhammad] the judge regarding the disagreement between them, then they shall find in themselves no impediment touching thy verdict, but shall surrender in full submission. (Q4:65)

Those who follow Muhammad will be successful:

> Whoso obeys Allah and His Messenger, and fears Allah and has awe of Him, those – they are the triumphant. (Q24:52)

They will also be counted among the blessed:

> Whosoever obeys Allah, and the Messenger – they are with those whom Allah has blessed ... (Q4:69)

Muhammad's manner of life is exemplary:

> You have had a good example in Allah's Messenger for whosoever hopes for Allah and the last Day, and remembers Allah oft. (Q33:21)

His moral character is most powerful:

> ... thou art not, by the blessing of the Lord, a man possessed. ... surely thou art upon a mighty morality ... (Q68:1-4)

---

1 To be fair, some anti-*hadith* movements seek to rely only on the Quran, but they are marginal.

He is not subject to deception or error:

> By the Star when it plunges, your comrade is not astray, neither errs, nor speaks he out of caprice. (Q53:1-3)

Opposing Muhammad's instruction and example is disbelief or *kufr*. This leads to a terrible fate, in this life and the next, a matter about which people are warned most severely:

> But whoso makes a breach with the Messenger after the guidance has become clear to him, and follows a way other than the believers', him We shall turn over to what he has turned to and We shall roast him in hell – an evil homecoming! (Q4:115)

> ... so confirm the believers. I shall cast into the unbelievers' hearts terror; so smite above the necks, and smite every finger of them! That, because they had made a breach with Allah and with His Messenger; and whosoever makes a breach with Allah and with His Messenger, surely Allah is terrible in retribution. (Q8:12-13)

> Whatever the Messenger gives you, take; whatever he forbids you, give over [i.e. abstain]. And fear Allah; surely Allah is terrible in retribution. (Q59:7)

> And whoso rebels against Allah and His Messenger, for him there awaits the fire of Hell; therein they shall dwell forever. (Q72:23)

This means that once someone accepts the Quran as a revelation from God, they are wedded to the example and teaching of Muhammad. A true Muslim must be committed to the *Sunna*: this theme runs throughout the Quran. Note that 'Allah-and-his-Messenger' are repeatedly referred to as a single unit by the Quran, as if their will was one, and to obey Muhammad is to obey Allah (Q4:80). For anyone who accepts the Quran, the *Sunna* of Muhammad is not an optional extra, but the very cornerstone of Islam.

The motivation to emulate Muhammad was already well established among his companions, who knew him personally and followed him during his lifetime. They took pains to observe Muhammad closely and copied his habits. One of Muhammad's companions gave the following explanation when he was questioned about his habits of wearing tanned leather shoes and dyeing his hair red with henna:

> ... regarding the tanned leather shoes, no doubt I saw Allah's Apostle wearing non-hairy shoes and he used to perform ablution while wearing the shoes (i.e. wash his feet and then put on the shoes). So I love to wear similar shoes. And about the dyeing of hair with Hinna [henna]; no doubt

I saw Allah's Apostle dyeing his hair with it and that is why I like to dye (my hair with it).[1]

It is useful to keep in mind that a great many of the beliefs and practices of Muslims are not mentioned in the Quran but can only be justified from the *Sunna*. Others may receive a brief reference in the Quran, but their specifics can only be found in the *Sunna*.

One example is the five times daily acts of worship (*salat*). The instructions for performing these prayers are found in the *Sunna*, not the Quran. Muslims who decided to rely solely on the Quran would not know how to say their prayers.

The Hadiths

As the *Sunna* of Muhammad is so important, this raises another question. Fourteen hundred years have passed since Muhammad was alive, so how can we know what Muhammad said and did?

According to the teachings of Islam, during Muhammad's lifetime people paid attention to what he said and did. They would then tell others what they had seen and heard. Over time, hundreds of thousands of sayings about Muhammad were passed on from one person to another, and eventually committed to writing. These sayings became the way in which the teaching and example of Muhammad was passed on to future generations of Muslims. Each individual saying is called a *hadith*.[2]

There were hundreds of thousands of *hadiths* but many of them were of dubious authenticity. Over time they were sifted and checked for authenticity. This became a critical issue around two centuries after Muhammad, when religious authorities were systematizing Islamic law, and debating the precise interpretations of legal issues. Some *hadiths* were believed to be authentic, and others were regarded as 'unreliable'.

The *hadiths* were compiled into large collections, of which the two most famous and authoritative for Sunni Muslims are known as the *Sahih al-Bukhari* and the *Sahih Muslim*. Altogether there are six canonical collections recognized by Sunni Muslims, but these two are regarded as the most reliable. Indeed these are the only two collections referred to

---

1   *Sahih al-Bukhari*. The Book of Ablution (*Kitab al-Wudu'*). 1:4:166.

2   An on-line database of *hadiths* can be accessed at <http://www.msawest.net/islam/ fundamentals/hadithsunnah/>. This includes the *Sahih al-Bukhari* and the *Sahih Muslim*. This collection can also be accessed through the Answering Islam website <http://www.answering-islam.com/hadith_search.htm>. The Muhaddith search engine allows English and Arabic language searches <http://www.muhaddith.org/cgi-bin/e_Optns.exe>.

as *sahih* in their titles, which means 'sound, authentic'. These collections are named after the people who compiled them. The *Sahih al-Bukhari* gets its name because its compiler came from the city of Bukhara in present-day Uzbekistan, and the *Sahih Muslim* is so-named because its compiler bore the name 'Muslim'.

Both these scholars were active around the middle of the ninth century AD, and Muhammad died in 632AD, so it was not until the third Islamic century that Muslims determined which *hadiths* were 'in' and which were 'out' of the canon.

Hadith collections are usually laid out in sections and subsections according to legal topics. This form of organization makes them handy as legal reference works. This reflects the primary reason for collecting them, which was to secure the basis for the Islamic legal code, the *Sharia*, which relies upon the *hadiths* for its foundations.

What kinds of sections and subsections are found in *hadith* collections? Consider, for example, the *Sahih al-Bukhari*. It is divided into 93 major sections known as *kitab* or 'books'. *Kitab* titles in the *Sahih al-Bukhari* include the *Book of Oaths and Vows*, the *Book of Tricks*, the *Book of Marriage*, the *Book of Manners*, and the *Book of Jihad*.

The *Book of Marriage* contains all sorts of *hadiths* which relate to marriage from an Islamic point of view. This includes many traditions relating to Muhammad's own marriages – because his is the best example – as well as his comments on the marriages of others.

Each book in the *Sahih al-Bukhari* is further divided into sections, all including at least one *hadith*.

Here is an example of a *hadith*, from *Sahih al-Bukhari*, Book 78, the *Book of Manners*. Chapter 125 of this book is entitled 'What is liked regarding sneezing, and what is disliked regarding yawning', and this chapter consists of just one *hadith*, number 6623:

> Narrated Abu Huraira:
>
> The Prophet said, 'Allah likes sneezing and dislikes yawning, so if someone sneezes and then praises Allah, then it is obligatory on every Muslim who hears him to say: "May Allah be merciful to you." But as regards yawning, it is from Satan, so one must try one's best to stop it as much as possible; if one says "*Ha*" when yawning, Satan will laugh at him.'[1]

---

1 *Sahih al-Bukhari*. The Book of Manners (*Kitab al-Adab*). 8:78:6623.

The *hadith* begins with an attribution 'Narrated Abu Huraira'. This is known as an *isnad* (shortened in this case to include just the first narrator). The *isnad* is important for evaluating the authenticity of a *hadith*, because it states who passed this tradition on. In sorting through all the *hadiths*, which were passed down over the centuries before they were standardized, the *isnad* attribution was regarded as valuable information, giving an indication of how reliable the *hadith* was. For example, if a *hadith* came from someone who knew Muhammad well and was considered to be a credible witness, and the subsequent names in the chain of transmission were reliable, it would be given more weight.

So what does this *hadith* mean for Muslims today? It says that Allah desires people to pronounce a blessing on anyone who sneezes, and to avoid yawning as something evil.

Ordinary Muslims are discouraged from analyzing *hadiths* for themselves. They should ask a scholar to make an interpretation on a particular issue, and the scholar is supposed to be qualified to apply what is in the *hadiths* (or the Quran) to everyday life. This may be done by writing a *fatwa* or legal opinion.

On the *Islam Online* website there is a *Fatwa Editing Desk* which offers rulings on Islamic matters online. Its discussion of suppressing a yawn illustrates how a *hadith* can be applied to derive rules of behavior:

> **Question:** Is it a sin to yawn, and what du'a (prayer) is there to say to stop you yawning? What happens if you do yawn?
>
> **Answer:** ... It is reported in several Prophetic hadiths that Allah likes sneezing and dislikes yawning. However, it is not a sin that one yawns especially when the act is beyond his/her control.
>
> Although there is no specific supplication to stop yawning, there are many ways to help one stop it such as attempting to face it by not allowing it to appear at first place [sic]. One can do that through bringing one's lips together to avoid it or else putting one's hand opposite to one's mouth to stop it.[1]

So, according to *Islam Online*, *hadiths* like this one imply that when a Muslim suppresses their yawn, they are not merely being polite: they are following the teaching and example of Muhammad and conforming to the dictates of Islam. Putting a hand over one's mouth is thus a religious act.

---

1 IslamOnline. General Fatwa Session, July 25, 2005, viewed 8 May 2009, <http://www.islamonline.net/livefatwa/english/Browse.asp?hGuestID=tQd69c>.

I was taught as a child to cover my mouth during a yawn – young Australians are often told that flies might go into their mouth – but this was not because of something Jesus taught. It was just a cultural tradition, something polite to do. In Islam many cultural practices, which might be non-religious in other cultures, exist and are maintained among Muslims in devotion to Muhammad's teaching and example. So when a Muslim mother teaches her young children to suppress and cover up a yawn, she is raising them up to be more than just polite: she is training them in Islam.

While the prohibition on yawning without covering one's mouth will seem understandable to most non-Muslims, a great many of the things Muhammad taught can seem quite strange. For example, he taught that a person should put on their right shoe before their left, take off their left shoe first, and never walk wearing only one shoe.[1]

Although the *hadiths* deal with matters such as this which might seem trivial, not all *hadiths* are like this. They also cover much more serious issues, such as marriage laws, punishment for serious crimes, and the rules of war.

Six basic beliefs and five pillars

Many of the most important things to know about Islam are based upon the *hadiths*, including the basic beliefs and the pillars of Islam.

Introductions to Islam will often give a list of basic beliefs, or 'articles of faith' of Islam. This list will have six items:

1. Belief in Allah
2. Belief in Angels
3. Belief in Scriptures
4. Belief in Apostles
5. Belief in the Day of Judgment
6. Belief in Predestination

How did this list arise? It is not the result of a conceptual analysis of Islam, nor is it the work of great scholars of Islam. This list of basic beliefs exists because one day, at a certain time and place, Muhammad said these were the basics. This is recorded in a *hadith*:

---

1 *Sahih al-Bukhari.* The Book of Dress. 7:77:5854-56.

It is narrated on the authority of Yahya b. Ya'mur ...

... He [an inquirer] said: 'Inform me about Iman (faith).' He (the Holy Prophet) replied: 'That you affirm your faith in Allah, in His angels, in His Books, in His Apostles, in the Day of Judgment, and you affirm your faith in the Divine Decree to good and evil.'[1]

In the same way, the famous five pillars of Islam are not listed in the Quran. Instead they derive from another *hadith*:

Narrated Ibn Umar,
Allah's Apostle said: 'Islam is based on (the following) five (principles):

1. To testify that *La ilaha illallah wa anna Muhammad-ar-Rasul Allah* (none has the right to be worshipped but Allah and that Muhammad is the Messenger of Allah).

2. To perform the (compulsory congregational) prayers.

3. To pay *Zakat* [a fixed proportion of wealth and property].

4. To perform *Haj*. (i.e. Pilgrimage to Makkah)

5. To observe ... fasts ... during the month of Ramadan.'[2]

The sira

Imagine a biography of Muhammad, which is cut up into thousands of small passages. All the pieces are then sorted and organized into piles according to categories. Passages on hunting go into one pile, references to taking a bath into another pile. Instead of a connected story, what you have before you is a collection of headings, with information about Muhammad grouped together under each heading. This is the nature of most *hadith* collections, including the six canonical collections. This arrangement makes it easy for a lawyer or a judge to look up what Muhammad said about taking a bath or going hunting, but because most *hadith* collections are not organized according to a story line, you cannot follow the thread of Muhammad's life from them.

Yet the story line is important for Islam, so to understand Muhammad's life, one must look to the *sira*, or biographies, which give a chronological account of his life.

For all who wish to refer to the *sira* or *hadith* literatures, a word of caution is in order.

---

1   *Sahih Muslim*. The Book of Faith (*Kitab al-Iman*). 1:1:1.
2   *Sahih al-Bukhari*. The Book of Faith (*Kitab al-Iman*). 1:2:8.

By the time the *hadith* collections were being standardized – two to three centuries after Muhammad – the life of Muhammad was what the scholar Guillaume has called a 'battlefield of warring sects, striving for mastery of men's minds and the control of their behavior with all the weight that Muhammad's presumed or fabricated example could bring to bear.'[1] Because of this, many *hadiths* were concocted or doctored to suit sectarian purposes. Since the *sira* literature predates the canonical *hadith* collections by a century, it could be regarded as more reliable (although not in the eyes of traditional Islam).

The earliest and most authoritative biography of Muhammad is the *Life of Muhammad* (*Sirat Rasul Allah*) by Ibn Ishaq (d. 767), a third generation Muslim who died 135 years after Muhammad.[2] Ibn Ishaq's original is lost, so we must rely mainly on a revision by Ibn Hisham made half a century later. However Ibn Hisham acknowledged in his introduction that he edited out passages of Ibn Ishaq's original because they were 'things which it is disgraceful to discuss' or 'matters which would distress certain people'.[3] In his English translation of the *Sirat Rasul Allah*, Guillaume also made use of other early Arab sources which quoted from Ibn Ishaq, especially the *sira* of al-Tabari, who included some of Ibn Ishaq's original, 'disgraceful' or 'distressing' material omitted by Ibn Hisham, such as the infamous 'Satanic verses' episode.[4]

Muhammad's character

Ibn Hisham's selective editing of Muhammad's life highlights something to be aware of when reading the *hadith* and the *sira* literature. While some aspects of Muhammad's life are positive, others are admirable, and many are quite intriguing and even fascinating, there are episodes which would, to say the least, be in conflict with contemporary ethical standards. Numerous statements and episodes in the *siras* and the *hadiths* are simply shocking.

As was seen with Ibn Hisham's treatment of Ibn Ishaq, there was a tendency among the *sira* and *hadith* compilers to 'airbrush' Muhammad's character by elevating material which lifted Muhammad's reputation, and suppressing material which reflected badly on him. Thus, one of the criteria for testing *hadiths* was to discount traditions which reflected

---

1 Guillaume, *The Life of Muhammad*, p.xxxiv.

2 Ibn Ishaq's *Life of Muhammad* has been translated into English by A. Guillaume. Another widely-cited biography (although dating well after Ibn Ishaq), is that of Ibn Sa'd, of which a translation has been made by S. Moinul Haq and H. K. Ghazanfar.

3 Ibid., p.691, note 10.

4 Ibid., pp.165-67.

badly on Muhammad's character: 'Traditions containing such remarks of the Prophet as ... are clearly unsuitable for him, should be rejected.'[1]

Despite this test, plenty of material survived in the *hadiths* and *sira* which could be used to cast Muhammad in a negative light.

An example of a shocking *hadith* is an account of how a man killed his wife for abusing Muhammad, after which Muhammad declared him innocent of any penalty for his action (otherwise to kill another person should have attracted the death penalty):

> Narrated 'Abdullah ibn 'Abbas:
>
> A blind man had a slave-mother [i.e. a concubine with whom he had fathered children] who used to abuse the Prophet and disparage him. He forbade her but she did not stop. He rebuked her but she did not give up her habit. One night she began to slander the Prophet and abuse him. So he took a dagger, placed it on her belly, pressed it, and killed her. A child who came between her legs was smeared with the blood that was there. When the morning came, the Prophet (peace be upon him) was informed about it.
>
> He assembled the people and said: 'I adjure by Allah the man who has done this action and I adjure him by my right to him that he should stand up.' Jumping over the necks of the people and trembling the man stood up.
>
> He sat before the Prophet and said: 'Apostle of Allah! I am her master; she used to abuse you and disparage you. I forbade her, but she did not stop, and I rebuked her, but she did not abandon her habit. I have two sons like pearls from her, and she was my companion. Last night she began to abuse and disparage you. So I took a dagger, put it on her belly and pressed it till I killed her.'
>
> Thereupon the Prophet said: 'Oh bear witness, **no retaliation is payable for her blood**.'[2]

Some of Muhammad's actions were wrong by almost any ethical standard, but other *hadith* material calls Muhammad's character into question in more subtle ways. For example, we find him celebrating his own excellence above all other prophets, stating that of all the prophets since the creation of the world, he was superior because, among other reasons, he had been given permission to take booty, and had been victorious over his enemies through terror:

---

1 Muhammad Zubayr Siddiqi, *Hadith Literature*, p.114.
2 *Sunan Abu-Dawud.* Prescribed Punishments (*Kitab al-Hudud*). 3:38:4348.

Abu Huraira reported that

> the Messenger of Allah said: 'I have been given superiority over the other prophets in six respects: I have been given words which are concise but comprehensive in meaning; I have been helped by terror (in the hearts of enemies); spoils have been made lawful to me; the earth has been made for me clean and a place of worship; I have been sent to all mankind and the line of prophets is closed with me.'[1]

Such material is not only disturbing as evidence of who Muhammad the individual was: it has implications for all Muslims. We must keep in mind that Muhammad's example was legislated by Allah as the best model to follow, so such incidents can be – and have been – used as standards for Muslims to follow. For example, because Muhammad celebrated his excellence in military conflicts, we find many Muslim scholars have regarded the military successes of Islam as God-given evidence of Islam's superiority over other religions.

The details given in the *hadith*s can also make Muhammad a target of humor, which is the last thing that Muslims would want.

It is perhaps because of this vulnerability that, in addition to declaring Muhammad to have a model character – for so the Quran teaches – Islam strictly forbids criticism of him. Indeed under *Sharia* conditions it is a capital offense to speak critically or sarcastically of Muhammad. To this day, few things can be calculated to offend Muslims more than saying bad things about their prophet, and in most Muslim countries there are laws in existence which are designed to prevent this from happening, such as the anti-blasphemy laws in Pakistan.

The Quran – Muhammad's personal document

Observant Muslims believe the Quran to be the letter-perfect revelation of Allah's guidance to humanity. Comparisons with the Bible can be misleading, for the Quran is a quite different kind of text from the Bible or any of its books. The Quran is a compilation of sayings, thought to be revealed word for word in quite short passages, progressively throughout Muhammad's life.

By contrast the Bible is a collection of many documents, produced over many centuries by a wide variety of authors, in three different languages (Hebrew, Greek and Aramaic), including letters, narratives, legal rulings, songs and prophetic texts.

---

1 *Sahih Muslim.* Book of Prayers (*Kitab al-Salat*). 1:4:1062.

The main thing to grasp about the manner of the Quran's production, is that Muhammad and the Quran are as intimately interconnected as a body is to its backbone. The *Sunna* is like the body and the Quran the backbone. Neither can stand without the other, and you cannot comprehend one without the other.

Understanding the Quran is not straightforward, for a number of reasons. Unlike much of the Bible, it is not in any kind of chronological, or logical order. Within the Quran the *suras* (chapters) are organized from longest to shortest, not from earlier ones to later ones.[1] Yet the chronology of the Quran is of vital importance. Many Muslims will say that Muhammad's life and the Quran are one, and inseparable. The Quran is in a very real sense Muhammad's personal document, addressed in the first place to him. Verses would be 'sent down' to Muhammad in the context of a particular issue or problem which he was facing. This means that to read the Quran with understanding requires the ability to be able to link particular passages with a specific context – or 'occasion of revelation' (*asbab al-nuzul*) – in Muhammad's career as a prophet of Islam. However the Quran does not provide any clear, consistent indication of these contexts. Consecutive verses from a single *sura* may come from distinct contexts which are completely unrelated to each other, and there will often be no way of knowing from the text of the Quran where the break occurs between one occasion of revelation and the next.

How then can the Quran be set in the proper context, which is Muhammad's life? For this one must look to the *hadiths* and the *sira* literature. Many *hadiths* explain how particular Quranic verses were revealed to Muhammad. For example, there is a section in the Book of Manners of *Sahih al-Bukhari* entitled 'Being good to a pagan father' which includes the following *hadith*:

> Narrated Asma bint Abu Bakr:
>
> My mother came to me, hoping (for my favour) during the lifetime of the Prophet. I asked the Prophet, 'May I treat her kindly?' He replied 'Yes.'
>
> Ibn 'Uyaina said, 'Then Allah revealed:
>
> > "Allah does not forbid you to deal justly and kindly with those who fought not against you on account of religion, and drove you not out of your homes, nor drove you out of your homes." ' (Q60:8)[2]

---

1 The same principle seems to apply with the sequence of Paul's letters in the New Testament: the longer letters precede shorter ones.

2 *Sahih al-Bukhari*. The Book of Manners (*Kitab al-Adab*). Vol.8:78:5978.

Note that this *hadith* includes within it a Quranic quotation. In this case the verse Q60:8 was revealed to Muhammad precisely on the occasion of answering a question posed to him about how to relate to a non-Muslim parent. This means that Q60:8 need not be related to the preceding and following passages, but finds its true context in a conversation reported elsewhere than in the Quran. In this case Q60:10, two verses later, relates to a completely different situation. When a woman known as Umm Kulthum fled to Medina to join the Muslims, her brothers came from Mecca to Muhammad and asked for her to be returned to them in accordance with the Treaty of Hudaybiyyah. Muhammad refused, declaring that Allah had revealed to him that 'if you know them to be believers, return them not to the unbelievers' (Q60:10).

As it happens, Q60 is a collection of verses which, taken as a whole, relate to the question of how to deal with relatives according to whether they are Muslims or not. However, for interpretive purposes, the immediate context of each verse is not the surrounding *sura*, but the occasion of revelation in which it was 'sent down' to Muhammad.

Finally, it is important to keep in mind that not all *hadiths* are equally sound or reliable. Specific details of *sira* biographies, and even of *hadiths*, can be thought by Muslims to be based on unsound traditions, and the soundness of *hadiths* is subject to critical evaluation in Islam. This is not the case however with the Quran, which Islam teaches is perfect in all its details and beyond criticism. This means the Quran plays a controlling role for interpreting the *hadith* traditions, even though it is the *hadiths* which supply the occasions of revelation for the Quran.

Abrogation

Different passages of the Quran can sometimes appear to be in conflict. What should the faithful do when they receive conflicting instructions?

Imagine you are a servant in someone's house. On Monday you are told to scrub the floor, but on Tuesday you are ordered to work in the garden. You receive no further instructions. What then should you do when you report for duty on Wednesday morning? The most sensible thing is to follow the last command received from your master. You decide to keep working in the garden.

Allah is like a master of servants in this respect, that where instructions appear to be in conflict, a later verse overrules a former verse. You stick to the last thing Allah has told you to do. The technical term for this is **abrogation** (*naskh*). The possibility of abrogation makes it important to know which verses came first, and which later, and for this one must study the life of Muhammad, in order to link episodes in his life to the verses in the Quran.

The theological basis for abrogation is found in the Quran, where it says that Allah can substitute one revelation for another, sending a 'better' one (Q2:106) to supersede the earlier verse, and he can 'blot out' (Q13:39) a previous revelation or cause it to be 'forgotten' (Q87:6):

> And for whatever verse we abrogate or cast into oblivion, We bring a better of the like of it; knowest thou not that Allah is powerful over everything? (Q2:106)

One of the disagreements between Muhammad and the Jews of Medina was that the Jews claimed the Torah did not allow abrogation.[1] It is related that Q2:106 was sent down to counter their claims. Concerning this verse, the renowned medieval Quranic commentator Ibn Kathir (d. 1373) observed:

> The statements of Allah here contain tremendous benefit, prove that the Jews are disbelievers and refute their claim that *Naskh* [abrogation] does not occur, may Allah curse the Jews.[2]

Other verses of the Quran which support abrogation include:

> Allah blots out, and He establishes whatsoever He will; and with Him is the Essence of the Book. (Q13:39)

> And when We exchange a verse in the place of another verse – and Allah knows very well what He is sending down – they say 'Thou art a mere forger!' Nay, but the most of them have no knowledge. (Q16:101)

> If We willed, We could take away that We have revealed to thee, then thou wouldst find none thereover to aid thee against Us, excepting by some mercy of thy Lord ... (Q17:86)

> We shall make thee recite, to forget not save what Allah wills: surely he knows what is spoken aloud and what is hidden. (Q87:6-7)

There are different kinds of abrogation. Muslim scholars have made a distinction between the canceling of meanings of a retained text, and the loss of the verse itself. Some verses continue in the Quran, although their meaning was cancelled by a later verse. In such cases the words of the verses still remain, although their meanings were later abrogated, and the verses remain in the text as a dead letter. In other cases, a later

---

1 For a discussion contrasting the Bible and the Quran in relation to whether God can change his revelations, see Mark Durie, *Revelation*, p.131ff.
2 *Tafsir Ibn Kathir*. Commentary on Q2:106. Vol. 1, p.327.

verse may merely qualify or impose restrictions on the interpretation of an earlier revelation.

There are even a few verses for which the words, but not the ruling, were said to have been abrogated. A famous example is the 'stoning verse' commanding the execution by stoning of married adulterers. 'Umar, when giving the first sermon after Muhammad's death, referred to this verse, which was somehow omitted from the Quran:

> God sent Muhammad and sent down the scripture to him. Part of what he sent down was the passage on stoning; we read it, we were taught it, and we heeded it. The apostle stoned (adulterers) and we stoned them after him. I fear that in time to come men will say that they find no mention of stoning in God's book and thereby go astray by neglecting an ordinance which God has sent down.[1]

The **wording** of this verse is said by most commentators to have been abrogated – so that the actual verse is no longer found in the Quran. However, the ruling – the **meaning** of the verse – is still considered to apply, so *Sharia* law requires that adulterers must still be stoned even though Allah caused the verse to be lost from the Quran.[2]

The Islamic doctrine of *jihad* is a noted example of the application of abrogation. Verses calling for warfare with unbelievers derive from Muhammad's militant Medinan period, while more peaceful verses derived from the earlier Meccan period, when the Muslims were weak and few in numbers. In accordance with the doctrine of abrogation, Medinan verses take priority over Meccan ones. For example, Q9:5 and Q9:29, both in the last chapter of the Quran to be revealed, call for virtually unlimited war against unbelievers. These have been regarded by some Muslim scholars as having abrogated more than a hundred earlier verses which commanded Muslims to deal peacefully with non-believers.[3] Consequently, for most Muslim scholars down the centuries the 'Medinan face' of Islam overshadows the 'Meccan face'.[4]

Al-Suyuti (d. 1505) refers to this as:

> The abrogation of a law based on a particular circumstance which subsequently disappears. This is the case with the call to patience and

---

1 Guillaume, *The Life of Muhammad*, p.684.

2 Ibn Kathir cites al-Suddi to give the erased wording as 'The married adulterer and the married adultress: stone them to death'. *Tafsir Ibn Kathir*. Commentary on Q2:106. Vol.1, p.325.

3 Reuven Firestone, *Jihad: The Origin of Holy War in Islam*, p.151, note 21.

4 David Bukay, 'Peace or Jihad? Abrogation in Islam.'

forgiveness during times of weakness or numerical disadvantages [in Mecca]. This was abrogated when fighting became obligatory [in Medina].[1]

It does help, in putting the chapters of the Quran into context, that some translations of the Quran state whether each sura belongs to Muhammad's Meccan period or his Medinan period. Many of the shorter *suras* which appear later in sequence in the Quran are Meccan, while the longer *suras* tend to be from Medina. However, some *suras*, including the second, are thought to include a combination of passages from Medina and Mecca.

Commentary (*tafsir*) – linking *Sunna* and Quran

A very useful tool for studying Islam is **commentary** (*tafsir*). A commentary connects the verses of the Quran with the *Sunna*. It links the Quran to episodes in the life of Muhammad, and clarifies issues related to apparent conflicts due to abrogation. As we have seen, this is absolutely essential in gaining a true understanding of Islam. A commentary will also report various views of scholars on the passage.

A great many commentaries on the Quran have been written and published down the centuries. In this section I have used illustrative examples from the medieval commentator Ibn Kathir, not only because his work is highly respected, but also because he is especially popular among Muslims all over the world today. Furthermore, an (abridged) translation of his commentary is easily accessible, either in book form, or on the world wide web.[2]

Abrogation of 'forgive and overlook' (Q2:109)

One of the many verses considered to have been abrogated is Q2:109, which tells Muslims to forgive and overlook unbelievers. On this verse Ibn Kathir commented:

> 'But forgive and overlook, till Allah brings his command.' [Q2:109] was abrogated by the *Ayah*, [verse] 'Then kill the *Mushrikin* [idolaters] wherever you find them' (Q9:5), and, 'Fight [the People of the Book – i.e.

---

1 *al-Itqan fi 'Ulum al-Qur'an*, chapter 3, 'The Abrogating and the Abrogated' <http://www. muneerfareed.com/itqan/rss.xml>, downloaded August 16, 2009. While acknowledging the common understanding of abrogation in this case, al-Suyuti goes on to suggest that the duty to wage war only applies when 'Muslims become stronger.' During times of weakness however, the rule is to forbear in the face of persecution.' Al-Suyuti concludes that this is not abrogation, but 'forgetting' (Q87:6): the duty of warfare may be set aside or 'forgotten' when Muslims are too weak to pursue it.

2 See http://www.tafsir.com. For other commentaries, see http://altafsir.com.

Christians and Jews] ...' [Q9:29]. Allah's pardon for the disbelievers was repealed ... It was abrogated by the *Ayah* of the sword [Q9:5] ...

... 'till Allah brings His command' [Q2:109] gives further support for this view. ... the Messenger of Allah and his Companions used to forgive the disbelievers and the People of the Book, just as Allah commanded ... until Allah allowed fighting them. Then Allah destroyed those who he decreed to be killed ...[1]

This passage of commentary interprets Q2:109 in the light of later verses which abrogated it (Q9:5 and Q9:29). It also sets the verse in the context of the life of Muhammad and his companions, referring to the change in Muhammad's treatment of non-believers from the earlier Meccan period, when in obedience to Allah he endured insults without taking revenge against his persecutors, to the later Medinan period, when he took up arms against disbelievers and killed them.

'Lawful to you in marriage' (Q5:5)

Another *tafsir* example from Ibn Kathir, on Q5:5, discusses marriage. This example illustrates how a commentator can draw upon the *Sunna* and cite views of other scholars to interpret a verse in the light of other verses in the Quran. The passage is:

> ...(Lawful to you in marriage) are chaste women from the believers and chaste women from those who were given the Scripture before your time [i.e. Jews and Christians] ... (Q5:5)[2]

In explaining this verse, Ibn Kathir first summarizes its meaning:

> The *Ayah* [verse] states: you are allowed to marry free, chaste believing women. This *Ayah* is talking about women who do not commit fornication, as evident by the word 'chaste'.[3]

The main interpretive problem which arises in connection with this verse is that there is an earlier verse in the Quran which states 'Do not marry idolatresses till they believe' (Q2:221). This would apply to People of the Book (Christians and Jews), because they are considered to be idolaters (literally 'associaters' *mushrik*): the Quran states in Q9:30 that Jews and Christians are alike guilty of claiming God has a son, which is considered to be a form of 'association' (*shirk*). The question which then arises is which of these two verses takes first place in regulating marriages between Muslim men and Christian (or Jewish) women? Can

---

1 *Tafsir Ibn* Kathir. Commentary on Q2:109. Vol.1, pp.333-34.
2 Ibid. Commentary on Q5:5. Vol.3, p.104.
3 Ibid. I have shortened Ibn Kathir's text by not including all the repetitions of the verse.

Muslim men marry Christian women or not? Is this practice forbidden because of Q2:221, or permitted because of Q5:5?

Muslim scholars have had differing opinions about this question, so Ibn Kathir reports their alternative interpretations. One view states that Q2:221 must be the one to overrule (although it is the earlier one) because the Christian faith is such a heinous case of idolatry:

> 'Abdullah Ibn 'Umar used to advise against marrying Christian women saying, "I do not know of a worse case of *Shirk* [association] than her saying that 'Isa [Jesus] is her lord, while Allah said 'And do not marry idolatresses till they believe.'" [Q2:221][1]

After reporting this opinion, Ibn Kathir cites a different opinion, which appeals to the example of the companions of Muhammad, considered to be a part of the *Sunna*:

> Ibn 'Abbas said that when this *Ayah* was revealed ... [Q2:221] the people did not marry the pagan women. When ... [Q5:5] was revealed ... they married women from the People of the Book. Some of the Companions married Christian women and did not see any problem in this, relying on the honorable *Ayah* ... [Q5:5]. Therefore, they made ... [Q5:5] an exception to ... [Q2:221] considering ... [Q2:221] to include the people of the Book in its general meaning.[2]

What Ibn Kathir is saying is that the earlier verse Q2:221 does indeed forbid marrying Christian women (as they are idolaters). However, based on the example of Muhammad's companions, the later verse Q5:5 is considered to allow an exception to the general rule. This is a type of abrogation where a later verse imposes a condition upon an earlier verse without cancelling it altogether. Thus a Muslim man could not marry a pagan woman (such as a Hindu, a western neo-pagan or an African follower of tribal pagan religions), based upon Q2:221, but could marry a Christian because of the abrogating exception allowed by Q5:5.

'Fighting is ordained for you' (Q2:246)

In the next example, Ibn Kathir uses *hadiths* to help reinforce the verse:

> Fighting is ordained for you [Muslims] ... [Q2:246]

Ibn Kathir explains the verse as follows, quoting two *hadiths*:

---

1 *Tafsir Ibn Kathir.* Commentary on Q5:5. Vol.3, p.104.
2 Ibid., pp.104-5.

In this *Ayah* [verse] Allah made it obligatory for the Muslims to fight in *Jihad* against the evil of the enemy who transgresses against Islam. [Then he cites an opinion from al-Zuhri:] It is reported in the Sahih [Muslim]:

> Whoever dies but neither fought (i.e. in Allah's cause), nor sincerely considered fighting, will die a death of *Jahiliyyah* (pre-Islamic era of ignorance).

On the day of Al-Fath (when he conquered Makkah), the Prophet said:

> There is no *Hijrah* (migration from Makkah to Al-Madinah) after the victory, but only *Jihad* and good intention. If you were required to march forth, then march forth.[1]

Ibn Kathir cites these two *hadiths* because they support and explain the message of the verse. He argues that fighting is obligatory for two reasons. First, if you do not fight and never even consider fighting, your Islam will be worthless to you and you could be considered no better than a pagan. Second, after the conquest of Mecca the earlier option of fleeing to a safe place (migration) was no longer allowed, so from this point on the Muslims' only permitted option was to fight in *jihad*.

The Islamic *Sharia* – the 'way' to be a Muslim

To follow the teaching and example of Muhammad, a Muslim must look to the Quran and the *Sunna*. However this raw material is too complex and difficult for most Muslims to access, understand and use for themselves. It became obvious to religious leaders in the early Islamic centuries that the majority of Muslims must rely on an expert minority who could codify and organize the raw materials of Muhammad's *Sunna* and the Quran into a systematic and consistent set of rules for living. So, based on the Quran and the *Sunna* of Muhammad, Muslim jurists derived what came to be known as the *Sharia*, the 'path' or 'way' to live as a Muslim.

The Islamic *Sharia* can also be referred to as the *Sharia* of Muhammad, because it is based upon Muhammad's example and teaching. This system of rules defines a total way of life. There can be no Islam without *Sharia*.

Westerners sometimes mistakenly think of *Sharia* as a medieval penal code, something from the dusty and irrelevant past. However the *Sharia* is intended to be simply what it says: the pathway for a Muslim to walk upon, an authoritative application of Muhammad's example

---

1 Ibid.. Commentary on Q2:246. Vol.1, pp.596-7.

in a comprehensive and consistent way, using rigorous principles of reasoning and Islamic case-law. This is much more inclusive in concept than any penal code.

Mustafa Cedric, the Grand Mufti of Bosnia, described the all-encompassing character of the *Sharia* in an interview:

> You know what Shariah means? It means to be kind to your neighbour, to be nice. To uphold certain moral standards ... And that means to tell the truth, to be just. To be pleasant to others. To be giving to others. This is Shariah. ... I cannot disavow myself from the Shariah ... asking me 'What do you think about Shariah?' is asking me 'Why are you Muslim?'[1]

Another thing to note about the *Sharia* is that, in contrast to the laws made by parliaments, which are devised by people and can be changed, the *Sharia* is thought to be divinely mandated, and therefore perfect and unchangeable. There are certain areas of flexibility – new circumstances keep arising so it is necessary for Muslim jurists to apply principles of reason and analogy to work out how the *Sharia* is to be applied – but these are adjustments around the margins of what is regarded as a pre-ordained, ideal system.

Let us consider a few examples of how the Islamic canon – Quran and *Sunna* – have been used to determine the principles of the *Sharia*.

Rules for using one's hands

In many Asian countries it is customary to use the right hand for eating, and the left hand for cleaning oneself after going to the toilet. However, for Muslims this is not merely a matter of hygiene or custom. It is a religious requirement, based upon both the example and teaching of Muhammad:

> Narrated Aisha, Ummul Mu'minin:

> The Prophet used his right hand for getting water for ablution and taking food, and his left hand for his evacuation and for anything repugnant.[2]

> Narrated Salman al-Farsi:

> It was said to Salman: 'Your Prophet teaches you everything, even about excrement.' He replied: 'Yes. He has forbidden ... cleansing with right hand ...'[3]

---

1 ABC Online radio interview with Mustafa Ceric, March 18, 2007, viewed 8 June, 2009, <http://www.abc.net.au/sundaynights/stories/s1874731.htm>.
2 *Sunan Abu Dawud*. Book of Purification (*Kitab al-Taharah*). 1:1:33.
3 Ibid. 1:1:7.

Stoning Amina Lawal

Another contemporary example of *Sharia* implementation relates to a report in *Time* magazine of June 17, 2002:

> An Islamic court in Nigeria has ordered that Amina Lawal, who bore a child more than nine months after her divorce, not be executed by stoning until 2003, when her baby is weaned.[1]

How did the judge come to this verdict? Why should the woman be stoned, and why should this be delayed until the child is weaned? Assuming he was making a ruling consistent with a *Sharia* legal code, our first question is whether this was upon the basis of comparable cases adjudicated by Muhammad. A search of the relevant sections of *hadith* manuals will turn up a tradition describing what happened to a woman who had committed adultery, and then came to Muhammad to confess, seeking atonement, so she could be 'purified':

> ... There came to him (the Holy Prophet) a woman from Gamid and said: 'Allah's Messenger, I have committed adultery, so purify me.' He (the Holy Prophet) turned her away. On the following day she said: 'Allah's messenger, why do you turn me away? ... By Allah I have become pregnant.' He said 'Well, if you insist upon it, then go away until you give birth.' When she was delivered she came with the child (wrapped) in a rag, and said 'Here is the child whom I have given birth to.' He said 'Go away and suckle him until you wean him.' When she had weaned him, she came to him (the Holy Prophet) with the child who was holding a piece of bread in his hand. She said 'Allah's Apostle, here is he as I have weaned him and he eats food.' He (the Holy Prophet) entrusted the child to one of the Muslims and then pronounced punishment. And she was put in a ditch up to her chest and he commanded people and they stoned her ...[2]

The woman coming to Muhammad asked for purification and instead he gave her death. What this *hadith* shows is that both the penalty against Amina Lawal and the delay until her baby was weaned was consistent with the example of Muhammad in his dealings with the woman from Gamid. It would seem that the Nigerian *Sharia* court judges had ruled in accordance with the principles of Islam.

---

1 Mark Durie, 'Amina Lawal and the Islamic Shari'a'.

2 *Sahih Muslim*. The Book pertaining to punishments prescribed by Islam (*Kitab al-Hudud*). 3:15:4206.

CHAPTER 4

Islam for Non-Muslims

Speak the truth, even if bitter.
Muhammad[1]

Classical Islamic law did not allow non-Muslims who lived in an Islamic state to gain a deep understanding of Islam. A famous early pact of surrender known as the 'Pact of Umar' stipulated that non-Muslims would agree not to teach their children about Islam.[2]

Johannes Jansen, Professor of Contemporary Islamic Thought at the University of Utrecht in the Netherlands, tells of his desire to undertake an investigation into the Coptic studies of Islam, and his discovery that he could not lay his hands on any such works.

> When I was still young and naïve, and while studying in Egypt for a year, I requested an audience with a local Coptic bishop in Cairo to inquire after books about Islam that were written by theologians of the Coptic Church. The Coptic Church is the indigenous, centuries-old Christian 'people's church' of Egypt. The Coptic language is the last form of the hieroglyphs from the Pharaohs' days. The Church's liturgy and sermons have been performed in Arabic for centuries. Its following has gradually dwindled since the conquest of Egypt by Islam in 636 ...
>
> It seemed unthinkable to me that Coptic theologians hadn't pondered Islam, and that there wouldn't be any books or articles about Islam from their vantage point. A good topic for a dissertation, I thought. But within three seconds, the bishop had set me straight. No, there were no such books.[3]

Today there can be considerable pressure upon non-Muslims not to investigate the primary sources of Islam for themselves, but to refer all their questions about Islam to a Muslim expert. Interfaith dialogue is an increasingly important forum for exploring Islam in Western countries, and these forums tend to follow principles of mutual respect,

---

1 SunniPath: the online Islamic academy. 'Is "Speak the truth even if bitter" a Prophetic hadith?' Answered by Shaykh Faraz Rabbani. Question ID:2285. July 06, 2005, viewed 8 May 2009, <http://qa.sunnipath.com/issue_view.asp?HD=7&ID=2285&CATE=120>.

2 *Tafsir Ibn Kathir*. Commentary on Q9:29. Vol. 4, p.407..

3 Johannes J.G. Jansen, 'Dhimmitude'.

emphasizing listening attentively to the other party and accepting their interpretations of their own faith. While this is a common-sense approach to sustaining productive and mutually satisfying relationships between people, it does however tend to have the same impact as traditional *Sharia* restrictions, inhibiting non-Muslims from studying about Islam for themselves.

If a Christian involved in interfaith dialogue wants to know what Islam teaches, they will often ask their Muslim dialogue partner, without devoting the effort needed to check what they are told. This can lead to serious problems of misunderstanding. At the same time, if a Christian does make investigations, and comes to conclusions which do not reflect positively on Islam, it can be a simple matter for a Muslim to cast doubt on the Christian's findings because of the inherent complexity of the Quran, and its relationship to the *Sunna* and the Islamic traditions of reflection on these texts. Among the strategies which have been used are to say that the non-Muslim has taken material out of context, that a particular *hadith* which was relied on is 'unsound', or that most authorities reject the interpretation offered.

One very good reason why Christians should study Islam for themselves is that Islam defines its spiritual identity, not merely in terms of Muslims' standing before Allah, but in opposition and contrast to Jews and Christians. This self-definition includes a deep rejection of Christianity and Judaism. It is a sad fact that incitement against non-Muslims, and specifically against followers of Biblical faiths, is an integral part of Islam, being hard-wired into the Quran and the *Sunna*.

Polemic against other faiths is part of Islam's message

Throughout its chapters, the Quran has much to say, not only about Jews and Christians, but other religions as well. Islamic legal terminology makes reference to four different religious categories:

1. First and foremost there are the **genuine Muslims**.

2. Then there is another category called **hypocrites**, who are renegade Muslims.

3. **Idolaters** were the dominant category amongst the Arabs before Muhammad appeared. The word for 'idolater' is *mushrik*, which literally means 'associater'. These are people who commit

shirk 'association' (from which the word *mushrik* is derived), which means saying that anyone or anything is like Allah.

4. The **'People of the Book'** are a subcategory of *mushrik*. This category includes Christians and Jews. They must be considered *mushrik*, because the Quran names both Christians and Jews as being guilty of *shirk* 'association' for claiming that Allah has a son:

> The Jews say, 'Ezra is the Son of Allah';
> the Christians say 'The Messiah is the Son of Allah.' (Q9:30)

The concept of 'People of the Book' signifies that Christianity and Judaism are related to and derived from Islam. Islam is regarded as the mother religion from which Christians and Jews had diverged over the centuries. According to the Quran, Christians and Jews follow a faith which was originally pure monotheism – in other words Islam – but their scriptures have been corrupted, and are no longer authentic. In this sense, Christianity and Judaism are regarded as distorted derivatives of Islam, and their followers have gone astray from the rightly guided path. Furthermore, Christians (and Jews) could not be freed from their ignorance until Muhammad came bringing the Quran (Q98:1). Muhammad was Allah's gift to Christians and Jews to correct misunderstandings. They should accept Muhammad as Allah's Messenger, and the Quran as his final revelation (Q5:15; Q57:28; Q4:47).

The Quran includes both positive and negative comments about Christians and Jews. In a positive light, it reports that some Christians and Jews are faithful and believe truly (Q3:113-14). However the same chapter says the test of their sincerity is that the genuine ones will become Muslims (Q3:199).

Although Jews and Christians are considered together in the one category of 'People of the Book', the Jews come off worse in the Quran. For example, the Quran says that it is Christians who will be 'nearest in love' to Muslims, but Jews and pagans will have the greatest enmity against Muslims. (Q5:82)

In the end, however, the Quran's final verdict is negative on both Jews and Christians alike. Condemnation is manifested in key theological claims, and incorporated into the daily prayers of every observant Muslim.

Daily prayers

The best-known chapter of the Quran is *al-Fatihah* 'The Opening'. This *sura* is recited as part of all the mandatory daily prayers – the *salat* – and repeated within each prayer. A faithful Muslim who said all their prayers would recite this *sura* at least seventeen times a day, and over five thousand times a year.

Al-Fatihah is a prayer for guidance:

> In the Name of Allah, the Merciful, the Compassionate
> Praise belongs to Allah, the Lord of all Being,
> the All-merciful, the All-compassionate,
> the Master of the Day of Doom.
> Thee only we serve; to Thee alone we pray for succor.
> Guide us in the straight path,
> the path of those whom Thou hast blessed,
> not of **those against whom Thou art wrathful**,
> nor of **those who are astray**.

This is a prayer asking Allah's help to lead the believer along the 'straight path'. As such it is true to the heart of Islam's message of guidance.

But who are those who are said to have earned Allah's wrath, or gone astray from the straight path? Who are these people who deserve to be stigmatized in every Muslim's prayers, each day, hundreds of thousands of times in many Muslims' lifetimes?

Ibn Kathir's commentary explains the meaning of this verse as follows:

> **These two paths are the paths of the Christians and Jews,** a fact that the believer should beware of so that he avoids them. ... the Jews abandoned practicing the religion, while the Christians lost the true knowledge. This is why 'anger' descended upon the Jews, while being described as 'led astray' is more appropriate of the Christians. ... We should also mention that both the Christians and the Jews have earned the anger and are led astray, but the anger is one of the attributes more particular of the Jews. Allah said about the Jews, 'Those (Jews) who incurred the curse of Allah and His wrath' (Q5:60). The attribute that the Christians deserve most is that of being led astray, just as Allah said about them, 'Who went astray before and who misled many, and strayed (themselves) from the right path' (Q5:77).[1]

Ibn Kathir goes on to cite a *hadith* in which Muhammad clarified the meaning of this *sura*:

---

1 *Tafsir Ibn Kathir*. Commentary on Q1:7. Vol. 1, p.87.

Imam Ahmad recorded that 'Adi bin Hatim said, ... he [Muhammad] said 'Those who have earned the anger are the Jews and those who are led astray are the Christians.'[1]

The verse from Q5 which Ibn Kathir refers to concerning Jews is:

Shall I tell you of a recompense with Allah, worse than that? Whomsoever Allah has cursed, and with whom He is wroth, and made some of them apes and swine, and worshippers of idols – they are worse situated, and have gone further astray from the right way. (Q5:60)

And the verse concerning Christians:

People of the Book, go not beyond the bounds in your religion, other than the truth, and follow not the caprices of a people who went astray before, and led astray many, and now again have gone astray from the right way. (Q5:77)

It is remarkable that the daily prayers of every Muslim, part of the core of Islam, include a rejection of Christians and Jews as misguided and objects of Allah's wrath.[2]

Theological claims about non-Muslims

Moving beyond solemn ritual, let us consider the Quran's theology of non-Muslims.

1. Christians and Jews who cling to their *shirk* and continue to disbelieve in Muhammad and his monotheism – i.e. those who do not convert to Islam – will go to hell:

   The unbelievers of the People of the Book
   and the idolaters shall be in the Fire of Hell,
   therein dwelling forever;
   those are the worst of creatures. (Q98:6)

2. Muslims are superior to other peoples, and their role is to instruct them concerning what is right and wrong, commanding what is honorable, and forbidding what is shameful. In contrast most Jews and Christians are transgressors:[3]

   You are the best nation ever brought forth to men, bidding to honour, and forbidding dishonour, and believe in Allah.
   Had the People of the Book believed, it were better for them;

---

1 Ibid., p.88.

2 It must be acknowledged that *al-Fatihah*'s slander against Jews and Christians is found in the *Sunna* and commentaries, not in the actual text of the verse, and it is possible that many Muslims pray these words without thinking of Jews or Christians.

3 The expression implies licentiousness, perversion, or iniquity.

some of them are believers, but the most of them are ungodly. (Q3:110)

3. Islam's destiny is to rule over all other religions:

> It is He who has sent His Messenger with the guidance and the religion of truth, that He may cause it to triumph[1] over every religion. (Q48:28)

This victory is the ultimate expression of Islam's promise of success.

4. To achieve this ascendancy, Muslims are to fight against Jews and Christians (the Peoples of the Book) until they are defeated and humbled, and forced to pay tribute to the Muslim community:

> Fight those who believe not in Allah and the Last Day
> and do not forbid what Allah and His Messenger have
> forbidden – such men as practise not the religion of truth, being
> of those who have been given the Book – until they pay the
> tribute out of hand and have been humbled. (Q9:29)

5. In the end-times Judaism and Christianity will be destroyed. Muhammad taught that when Isa, the Islamic Jesus returns to the earth, he will destroy Christianity ('break the Cross'), and make an end of the legal tolerance of Christians to live under Islamic rule ('there will be no *jizya*'). Scholars interpret this *hadith* to mean that Isa the Muslim prophet (i.e. Jesus) will force all Christians, and followers of all other faiths, to convert to Islam at the point of the sword:

> Narrated Abu Huraira:
> Allah's Messenger said, 'By Him in Whose Hands my soul is,
> surely (Jesus,) the son of Maryam (Mary) will shortly descend
> amongst you (Muslims) and will judge mankind justly by the
> law of the Qur'an (as a just ruler); he will break the Cross and
> kill the pigs and there will be no *jizya* (i.e. taxation taken from
> non Muslims). ...'[2]

6. In addition to all this, there are numerous specific theological claims about the Jews. For example, Muhammad taught that at the end, the very stones will lend their voices to help Muslims kill the Jews:

---

1 Arberry translates this as 'uplift it', however the expression actually means 'cause to be victorious over', 'cause to triumph over' or 'prevail over'.

2 *Sahih al-Bukhari.* The Book of the Stories of the Prophets. 4:60:3448. See also *Sahih Muslim.* The Book of Faith (*Kitab al-Iman*) 1:1:287.

Narrated Abu Huraira:

Allah's Apostle said, 'The Hour will not be established until you fight against the Jews, and the stone behind which a Jew will be hiding will say. "O Muslim! There is a Jew hiding behind me, so kill him."'[1]

See chapter 5 for further discussion of the Quran's teachings on Jews.

An important question is how Muslims actually apply these principles when relating to people of other faiths today. The answer of course is that Muslims are not all the same. They adopt a wide variety of attitudes to Christians and Jews. Yet at the same time, it is clear that the theological foundations of Islam are antagonistic to both Christianity and Judaism, and where negative attitudes arise, even in modern-day societies, they are influenced by the anti-Christian and anti-Jewish themes found in the Quran and the *Sunna*. The compass of faith exerts its influence even across vast distances, and across cultural divides. Thus it is that these passages are of critical importance in driving persecution of Christians and other non-Muslims in Islamic societies.

Because Islam defines itself in relation to Christians and Jews, it is incumbent upon the followers of Biblical faiths to study Muhammad's teaching and example and to make up their own minds about it, for themselves. The only way to do this properly is to be well informed about the teachings found in the Quran and the *Sunna*, because Islam is based upon these foundations.

Sharia implementation and Islamic reformation

Another reason why it is essential for non-Muslims to study Islam for themselves has to do with the nature of *Sharia* law.

Although it does include personal faith and devotion with its scope, for the *Sharia* to be followed consistently and comprehensively – and this is most important – it requires an Islamized society. This has been the general consensus of scholars for centuries, and it remains a view widely held by most, if not all, Muslims today. Thus there are very few majority Muslim nations that have not embedded the *Sharia* into their national constitutions, often by a reference which names the *Sharia* as the source of all lawful authority. Even the new Iraq and Afghanistan

---

1 *Sahih al-Bukhari.* Book of *Jihad* (Fighting for Allah's Cause). 4:56:2926.

constitutions, created under the conditions of non-Muslim military occupation, cite the *Sharia* as the source of law.

Why is this so? The simple theological explanation is that in his person Muhammad combined religious, political, juridical and military authority for the early Islamic community, and since Muhammad's example is the best example, making no distinction between religion and politics has become normative for all Muslims. Based on Muhammad's example, orthodox Islam has always taught that the *Sharia* should be enforced by the state, with Islam acting as the dominant faith in public affairs. Today most, but not all, Muslims believe that the *Sharia* should be a source of legislation for the state.[1] From this perspective, Islam is not just a religion, but a total way of life for a nation, and it is for this reason that many constitutions of Muslim-majority countries explicitly acknowledge the *Sharia*.

Is the truly Islamic state something to be sought, or shunned? It could be argued that certain recent experiments at *Sharia* implementation have failed spectacularly. Four of the strictest *Sharia*-observant societies in modern times have been Iran, Afghanistan under the Taliban, Saudi Arabia and Sudan. None of these are model states. The Islamic revolution in Iran did not usher in a *Sharia* utopia, but a society plagued by homelessness, drug use, prostitution and suicide.[2] As a result, many young Iranians are rejecting Islam. The Taliban, once hailed by the Muslim diaspora around the world as heroes of the global Islamic movement, turned out to be cruel tyrants. The Sudanese Islamic government's strategy of unleashing the Islamic *jihad* against its own citizens has fueled one of the bloodiest civil wars of the late 20th and early 21st century, causing the deaths of millions. Saudi Arabia is notorious for its human rights abuses, including discriminating against women and religious minorities.

The utopian dream

Despite the two glaring failures of Iran and Afghanistan, ongoing abuses of human rights in Saudi Arabia, and the genocidal *jihad* campaigns of

---

1 Dalia Mogahed, 'Islam and Democracy,' Gallop Special Report: Muslim World, 2006, downloaded 8 May 2009, <http://www.muslimwestfacts.com/mwf/File/109489/Islam_and_Democracy.pdf>.

2 Chris Hedges, 'Iran's Old Soldiers Die, as suicides.' *New York Times*, July 12, 1993, viewed 8 May 2009, <http://query.nytimes.com/gst/fullpage.html?sec=health&res=9F0CE5D71331F93 1A25754C0A965958260>; Morteza Aminmansour, 'Street children, women trafficking in Iran. Part 2.' *Persian Journal*, December 21, 2004, viewed 8 May 2009, <http://www.iranian.ws/cgi-bin/iran_news/exec/view.cgi/2/5052>.

the Sudanese government, a rosy and convenient view of past Islamic eras as golden ages of tolerance and prosperity is deeply embedded in the historical world view of many Muslims. More than this, a utopian future, where power is exercised only for and by Islam, has been vigorously promoted for decades through the teaching of radicals such as Sayyid Qutb and Mawdudi.

Historian Bernard Lewis has also argued that a sense of disappointment over the loss of Muslim power and the advance of the West fuels the reformist vision of a pure Islamic society, based upon the conviction that when Muslims finally implement Islam properly, Allah will be pleased with them and once again grant them success.[1]

This utopian dream props up confidence in the *Sharia* as the best form of governance for mankind, countering the evidence to the contrary. However, for non-Muslims, implementation of *Sharia* law implies state-legislated inferiority, so the will among Muslims to establish *Sharia* law is a matter of great interest and relevance for non-Muslims, something they should seek to be informed about, and about which they should expect to have their views heard.

To Sharia or not to Sharia?

The *Sharia* needs to be fully understood. While many of its principles can be directly inferred from the Quran and the *hadiths*, a full grasp of what *Sharia* law means can only be gained from reviewing a *Sharia* manual. These are systematic reference works giving all the rules to live by in a particular school of *Sharia*. Such a manual is comparable to a summary of the whole legal code of a nation.

It must be acknowledged that there is a debate going on in the Muslim community concerning the applicability in the modern world of the traditional schools of Islamic law. Some, such as *salafi* Muslims, argue for a return to the fundamental foundations of the Quran and the *hadiths*, stripping away the accretions of medieval scholarship which are reflected in the *Sharia* legal traditions. However the various traditional schools of *Sharia* simply represent a rigorous attempt to adhere to the teachings of Muhammad. Although one may disagree with individual rulings, and argue – as some radicals do – that they are over-loaded with human accretions, the reality is that the schools are built upon the fundamental foundations of Islam, and therefore *salafi* attempts will themselves fail or only produce more of the same.

---

1 This is Bernard Lewis' core argument in, *What went wrong?*

Accessing information about Muhammad's life

Anyone can read all the primary historical evidence about the life, character and mission of Jesus by reading the gospels. This can be done in the course of one afternoon. The gospel biographies of Jesus could be called 'public truth', for they are the most widely published and readily available texts in the world today.

Not so with Muhammad's life. While millions of Muslims do seek to imitate Muhammad, detailed information about him is not readily accessible to them. It must ultimately be derived from the Quran, from thousands of *hadiths* and from biographies, the *sira*. The full extent of this material is vast and much of it is only available in classical Arabic. The difficulties in accessing this information have already been described.

It is quite understandable that so many Muslims have only a limited understanding of Muhammad's life, and do not have a detailed working knowledge of the Quran and the context in Muhammad's life that specific passages relate to. The Muslim community has always relied heavily upon scholars to make this knowledge available. A great deal is taken on trust. Only in the last 20-30 years have key primary source texts become available in English.

A sanitized life

Versions of Muhammad's life made available to the general public could be said to be sanitized. For example, it is commonly emphasized that Muhammad married Khadijah, an older widow, and was faithfully and monogamously married to her for 20 years. But it is not normally reported that Muhammad married Aisha, his close friend's daughter, when she was 6 (or 7 by some accounts), and consummated the marriage when she was 9.[1] At that time Muhammad was in his 50's.

Based on this example, and the Quranic verse Q65:4, Islamic scholars even developed regulations for remarrying young girls, namely that a divorced prepubescent girl would need to wait three months before remarrying (this waiting period is known as the *'idda*). Thus the *Sahih al-Bukhari* includes the following passage in the Book of Marriage:

(39) CHAPTER. Giving one's young children in marriage (is permissible)

By virtue of the Statement of Allah '... and for those who have no (monthly) courses (i.e. they are still immature) (V.65:4).

---

1 As the Islamic reckoning refers to lunar years, by Western reckoning she was perhaps still 8.

And the *'Idda* for the girl before puberty is three months (in the above Verse).

5133. Narrated A'isha that the Prophet married her when she was six years old and he consummated his marriage when she was nine years only, and then she remained with him for nine years (i.e. till his death).[1]

Ibn Kathir, in his commentary on Q65:4 states:

The same is for the young, who have not reached the years of menstruation. Their *'Iddah* is three months like those in menopause. This is the meaning of the saying 'and for those who have no courses' [Q65:4][2]

Such reports of Muhammad's life are found in the *hadith* and *sira*, and should be well known to trained scholars of Islam, but they are not meant to be discussed publicly, especially not before non-Muslims. Nevertheless they have enormous practical consequences. Setting a marriage age of nine for girls is no matter of obscure theological interest or polemical debate, but an intensely practical issue of enormous consequence for the lives of countless young girls in Muslim nations. The Ayatollah Khomeini, then in his late 20's, married Batoul Saqafi Khomeini when she was eleven years old, following his prophet's example. Today some Muslim countries make 9 the minimum age of marriage for girls, and in others such marriages are not prevented, even though they may be illegal. Countless thousands of young girls' lives are affected by Muhammad's example in marrying Aisha.

Another example is Muhammad's treatment of female captives, which served as the precedent down the centuries for Muslim men to use captive women for sexual purposes. This principle is clearly stated in the Quran (Q4:24), and it has been repeatedly reaffirmed by legal authorities. Book 8, chapter 567 of the *Sahih Muslim* is headed:

It is permissible to have sexual intercourse with a captive woman after she is purified (of menses or delivery). In case she has a husband, her marriage is abrogated after she becomes captive.

Abdul Hamid Siddiqi, distinguished Fellow of the Islamic Research Academy of Karachi, and translator of the *Sahih Muslim*, adds the following note to this section:

... the expression *malakat aymanukum* (those whom your right hands possess [in Q4:24]) denotes slave-girls, i.e. women who were captured in the Holy War. **When women are taken captive their previous marriages**

---

1 *Sahih Muslim*. Book of *An-Nikah* (The Wedlock), Chapter 39, p.57.
2 *Tafsir Ibn Kathir*. Commentary on Q65:4. Vol. 10, p.43.

are automatically annulled. It should, however, be remembered that **sexual intercourse with these women is lawful** with certain conditions.[1]

Muhammad married Safiya, a Jewish captive from Khaybar, immediately after torturing her husband and killing him and her father. Safiya was even led to Muhammad by Bilal past the dead bodies of her male relatives, including her husband. Later Muhammad rebuked Bilal for his insensitivity![2]

In Medina, Muhammad had already taken Rayhana, another Jewish woman, for his concubine under similar circumstances. However Rayhana asked to stay as a slave in Muhammad's house rather than convert to Islam and marry her owner.

Because Muhammad's *Sunna* is the foundation of *Sharia* law, it is important not to relativize or gloss over the recorded details of what he did and said as recorded in the *hadiths* and the *sira*. Ignorance about Muhammad is ignorance about *Sharia*, and therefore about the human rights of people living under Islamic conditions. What Muhammad did, *Sharia* law commends to Muslims to emulate, and the lives of hundreds of millions are affected, both Muslims and non-Muslims. The relationship between Muhammad's life and the lives of people today may not always be a direct one, but it remains extremely powerful and significant.

For this reason, anyone who wants to form an independent and accurate opinion of Islam, for whatever reason, should first read Ibn Ishaq's *Life of Muhammad* and then one of the major *hadith* collections such as *Sahih Muslim* or *Sahih al-Bukhari*. The Quran may then be read in the light of Muhammad's life. Secondary derivative sources should not be assumed to be reliable guides.

Blasphemous truth

The very existence of controversial material in Muhammad's life story means any public representation of his life and character is going to be selective. It will either include offensive material and become polemical in nature, or it will censor it and risk becoming nothing more than propaganda. This is a serious practical difficulty for non-Muslims who wish to study and critique Islamic canonical texts. When primary historical source traditions about Muhammad are made known, ordinary Muslims can react with shock, denial and anger, because they

1 *Sahih Muslim.* Vol. 2, note p.897.
2 Guillaume, *The Life of Muhammad*, p.515.

are not comprehensively educated in the realities of Muhammad's life and are unable to process this confronting material as a truthful report. An example of this was the conviction in 2001 of Pakistani Christian school principal Pervaiz Masih of blasphemy, apparently for referring to Muhammad's marriage to Aisha when she was six, and saying – as is indeed the case – that this is recorded in the *Sahih al-Bukhari*.[1] Masih was acquitted on appeal in 2006, after five years in detention.

Another example was a civil complaint, made in Australia against Christian pastor Daniel Scot, for teaching – among other things – the fact that apostasy from Islam requires the death penalty. The complaint stated: 'Pastor Scot intimated that Muslims are killed by other Muslims if they leave the Islamic faith.'[2] In fact Islamic law does indeed impose the death penalty for apostasy, and there have been many examples of this penalty being carried out in recent years.[3]

The problem of misinformation

Misinformation about Islam is a constant issue for non-Muslims. A report in the *Herald Sun*, a major Melbourne daily newspaper, was published on August 8, 2005 stating that the senior Muslim Imam of Victoria, Sheikh Fehmi (subsequently appointed as Australia's mufti) reassured non-Muslims in Victoria that Muslims wish only to live in peace with their non-Muslim neighbors:

> 'Muslims live cheerfully and happily with all denominations', Sheik Fehmi said. 'This is what Islam is. The Prophet has lived among Jews and Christians. In many parts of the world Muslims, Jews and Christians are living happily.'

Who would not applaud Sheikh Fehmi's desire for people of different faiths to live together in harmony? The problem arises when he appeals to Muhammad's example as the basis for non-Muslims to have confidence that Muslim neighbors represent no threat to peaceful coexistence. Although there was a time early in Muhammad's life when he lived peacefully alongside non-Muslims, large sections of Muhammad's biographies and the Quran deal with periods when he was embattled

---

1 Barbara G. Baker, 'Christian Principal accused of blasphemy.' *Christianity Today*, 21 May, 2001, viewed 8 May 2009, <http://www.christianitytoday.com/ct/2001/may21/25.31.html>.

2 Complaint lodged in 2002 with the Equal Opportunity Commission of Victoria by the Islamic Council of Victoria.

3 See Christine Schirrmacher, *The Islamic View of Major Christian Teachings*; Mark Durie, 'The Apostasy Fatwas', viewed 8 May 2009, <http://acommonword.blogspot.com/2008/02/apostasy-fatwas-and-common-word-between.html>; Sayyid Abul A'la Mawdudi, *The punishment of the apostate according to Islamic law.*

with his non-Muslim Jewish neighbors. As we shall see in the next chapter, Muhammad ordered assassinations of Jewish women and old men, and oversaw a mass decapitation and enslavement of hundreds of his Jewish neighbors. This darker material Sheikh Fehmi could not fail to be familiar with, as these victories of Islam over the Jews of Arabia are as well known to Muslim children as Joshua's conquest of Jericho is to Christian Sunday School children.

How then are Fehmi's non-Muslim, fellow Victorians to interpret his reassurances that they can have nothing to worry about, because Islam takes Muhammad as its example?

If a non-Muslim were to write in response to Sheikh Fehmi's comment in the *Herald Sun*, pointing out Muhammad's less than happy, and indeed fatal, relationships with his non-Muslim neighbors, how could this be done without sounding like incitement of interfaith conflict and a rejection of Fehmi's apparently moderate and peaceful stance? By relying on acceptance of the excellence of Muhammad's example as a pre-condition of interfaith harmony, Sheikh Fehmi's words serve to lock up the truth about Muhammad even more tightly in the dark box of ignorance.

These are not easy subjects to deal with, but deal with them we must, and one of the keys to a free and frank conversation with Muslims about such matters of importance is that non-Muslims must study Islam for themselves. They cannot rely on Muslim spokespeople as their only source of information on Islam. The same can be said for Muslims: they also should not rely solely on secondary sources, not even on Islamic clerics, to understand their faith.

Lawful lying, misleading impressions and harm prevention

On Friday 20 March 2001, Zachariah Matthews, a prominent Australian Muslim youth leader, presented a lecture to the Muslim Society at the University of Western Sydney. His subject was the proper method of establishing Islam in the lands of immigration. He argued that it was necessary to adhere to principles derived from the example of Muhammad's *Hijrah* 'migration' to Medina, since 'The Prophetic Method of *Dawah* is the only method that will bring us success.' Matthews listed six 'Hijrah Management Principles', which were based upon episodes in Muhammad's life. Of these the third was 'secrets should be hidden' and the sixth 'deception is necessary'.[1]

Is it true that the use of deception is a legitimate part of establishing Islam?

While it must be acknowledged that lying is considered a very serious sin in Islam, there are situations where lying is permissible, according to Islamic authorities, based, of course, upon Muhammad's example. For example, a chapter in the *Sahih al-Bukhari* is headed 'He who makes peace between people is not a liar.' The *hadith* given is:

> Narrated Umm Kulthum bint Uqba that
>
> she heard Allah's Messenger saying, 'He who makes peace between the people by inventing good information or saying good things, is not a liar.'[2]

According to this teaching, one of the circumstances in which Muslims are permitted to say untrue things is when reconciling people, if the lies are of a positive nature.

Harm prevention

According to the Quran, another circumstance for deception is when Muslims are in danger from non-Muslims.

> Let not the Believers take for friends or helpers Unbelievers rather than Believers: if any do that, in nothing will there be help from Allah, **except by way of precaution, that ye may guard yourselves from them**. But Allah cautions you (to remember) Himself; for the final goal is to Allah. [Q3:28 – Yusuf Ali's translation[3]]

The word translated 'guard' here is based upon the root *w-q-y*, which means to prevent harm. From this is derived the term *taqiyya*,[4] which refers to the practice of deception in order to keep Muslims safe. The expression 'friends or helpers' translates *auliya*, which, despite Yusuf Ali's choice of words, implies guardianship or legal subjection. Thus Sunni

---

1 Zachariah Matthews, 'The Hijrah: a necessary phase in the Dawah.' *Salam Magazine*, March/ April 2001. The article is archived at <http://web.archive.org/web/20050615002854/www. famsy.com/salam/Hijrah41.htm>. It must be acknowledged that after being publicly criticized for this teaching, Matthews delivered an address emphasizing that Islam regards lying as wrong.

2 *Sahih al-Bukhari*. The Book of Peacemaking (or Reconciliation). 3:53:2692.

3 For Q3:28 Arberry's translation is so far from the standard interpretation that it is unusable.

4 It is not correct to use the term *taqiyya* to refer to lawful deception in general. *Taqiyya* involves lying about one's beliefs in order to prevent harm, but the teaching and practice of lawful deception in both Sunni and Shi'ite Islam are more extensive than this. Also, it should be noted that although some claim lawful deception to be only a Shi'ite, and not a Sunni doctrine, this claim is not true.

commentaries on Q3:28 take the view that *taqiyya* is permitted when Muslims are subject to the power of non-Muslims (so that Muslims could have reason to fear them):

> It was permitted for [Muslims] to take [non-Muslims] as guardians [i.e. to accept non-Muslims in a position of power] if they feared them. What is meant by this guardianship is the contrary of the apparent relationship [i.e. the relationship is not what it seems]; the heart is comforted by enmity and hatefulness [towards the non-Muslims] ... (al-Zamakhshari, d. 1143)[1]

> If the believer is living amongst the infidels and he is afraid of them, he may praise them with his tongue while his heart is comforted with faith, to avoid harm to himself [i.e. from the infidels] ... *Taqiyya* is not to be used except when in fear for one's life. (al-Baghawi, d. 1122)[2]

> ... if the infidels have apparent authority over [Muslims], then [the Muslims] show them kindness but oppose them in religion [i.e. in their heart's convictions] (al-Suyuti, d. 1505).[3]

> ... believers who in some areas or times fear for their safety from the disbelievers ... are allowed to show friendship to the disbelievers outwardly, but never inwardly. For instance, al-Bukhari recorded that Abu Ad-Darda' said, 'We smile in the face of some people although our hearts curse them.' Al-Bukhari said that al-Hasan said, 'The *Tuqyah* [*taqiyya*] is allowed until the Day of Resurrection.' (Ibn Kathir)[4]

> ... it is lawful for a believer ... to keep his faith concealed and to behave in such a manner as to create the impression that he is on the same side as his enemies. A person whose Muslim identity is discovered is permitted to adopt a friendly attitude towards the unbelievers in order to save his life. ... he may even state that he is not a believer. ... If one is constrained in extraordinary circumstances to resort to a prudent concealment of faith (*taqiyah*) in order to save one's life, this concealment should remain within reasonable limits. (Mawdudi, d. 1979)[5]

Al-Khazin (c. 1340) reports that some scholars say *taqiyya* was only for the early stages of Islam, before Muslims gained power, so the doctrine no longer applied after Muslims gained the upper hand.[6] However the logic of this view would imply that when Muslims are no longer in power, the concession for *taqiyya* must come back into force.

---

1 *al-Kashshaf,* Commentary on Q3:28, viewed 21 February 2008, <http://altafsir.com>.

2 *Ma'alam al-tanzil.* Commentary on Q3:28, viewed 21 February 2008, <http://altafsir.com>.

3 *Dur al-Manthur.* Commentary on Q3:28, viewed 21 February 2008, <http://altafsir.com>.

4 *Tafsir Ibn Kathir,* vol. 2:142. (Commentary on Q3:28.)

5 Mawdudi, *Towards understanding the Qur'an,* p.130. Commentary on Q3:28.

6 *Tafsir Lubab al-Ta'wil.* Commentary on Q3:28, viewed 21 February 2008, <http://altafsir.com>.

The consensus of Sunni commentaries is that Muslims, when living under the political dominance of non-Muslims, are allowed to show friendliness and kindness to non-Muslims as a protective measure, so long as they hold fast to their faith (and enmity) in their hearts.

One implication of this doctrine is that observant Muslims' behavior towards non-Muslims might be expected to become less friendly, and their beliefs less veiled, as their political power increases.

Misleading impressions

In Islam deception is not limited to contexts where Muslims fear persecution. An extended discussion of the subject of lawful lying is found in the *Sharia* manual, the *Reliance of the Traveller*, in four sections:

> r8.1 LYING,
> r8.2 PERMISSIBLE LYING,
> r9 EXAGGERATION and
> r10 GIVING A MISLEADING IMPRESSION.

After first emphasizing that lying is 'among the ugliest sins', the *Reliance of the Traveller* goes on to say that '... lying is sometimes permissible for a given interest, scholars having established criteria defining what types of it are lawful.'[1] A *hadith* is then cited which reports that Muhammad permitted untruth in warfare, settling disputes (as shown by the *hadith* cited above), and between husband and wife to 'smooth over differences'.

The *Reliance* then quotes the renowned Islamic authority al-Ghazali:

> Speaking is a means to achieve objectives. If a praiseworthy aim is attainable through both telling the truth and lying, it is unlawful to accomplish it through lying because there is no need for it. When it is possible to achieve such an aim by lying but not by telling the truth, **it is permissible to lie if attaining the goal is permissible ... and obligatory to lie if the goal is obligatory.** ... Whether the purpose is war, settling a disagreement, or gaining the sympathy of a victim legally entitled to retaliate against one so that he will forbear to do so; it is not unlawful to lie when any of these aims can only be attained through lying. But **it is religiously more precautionary ... in all such cases to employ words that give a misleading impression,** meaning to intend by one's words something that is literally true, in respect to which one is not lying ...

> One should compare the bad consequences entailed by lying to those entailed by telling the truth, and if the consequences of telling the truth are more damaging, one is entitled to lie ...[2]

---

1   Nuh Ha Mim Keller, ed. and trans., *Reliance of the Traveller*, p.745.
2   Ibid., p.745-46, paragraph r8.2.

Essentially al-Ghazali is advocating a utilitarian ethic, that in lying, the end justifies the means.

The editor of the *Reliance of the Traveller*, Nuh Ha Mim Keller, cites 'Abd al-Wakil Durubi to offer an example of the difference between lying and giving a misleading impression. If someone asks you whether a particular person is present in your house, and you do not want to give the person's whereabouts away, you could lawfully give a misleading impression by saying 'He is not here', meaning the empty space between you and the questioner, but intending that the questioner would think you are referring to the house.[1]

The need to pay attention

How might this work in the public sphere? Suppose, for example, a Muslim leader in a Western country gave a sermon in Arabic, which was translated by the media into English, and certain statements in it were found to be inflammatory. A spokesperson for the leader might issue a media release saying, 'the translation was not accurate', meaning that some incidental aspects of the translation, which were not in fact relevant to the statements at issue, were inaccurate, but intending thereby to give the misleading impression that the inflammatory material itself was being disavowed. The purpose of such deception would be to prevent harm to the Muslim community and the Islamic cause.

Because of the potential for misleading impressions to arise, it can be important to pay very careful attention to what is and is not said, when interpreting statements by Muslim apologists.

During June 2008, the Australian Muslim commentator Keysar Trad issued a statement commending the United Kingdom for giving formal recognition to polygamy.[2] This resulted in a storm of media commentary.

The issue of the woman's consent to such marriages is a key point in *Sharia* law. While a woman is normally required to consent to her own marriage, a husband is **not** required to reveal any pre-existing marriages when taking an additional wife, nor is he required to inform his previous wives, or seek their consent for the new marriage.[3] Keysar Trad wrote:

---

1 Ibid., p.748.

2 Jonathan Wynne-Jones, 'Multiple wives will mean multiple benefits.' *The Daily Telegraph*. 18 April, 2008.

3 See for example the ruling 'He married a second wife and they became Muslim – what should he do with his first wife?' viewed 26 September 2009, <http://www.islamqa.com/en/ref/20849>.

There are many rules and regulations that govern plural unions which some Muslim men and women say make it almost beyond the capacity of ordinary males. Marriage being a union that requires consent, males can only enter into it when they find a willing woman. A man cannot pick and choose if the woman doesn't.[1]

Australian media commentators were quick to interpret Trad as saying that Islamic polygamous marriages are voluntary on the women's part – that it is the woman's choice – because of Trad's words 'males can only enter into it when they find a willing woman'. In fact all that Trad had said was that the woman must be willing to marry. What he did **not** say was that the woman (or any of the pre-existing wives) must give their consent to the polygamy.

Getting caught out

Sometimes Muslim leaders can be 'caught out' saying one thing to a non-Muslim audience, and something else altogether to a Muslim audience. For example, at a time when negotiations between the Palestinian Liberation Organization and the Israeli authorities had appeared to be going well, and international optimism was riding high, Yasser Arafat gave an inflammatory off-the-record speech in a Cape Town mosque in which he exhorted his hearers 'to come and to fight a *jihad* to liberate Jerusalem'.[2] He also compared the treaty recently contracted with the Israelis to Muhammad's treaty with the Quraysh tribes people of Mecca (known as the Treaty of *al-Hudaybiyyah*): 'I see this agreement as being no more than the agreement signed between our Prophet Muhammad and the Quraysh in Mecca.'[3] This treaty Muhammad subsequently rejected, after which the Muslims secured a great victory over the Meccans.

A secret recording of Arafat's speech was made by journalist Bruce Whitfield. When the speech was relayed to the world, Arafat's words created a storm of protest. Yet Arafat defended himself by saying that he had only been speaking of his peacemaking efforts: 'I will continue my *jihad* for peace.'[4]

---

1 Keysar Trad, 'UK is right to recognize polygamy,' viewed 8 May 2009, <http://www.crikey.com. au/Politics/20080625-UK-is-right-to-recognise-polygamy.html>.

2 Clyde Haberman, 'Rabin says Arafat "Jihad" remark set back peace effort.' *The New York Times*, May 20, 1994, viewed 8 May 2009, <http://www.nytimes.com/1994/05/20/world/rabin-says-arafat-s-jihad-remark-set-back-peace-effort.html>.

3 Daniel Pipes, '[Al-Hudaybiya and] lessons from the Prophet Muhammad's diplomacy.' *Middle East Quarterly*, September 1999, viewed 8 May 2009, <http://www.danielpipes.org/316/al-hudaybiya-and-lessons-from-the-prophet-muhammads>.

4 Clyde Haberman, op cit.

In another example, Dan Sytman of Seattle's KTTH radio compiled an audio collage of Azzam Tamimi, of the Institute of Islamic Political Thought in London, in which Tamimi's calm and reassuring statements on American National Public Radio alternated with excerpts from a fiery street speech delivered to a mainly Muslim audience. Here are two such contrasting passages from the two recordings:

National Public Radio
Interviewer: 'Do you think there is significant support in the British Muslim Community for using violence to express opposition to British policy?'
Tamimi: 'Not at all. **The majority of Muslims are absolutely opposed to the use of violence. It is illegitimate. It's not acceptable.** ... We have the responsibility to explain this to our youngsters, that they cannot resort to force.'

Tamimi's street speech (shouting)
'And We say, we say we are willing to bring it to an end peacefully. **But if they don't want peace, we have another language! We have another language! And we have every right to use that language!** And time will tell! And history will tell! *Allahu Akbar! Allahu Akbar! Allahu Akbar!'*[1]

On national radio Tamimi declares that Muslims are opposed to violence, but in the street he loudly proclaims their right and readiness to use it.

Lost in translation

Because of the potential for deception, hard questions need to be asked about some translations of Islamic texts into English. There can be a tendency to 'soften' the original meaning of texts in translation. This is hardly an issue which is unique to Islam, but the reality of lawful dissimulation in Islam establishes an ethical framework which appears to encourage such practices.

An example of important information becoming lost in translation occurs in relation to Q4:34, which states that husbands may beat their wives as a punishment. The Arabic expression just says 'beat' or 'hit'. The range of possible meaning is very wide: this could mean anything from a light blow through to a flogging, but the normal understanding

---

1 Admittedly Tamimi is referring here to two different contexts – Britain and the Palestinians' conflict with Israel – but his rejection of violence on NPR is unqualified and does not specific any limitations of context. See <http://littlegreenfootballs.com/weblog/?entry=22136_Azzam_Tamimis_Duplicity_Exposed>, downloaded 8 May 2009. The quotation here is from the video, posted at <http://www.youtube.com/watch?v=zh6q02J6dJk>, viewed 8 May 2009.

would be a beating.[1] Yusuf Ali's original 1934 translation of the Quran rendered this as 'beat them (lightly)', adding the 'lightly' to make clear the style of corporal punishment Yusuf Ali believed was indicated. However a more recent edition of Yusuf Ali[2] has changed this to 'chastise them (lightly)' which is misleading, as *chastise* need not imply any use of force, and could simply mean a verbal rebuke, which is not at all what the Arabic says.

Another apparent example of a misleading impression being given by translation comes from Keller's translation of the *Reliance of the Traveller*, in a section dealing with female circumcision.

The term 'female genital mutilation' was coined at a World Health Organization seminar held in Khartoum in 1979. An NGO report by the Association for World Education to the United Nations Commission on Human Rights in July 2005 stated, concerning female circumcision:

> ... two million female children and girls in more than 30 countries – including more and more thousands in Europe from an immigrant population – are being brutally mutilated each year.[3]

Over the years countless public statements have been made alleging that female circumcision has no basis in the teachings of any religion. Nevertheless in 1981 Sheikh Gad al-Haq, of Al-Azhar University, a supreme authority in Sunni Islam, issued a *fatwa* stating that circumcision of girls was a religious obligation.[4]

Circumcision is one of the matters dealt with in the *Reliance of the Traveller*, a manual of Shafi'i law, in which the original Arabic text is published facing Keller's English translation.[5] The English translation of the section on circumcision conceals the Arabic instructions for circumcising girls by excising the clitoris. The Arabic is translated by Nuh Hah Mim Keller as follows:

---

1   The argument that the root *d.r.b* 'hit, beat' can be used metaphorically in the Quran (for example, Q14:29 where Allah 'strikes' a simile) is hardly relevant. Such uses can only be read as metaphors because of their context: because the physical interpretation is impossible, the non-literal reading is mandatory. Conversely, when a physical interpretation is the obvious one, the metaphorical reading will not be available. Just because in English a conductor can 'beat time' does not mean that if a husband 'beats his wife' she is having a musical experience!

2   Yusuf Ali, *The Holy Qur'an*, p.219.

3   'Specific Human Rights Issues: Women and Human Rights.' NGO written statement by the Association for World Education to the Sub-Commission on the promotion and protection of Human Rights, 57th session, 2005 (E/CN.4/Sub.2/2005/27).

4   Sheikh Gad al-Haq 'Ali Gad al-Haq, 'Khitan al banat.' See also Sami Awad Aldeeb, *Mutiler au nom de Yahve ou d'Allah.*

5   Nuh Ha Mim Keller, ed. and trans., *Reliance of the Traveller*, p.59 (§e4.3).

Circumcision is obligatory (O: for both men and women.[)][1] For men it consists of removing the prepuce from the penis, and for women, removing the prepuce (Ar. bazr) of the clitoris (n: not the clitoris itself, as some mistakenly assert). (A: Hanbalis hold that circumcision of women is not obligatory but sunna, while Hanafis consider it a mere courtesy to the husband.)[2]

However what the facing Arabic on the same page actually says is:

'Circumcision is obligatory (for every male and female) (by cutting off the piece of skin on the glans of the penis of the male, but circumcision of the female is by cutting out the *bazr* 'clitoris' [this is called *khifadh* 'female circumcision'])'.[3]

e4.3 وَيَجِبُ (على كل من الــذكر والأنثى) الخِتَـانُ (وهـو قطع الجلدة التي على حشفـة الـذكر وأما ختان الأنثى فهو قطع البظر [ويسمى خفاضاً]) .

Apologetics: Versions of the Quran

Perhaps as a result of the 'need to know' basis of knowledge in Islam, certain beliefs can be widely and even vehemently announced to the world, which are without foundation. For example, it is often stated that the Quran has never been altered, and exists without variation. This is a point frequently made in anti-Christian and anti-Jewish apologetics, a reason given for the alleged inferiority of the Bible. A widely used Islamic publication put it like this:

> No other book in the world can match the Qur'an ... The astonishing fact about this book of ALLAH is that it has remained unchanged, even to a dot, over the last fourteen hundred years. ... No variation of text can be found in it. You can check this for yourself by listening to the recitation of Muslims from different parts of the world.[4]

In fact there are several different versions of the Quran, with variations which affect virtually every page, and at least four of these are in print in different parts of the world today,[5] so recitations of the Quran are not the same all over the world. In addition there are also divergent Shi'ite

---

1 A closing bracket appears to be missing in Keller's text.

2 Note that *bazr* is, in fact, the Arabic word for 'clitoris'. In this context *sunna* means 'recommended'. The square brackets in this quotation are Keller's. O = excerpt from the commentary of 'Umar Barakat; Ar = Arabic; n = remark by translator; A= comment by Sheikh 'Abd al-Wakil Durubi

3 Peter Antes, 'Islam in the *Encyclopedia of Religion*,' confirms this view, reporting that clitoridectomy is obligatory only in the Shafi'i school of Sunni Islam. The word *khifadh* literally means 'making calm, gentle, submissive' or 'lowering'.

4 *Basic Principles of Islam.*

5 Samuel Green, 'The different Arabic versions of the Qur'an,' viewed 8 May 2009, <http://www.answering-islam.org/Green/seven.htm>.

readings of the text.[1] There were once even more variants, but under the caliph 'Uthman many variant Qurans were burnt in order to eliminate the variation.[2]

Obscuring the meaning of jihad

Certain Islamic teachings appear to be the special focus of efforts at misrepresentation. A commonly heard claim is that the word *jihad* does not primarily refer to military conflict, but to personal struggle with oneself.[3] This claim is based upon a *hadith* which speaks of military activity as the 'lesser *jihad*' and is often cited to justify the primacy of the spiritual *jihad*. However this *hadith* was not included in any of the six canonical *hadith* collections, and has been rejected as a fabrication.[4] In contrast, an authentic, secure *hadith* declares that internal or spiritual resistance is the 'least' expression of faith, and the use of force should be a Muslim's first preference:

> He who amongst you sees something abominable should modify it with the help of his hand; and if he has not strength enough to do it, then he should do it with his tongue, and if he has not strength enough to do it, (even) then he should (abhor it) from his heart, and that is the least of faith.[5]

An examination of the *Kitab al-Jihad* ('book of *jihad*') in the *Sahih al-Bukhari*, or for that matter any of the canonical *hadith* collections, reveals that the principal meaning of *jihad* in the *hadiths* is the use of military force against unbelievers to make Islam victorious and dominant.[6] This is most significant, because Islamic law is based upon the *Sunna*.

We also find that military *jihad* is given very extensive treatment in the Quran, with several *suras* being named after battle practices, such as The Spoils of War (Q8).[7]

Within *Sharia* legal traditions, a chapter in a legal manual on *jihad* would be concerned with military jurisprudence, dealing with warfare against unbelievers, and discuss such topics as the rules of engagement,

---

1 Daud Rahbar, 'Relation of Muslim Theology to the Qur'an.'
2 Samuel Green, 'How and why the Qur'an was standardized,' viewed 8 May 2009, <http://www.answering-islam.org/Green/uthman.htm>.
3 See Daniel Pipes 'Jihad and the professors' for a critique of this mythology.
4 Abu Fadl, 'Greater and "Lesser" Jihad.'
5 *Sahih Muslim*. Book of Faith. 1:1:79.
6 For an extensive treatment of this subject, see Andrew Bostom, *The Legacy of Jihad*.
7 See also 'Abdullah bin Muhammad bin Hamid, Sheikh of the Sacred Mosque of Mecca, 'The call to Jihad (holy fighting for Allah's cause) in the Holy Quran.'

the division of booty, and treatment of captives.[1] In the worldview of classical Islam, which unites the military, legal, political and religious domains, any justifiable military action by the Islamic state is *jihad*, a religious conflict to secure and extend Islam, and any soldier who dies fighting in the army of an Islamic nation is a martyr to his faith. In the long and bitter war between Iran and Iraq, both sides claimed that their vast casualties died as martyrs in *jihad*.[2]

All Islamist terrorist groups espouse the military understanding of *jihad*. Their political literature is packed with Quranic quotations and references to *hadiths*. Al-Qaida proclaimed that the 9/11 attack was a *ghazwa*, an Islamic military expedition.[3] *Fatwas* prepared by religious scholars who support these groups define with great precision what is or is not permitted for the terrorist assassins.[4]

Deceptive da'wah

It is instructive to consider a successful 20th century example of the use of strategic deception in promoting Islam. In October 2002 the Arabic-language quarterly *Al-Manar Al-Jadid Magazine* (published under the auspices of the Ann Arbor-based Islamic Assembly of North America) included a biographical essay by Muhammad 'Abduh on the achievements of Abdul-Hamid ibn Badis.[5] The essay bore the title 'The Understanding of Abdul-Hameed Ibn Baadis of the Phases of *Da'wah*'. The wording of the title is important. Like Zachariah Matthews' lecture, Muhammad 'Abduh's essay was concerned with the correct method of *da'wa*, or 'summoning' a community to Islam. 'Abduh describes the role of Ibn Badis in leading the Islamic revival in Algeria before World War II, through a carefully planned series of phases.

---

1 See, for example, the chapter entitled *al-Jihad* in Nuh Ha Mim Keller, ed. and trans., *Reliance of the Traveller*, p.599 (§o9.0).

2 For Iraq, see 'Martyr's Monument.' *Encyclopædia Britannica*. 2009. Encyclopædia Britannica Online, viewed 8 June 2009, <http://www.britannica.com/EBchecked/topic/907269/Martyrs-Monument>. For Iran, see Kevin Toolis, 'A million martyrs await the call.' *The Times*, November 19, 2005, viewed 8 May 2009, <http://www.timesonline.co.uk/tol/comment/columnists/guest_contributors/article591773.ece>.

3 Hans G. Kippenberg, 'Consider that it is a Raid on the Path of God: the Spiritual Manual of the Attackers of 9/11.' Walid Phares, 'Exclusive: the inevitability of 9/11'. *Family Security Matters*, 11 September 2008, viewed 8 May 2009, <http://www.familysecuritymatters.org/publications/id.1141/pub_detail.asp>.

4 See e.g. Abu Ruqaiyah, 'The Islamic Legitimacy of Martyrdom Operations.'

5 Muhammad 'Abduh, 'The Understanding of Abdul-Hameed Ibn Baadis of the Phases of Da'wah.' *Al-Manar Al-Jadid*, October 2002. Trans. into English by the Islamic Information & Support Centre of Australia (IISNA), posted on their website in 2003: <http://web.archive.org/web/20030208010959/www.iisca.org/knowledge/misc/ibnbaadis.htm>.

Ibn Badis is praised in the essay for his skilful use of deception. Early in his career he focused on training the young. During this initial phase he would assure the French authorities that his efforts were apolitical, and he supported French political ideals:

> We are Algerian Muslim people in the colonial province of the French Republic. So because we are Muslims we act for the preservation of the traditions of our religion. And indeed, a government who is ignoring the people's religion cannot manage it properly. **We are not intending by this to mix religion and politics** into all of our matters ... And because we are a colony, we seek to fasten the bonds of friendship between us and the French nation. And we call on France to adhere to its three foundational principles: Freedom, Equality and Brotherhood.[1]

Later, when Ibn Badis formed an association of Algerian ulamas, he was careful to include in the constitution the stipulation that 'It is not permitted for the *Jam'iyyah* [Association], under any circumstances to get involved in political matters.'[2] When Ibn Badis was challenged for inciting people against the French authorities, he protested that he had no interest in politics:

> Then what business has the *Jam'iyyatul 'Ulamaa* [the Association of Ulamas] in this matter, when **it is a religious organisation, merely corrective, and completely far away from politics?!'**[3]

Muhammad 'Abduh comments:

> **And that was just to conceal the real activities that were happening**. Indeed, the *Jam'iyyah* got involved into politics by another avenue ... his plan was to encircle [colonialism] and to destroy [it] ... step by step.[4]

'Abduh praises Ibn Badis' patient strategy, pursued over three decades, which began with a focus on religious education, then progressed through formal organization of the Muslim community to the phase of political engagement and resistance. The movement was being prepared for a fourth phase, the use of force, when Ibn Badis passed away in 1940: the bloody Algerian War of Independence commenced in 1954.

This essay eulogizes Ibn Badis for strategically deceiving the French authorities over a period of almost thirty years. He pretended that his religious ideals had nothing to do with politics, while his religious vision was always thoroughly political. He pretended to support

---

1 Ibid.
2 Ibid.
3 Ibid.
4 Ibid.

French political ideals, while being fundamentally opposed to them. He pretended friendship with France, while being determined to drive the French from Algeria. Even the constitution of the peak body of Algerian ulamas led by Ibn Badis was a fabrication, designed to lull the French into a false sense of security.

An ethically damaged community

A utilitarian ethic for lying and truth-telling can be very damaging. It destroys trust and creates confusion, damaging domestic and political cultures. If husbands habitually lie to their wives, to 'smooth over differences', this will erode trust within marriage. On a societal level, a culture of lawful deception will incite suspicion and stimulate conspiracy theories. If it is taken for granted that enemies lie to each other – because religion makes a virtue of such behavior – then conflicts will be more prolonged, and lasting peace harder to achieve.

The *Sharia* principle that lying is a means to an end can also drive a cycle of mistrust between Muslims and non-Muslims. This cycle can be observed in media reports of Islamic hate-speech. An Islamic leader is quoted in the media as having incited contempt for gays, Jews, Christians, women or democracy. The media report is then condemned by Muslim groups, who dismiss it as defamatory: the material was selectively taken out of context; the directors of the mosque were not aware that these views were being promoted; the group in question were only renting the facilities; the Arabic was mistranslated; the report is an attempt to demonize Muslims and exemplifies Islamophobia and racism in the media; other faiths hold similar views but only Muslims are targeted by the media; the report must be false because Islam requires Muslims to deal positively with others; and so forth.

Whatever the particularities, the essence of the dissimulation is the implication that the report was defamatory – that is to say, it was false – so the Muslims involved have nothing to answer for. However some months or years later, the same preacher or the same mosque is implicated in the same kind of hate-speech, mistrust increases, and community relations go from bad to worse. This cycle could be observed in responses to Channel 4's Undercover Mosque documentaries[1] in

---

[1] Sarah Hassan, 'Preachers of separatism at work inside British mosques.' *The Daily Telegraph*, 31 August, 2008, viewed 8 May 2009, <http://www.telegraph.co.uk/news/uknews/2653266/Preachers-of-separatism-at-work-inside-Britains-mosques.html>.

January 2007 and August 2008, which repeatedly exposed preachers of hate in some of Britain's leading mosques.[1]

The best way to break the cycle would be for Muslims together to acknowledge the problem, as Ghayasuddin Siddiqui, head of the Muslim Parliament of Great Britain proposed soon after the first Undercover Mosque documentary: 'British Muslims have a problem and it needs to be recognized.'[2]

Muslims or Islam?

Many observers have remarked that Muslims do not all hold the same views about what Islam teaches. Sometimes the differences in views can seem surprising, especially when particular opinions are put forward with great confidence and even with insistence that no other opinion can be countenanced. Faced by the reality of disagreements and debates between Muslims about their faith, many people – both Muslims and non-Muslims alike – can feel the need to know what Islam 'really' teaches on certain subjects. Does Islam really promote violence? Does Islam really advocate the death penalty for apostates? Does Islam really reject female circumcision? Will the real Muslim please stand up!

The primary sources of Islam are large and complex, and the process of deriving *Sharia* rulings from the source materials of the Quran and the *Sunna* is considered to be a highly skilled one, requiring long years of training, which the vast majority of Muslims are not able to undertake. This means that, from a practical point of view, it is expedient for Muslims to rely on their scholars for guidance in matters of faith. Indeed Islamic jurisprudence instructs Muslims to seek out and follow someone who is more knowledgeable about matters of faith than themselves, and to follow that person. If Muslims have questions about *Sharia* law, they are supposed to ask someone who has the required expertise.

---

1 For two initial Muslim responses, see 'Channel 4's "Dispatches: Undercover Mosque" another example of anti-Muslim hostility as discussed in forthcoming IHRC report.' The Islamic Human Rights Commission, press release January 15, 2007 <http://www.ihrc.org.uk/show. php?id=2414> (viewed 8 May 2009); and Muslim Council of Britain letter to affiliates and press release, January 15, 2007, downloaded 8 May 2009, <http://www.mcb.org.uk/downloads/ MCB%20Letter%20&%20Press%20Release.pdf>. See also 'Muslim Groups Organised Campaign to Silence Critics Over Channel 4's Dispatches,' *The Daily Pundit*, January 21, 2007, viewed 8 May 2009, <http://the-daily-pundit.blogspot.com/2007/01/muslim-groups-organised-campaignto.html>.

2 Tom Harper. 'TV "preachers of hate" escape police action'. *The Sunday Telegraph*, 20 January, 2007, viewed 8 May 2009, <http://www.telegraph.co.uk/news/uknews/1540081/TV%27 preachers-of-hate%27-escape-police-action.html>.

The modern scholar Muhammad Sa'id Buti interprets Q16:43 – 'question the people of the Remembrance, if it should be that you do not know' – as evidence that if 'someone does not know a ruling in Sacred Law or the evidence for it' they must 'follow someone who does'.[1] He has stated that a formal opinion from a scholar is as binding for the ordinary person as the words of the Quran are for the scholar.[2]

There are degrees of expertise in Islam, and even trained scholars will at times need to refer to someone more knowledgeable than themselves. For example, *Sunni* Imams in different parts of the world may refer matters they cannot resolve to Al-Azhar University in Egypt.[3]

All this helps account for the great popularity of websites such as fatwa-online.com, and TV programs where scholars offer *fatwas* in response to questions from ordinary Muslims.

In part because of the culture of reliance on the religious expertise of others, many Muslims hold views about their faith without being able to justify or give evidence for these views. They have simply taken them on trust. This lack of acquaintance with the reasons for an opinion does not seem to mean that the opinion is held with any less confidence.

Overcoming the 'need to know basis'

From a historical perspective, while there are many subjects which have been open to debate within Islam, many important issues have been resolved long ago, and were settled through a consensus developed by scholars working within various schools of Islamic law. Sunni Islam has four recognized schools of *Sharia*: Maliki, Shafi'i, Hanbali and Hanafi, each named after an Islamic scholar regarded as the school's founder. There are also various Shi'ite schools of law.

Within the range of issues which Islam has had to deal with, very many questions have been settled in such a clear and decisive way that all the classical traditions are in complete agreement. For example, all four schools of Sunni law agree that a man may marry up to four wives. However other issues can be subject to dispute and variations in opinion. In addition to this, ordinary Muslims can hold views which are different again from the rulings of jurists.

---

1 Nuh Ha Mim Keller, ed. and trans., *Reliance of the Traveller*, p.17 (§b2.1).

2 Ibid., p .20 (§b5.1).

3 A formal statement to this effect was part of a 2003 submission by the Imams of Victoria to the Victorian Civil and Administrative Tribunal, in connection with the case between the Islamic Council of Victoria and Pastors Daniel Scot and Danny Nalliah.

There are a number of complicating factors which compound the difficulties associated with the diversity of views among Muslims about Islam.

The problem of immoral teachings

The first complicating factor is the moral unacceptability of some Islamic teachings. Some rulings, which in the past were even universally accepted by Muslim scholars, can present great difficulties for Muslims living in modern society. Muslims who advocate or follow these rulings may find their faith coming under attack, and they may be pursued by the full force of the law. For example, there is a ruling in Islam that apostates should be killed, and no one who kills an apostate should be held accountable for their blood. However to promote such a belief openly in a non-Muslim society invites contempt and rejection. Anyone who kills an apostate – in a so-called 'honor killing' – risks a long sentence in prison for murder, or worse. (This risk is less in an Islamic state.) In non-Muslim countries, even advocating this doctrine could legitimately be regarded as incitement to murder, and a criminal act. Consequently, the penalty for apostasy may not be taught freely among Muslims who live in a non-Muslim society. This can mean that a group of Muslims could develop – such as recent converts – who are unfamiliar with this law.

The problem of Muhammad's example

It is not only specific Islamic rulings which risk offense in the eyes of non-Muslims. Many aspects of the life of Muhammad, or of the Quran, raise concerns. As a result there are large 'no-go' areas in Muhammad's life which, even among Muslims, only scholars know about. Such subjects could not traditionally be debated openly. For example, in the *hadiths* there are several reliable references to Muhammad instructing a woman to suckle a grown man so that he could be considered her foster son. The reason for doing this was that the man would then become someone she was allowed to be alone with, and before whom she did not have to wear the veil.[1]

In May 2007 Ezzat Attiyya, head of Al-Azhar University's Department of Hadith, issued a *fatwa* based on this tradition to enable an unrelated man and woman to work together in private. If she suckled him, he would become her foster son, and they could be together without a chaperone. This ruling, although logically consistent with the *Sunna* of

1 *Sahih Muslim.* Book of Marriage (*Kitab al-Nikah*). 1:3:3424-31.

Muhammad, caused considerable public embarrassment, and the matter was even debated in the Egyptian parliament.[1] As a result Attiyya had to face an Al-Azhar disciplinary panel.[2]

Such 'no-go' areas mean Muhammad's story gets selectively edited and re-edited in the re-telling, so many Muslims develop ill-informed understandings about his controversial acts and statements. When ignorance abounds, disputes can easily arise, and offense can all too easily be taken.

On the other hand, Muslims and others who expose such material to public scrutiny can find themselves being severely censured, whatever their motives, as Ezzat Attiyya was, because of the requirement that Muslims maintain a positive image for Islam.

The problem of historical consciousness

Another dimension of the problems of the connection between Muslims and Islam concerns the place of history in the Islamic consciousness. Like other conquering ideologies, Islam has tended to appropriate history for itself. One of the effects of this process can be the promotion of ahistorical mythologies, such as the belief that the expansion of Islam was a comparatively peaceful series of 'liberations' of grateful peoples across the Middle East.

One myth is that of the Andalusian golden age, a time when, so the story goes, Muslims lived in peaceful and admired coexistence with Christians and Jews, and did not engage in *jihad* aggression against their Christian neighbors. Although this myth has no foundation in history,[3] it can be most fervently held, and Muslims will sometimes appeal to it to counter ideological challenges.

If someone were to propose that the Quran advocates violence, or, for example, that Palestinian hostility to Israel is theologically motivated, the response may be along the lines of: 'Consider Andalusia, when Muslims lived in peace with their neighbors. History proves that Islam does not advocate violence and bears no hostility to Jews or Christians.'[4]

---

1 A report in *Al-Arabiyya* newspaper, May 16, 2007, viewed 8 May 2009, <http://www.alarabiya.net/articles/2007/05/16/34518.html#007>.

2 'Egypt: Fatwa allows breast-feeding among adults'. 21 May, 2007. *Jerusalem Post*, viewed 8 May 2009, <http://www.jpost.com/servlet/Satellite?cid=1178708655924&pagename=JPost%2FJPArticle%2FShowFull>.

3 See, for example, chapter 13 'The Andalusian Utopia', in Bat Ye'or, *Eurabia*.

4 Just such an argument was put by Bilal Cleland, spokesperson for the Islamic Council of Victoria, in a letter to the editor published in the *Australian Jewish News*, 21 February, 2003. Cleland wished to show that Muslim's present-day hostility to the Jews was because of Israel.

The problem of lawful deception

Another compounding factor is the Islamic doctrine of lawful deception, which we have already considered. This makes the problem of discerning the truth about Islamic teachings much harder. For example, if a Muslim community living in a western nation conceals some of its beliefs about *jihad*, as an exercise in self-protection, this can promote ignorance, not only among non-Muslims, but also among Muslims themselves. If Muslim leaders, who may be familiar with the basis for lawful deception, promote untruths about Islam in public forums, less knowledgeable Muslims can also fall victim to these deceptions.

We have already referred to Zachariah Matthews' lecture on the proper method for propagating Islam. Another principle he proposed in that lecture was that it can be necessary to apply a 'need to know' basis for revealing the plans of Islam, **even to Muslims**:

> **Secrets should be hidden**: The Prophet … hid the secrets of his journey and only disclosed them to those with strong ties to him. And, then **they were only told what they needed to know in order for them to act** – they were 'on a need to know' basis. Today we talk about issues that don't need to be talked about to the general public – what is needed is 'less talk and more action'.[1]

Islamic religious knowledge is not democratized in the way Biblical knowledge has been in recent centuries. In Islam certain things are just not discussed if there is no need to mention them, or it might put Islam in a bad light to do so: information about Islam is made available on a need-to-know basis.

A 'crack in the wall'?

This 'need-to-know' principle is not going unchallenged today. The increasing availability of satellite television, printed translations, internet resources, and search engines is now overthrowing traditional constraints on religious knowledge in Islam. Scholars are debating issues openly on television which in the past would never have seen the light of day.

Some Muslims will be radicalized by access to this material. Others will find cause to question their faith. Many are questioning whether the example of Muhammad is the best example after all.

---

1 Zachariah Matthews, 'The Hijrah: a necessary phase in the Dawah.' *Salam Magazine*, March/April 2001. The article is archived at <http://web.archive.org/web/20050615002854/www.famsy.com/salam/Hijrah41.htm>.

All these factors, when combined together, can accentuate the remarkable diversity of beliefs among Muslims. It can be hard to distinguish the deceiver from the deceived, and the victims of untruth from its perpetrators. Under such confused and confusing conditions, the truth is all the more precious, and seeking after it can be very costly, requiring courage, a strong will and a steadfast heart, as Pastor Damanik pointed out.

The danger of stereotyping

One of the challenges of the search for truth is to avoid stereotyping. Stereotyping is imputing (or denying) characteristics to a whole group based upon information which may be true for only a minority of the group or for none at all. We do this all the time in everyday discourse: it is a natural human tendency to generalize. However, there are risks, when considering Islam, of stereotyping Muslims with more ideological baggage – whether positive or negative – than they actually carry. On the one hand it is crucial to be wary of falsely imputing evil motives to Muslims, and on the other hand there is the danger of naïvely accepting every pleasant statement one is told.

A case study: Muslims debate female circumcision

Female circumcision is a highly sensitive topic among Muslims. Yet it has been discussed on Arab language television stations throughout the Middle East, as an issue which ordinary Muslims want to know about. A debate was held on Al-Arabiya TV on February 12, 2007 between two religious scholars, Sheikh Mahmoud Ashur, and Dr Muhammad al-Mussayar, both of Al-Azhar University, which is Sunni Islam's premier higher educational institution. The debate was recorded, and subtitled in English by the MEMRI TV project.[1]

Sheikh Mahmoud Ashur argued that 'Female circumcision is not part of Islam. Rather it is a traditional custom.' He rejected it on grounds of Islamic sources (*hadiths*), and also on medical and psychological consideration of the trauma it causes to young girls.

Dr Muhammad al-Mussayar responded, referring to reliable *hadiths* from Muslim and al-Bukhari:

> All jurisprudents, since the advent of Islam and for 14 centuries or more, are in consensus that female circumcision is permitted in Islam. But

---

1 'Al-Azhar University Scholars Argue over the Legitimacy of Female Circumcision Practiced in Egypt,' Clip #1392 Broadcast: February 12, 2007, viewed 8 May 2009, <http://www.memritv.org/clip/en/1392.htm>.

they were divided as to its status in the sharia. Some said that female circumcision is required by the sharia, just like male circumcision. Some said this is a mainstream practice, while others said that it is a noble act. But throughout the history of Islam, nobody has ever said that performing female circumcision is a crime. There has been a religious ruling on this for 14 centuries.

Much the same position was put on August 14, 2004 on Dubai TV by Dr 'Omar al-Khatib of the Dubai Ministry of Religious Endowment, who stated:

I say that whoever performs this procedure of circumcising his daughters in a legitimate way, and according to accepted religious principles – there is nothing wrong with this. Also whoever does not perform this procedure – there is nothing wrong with this either.[1]

In contrast, Aminah Assilmi, a western convert to Islam and activist for women's rights, stated on Islam Studios 'It absolutely has nothing to do with Islam. In fact, it's absolutely prohibited in Islam. And that's why it's decreasing as people are becoming more educated about Islam.' She suggested that as more Muslims read the Quran for themselves, 'this is a practice that will be abolished before long'.[2]

In June 2007, after an eleven year old Egyptian girl Budour Ahmed Shaker died as the result of a circumcision conducted under medical supervision, the mufti of Egypt, 'Ali Gomaa, issued a statement rejecting female circumcision: 'The harmful tradition of circumcision that is practiced in Egypt in our era is forbidden.'[3] The mufti explained his reasons on Egyptian TV:

... [female circumcision] is not permitted today. One may ask: 'Are the laws of God subject to change?' As I told you, there is no divine law on this matter. It is a custom, and not a religious practice. That's one thing. The second thing is that the world has changed. ... The medical knowledge at the time concluded that this cut is useful. It may have been – I wasn't alive 100 years ago. But when the current medical knowledge tells me this is disastrous, and I can see that the environment has changed – by God, how

---

1 'Dubai Government Official: Female Genital Mutilation of Daughters is Optional from the Religious Point of View,' MEMRI TV Clip #217 Broadcast: August 15, 2004, viewed 7 October 2009, <http://www.youtube.com/watch?v=jFGLqZUGeS0>.

2 Aminah Assilmi, Islam on Female Genital Mutilation, uploaded onto YouTube: <http://www.youtube.com/watch?v=QPVYxvHWVHc>, viewed 8 May 2009.

3 'Egypt mufti says female circumcision forbidden.' Reuters news alert, June 24, 2007, viewed 8 May 2009, <http://www.alertnet.org/thenews/newsdesk/L24694871.htm>.

can one avoid changing one's fatwas in order to reach the intention of the religious law, and prohibit ... female circumcision as well?[1]

A few days later on MBC TV, the Egyptian cleric Safwat Higazi responded:

> Female circumcision is allowed. It does exist in Islam. It existed before the advent of Islam, and Islam and the Prophet Muhammad have recognized it. In my opinion, it is likely that the Prophet had his daughters circumcised. ... If it reaches the point that someone prohibits something that existed in the days of the Prophet, and was not prohibited by him – this is completely unacceptable, whether it is the Mufti or anyone else.[2]

These debates illustrate four distinct strategies which are widely representative of faithful Muslims' attitudes to some of the questionable practices of the *Sharia*:

1. **Canonical support.** Some, like Muhammad al-Mussayar, 'Omar al-Khatib and Safwat Higzai understand and support the practice, accepting the traditional interpretations of the Islamic canon (Quran and *Sunna*).

2. **Canonical reform.** Others, like Mahmoud Ashur seek reasons from within the canon of Islam to reject it.

3. **Denial without evidence.** Others, like the convert Aminah Assilmi, seem to be ignorant of the authorities. Finding the practice contrary to conscience, and perhaps also just contrary to what they believe about Islam, but citing no evidence, they deny that it is a part of Islam at all.

4. **Reform by appeal to external criteria.** Some, like Mahmoud Ashur and 'Ali Gomaa appeal to criteria external to Islam, such as the modern medical findings, or human conscience.

What should non-Muslims make of debates of this kind? First, we should pay attention, and acknowledge the different views, and that a debate is going on.

We also need to understand that it can be very difficult for Muslims to make progress with issues when the *Sunna* essentially fails them as a model to follow. In the case of female circumcision, the religious evidence cannot be easily dismissed: the Islamic authorities do support

---

1 'Mufti of Egypt, Ali Gum'a, Encounters Opposition after Ruling that Female Circumcision is Prohibited,' Clip #1509 Broadcast: July 3, 2007, viewed 8 May 2009, <http://www.memritv.org/clip/en/1509.htm>.
2 Ibid.

'Omar al-Khatib, Muhammad al-Mussayar and Safwat Higzai. In essence:

- Female circumcision is described with the same word in Arabic as male circumcision. When Muhammad commended circumcision in the *hadiths*, he did not distinguish male circumcision from female circumcision.
- Although it is not in the Quran, there is clear evidence in the *hadiths* that female circumcision is assumed. In reliable *hadiths*, attributed to his wife Aisha, Muhammad stated that lawful intercourse takes place when the 'circumcised parts touch each other', implying that women are circumcised (as Aisha must have been, for her report to make sense).[1] Also Muhammad recommended, when circumcising girls, not to cut too deep, which implies he endorsed the practice.[2]
- Circumcision (of both sexes) had traditionally been regarded as at the very least 'recommended' (*sunna*) by all schools: something which gains merit if done, but is not punished if omitted.
- Apart from this, Muslim scholars and schools disagree about whether female circumcision is obligatory or optional. The Shafi'i school teaches that it is obligatory, so it not surprising that the practice is more frequent in areas where Shafi'i jurisprudence is followed, such as Egypt and Indonesia.

This continuing debate about female circumcision is a matter of the utmost importance for the human rights of millions of women and girls living under Islamic conditions. All four strategies for resolving the question deserve to be listened to.

The first, canonical support, has appalling consequences for millions of women, however sincere its advocates may be in their convictions.

The second, canonical reform, might offer hope, if someone with genuine knowledge is able to construct arguments from within Islam to reform the practice. However this requires a re-think of centuries of religious policy, and may in the end be impossible without some sleights of hand, when the evidence of the *Sunna* is clearly in opposition to the proposed reform.

---

1 When Aisha was asked about intercourse and bathing, she replied that Muhammad had said 'when the circumcised parts touch each other a bath becomes obligatory.' *Sahih Muslim.* Book of Menstruation (*Kitab al-Haid*). 1:3:684. This way of defining intercourse implies that Muhammad presupposed that both men and women would be circumcised, and also that both Muhammad and Aisha had been circumcised.

2 *Sunan Abu Dawud.* Book of General Behavior (*Kitab al-Adab*). 3:41:5251.

The third position of denial without evidence is unsustainable, and will be ineffective in the long term because it involves rejection of the truth. Policy initiatives launched by international agencies whose approach is to teach that female circumcision is not a part of Islam will ultimately be ineffective because local religious leaders will easily be able to refute their claims, citing good reasons that it **is** part of Islam. If people are to embrace reform without neglecting their faith, something better must be offered to them than ignorant denial.

Of course many Muslims are contemplating the implications of the fourth position, of reform by appeal to external criteria. This may be regarded as privileging mutable non-Islamic authorities, such as science, over the *Sunna*, which is regarded as perfect and immutable. However claiming the external criteria as a part of Islamic knowledge can minimize this difficulty.

There are a number of traps for non-Muslims in relation to an issue like this. Is a non-Muslim to accept that the practice is not a part of Islam, just because someone has told them so? This kind of unthinking response is all too common, but it is unacceptable and can easily lead to failure. It is essential to ask the 'Why' question where Islam is concerned, and to be able to weigh up the reasons given. One must ask questions like: 'Which part of Islam prohibits female circumcision?'

Another trap is to be too ready to think the worst of Muslims. Just because someone has read or been told about a *hadith* supporting female circumcision, they may leap to the conclusion that all Muslims want to circumcise their daughters and support this practice. Another mistake is to allow oneself to remain ignorant of the on-going debate, and the fact that the outcome of the debate is far from certain.

This is undoubtedly a difficult and painful debate for Muslims. Some will find it embarrassing and will only enter it reluctantly. The stakes are high, both human and theological. The ideological obstacles to relativizing Muhammad's example in the light of modern conditions are profound. Yet, for the sake of many millions of Muslims and non-Muslims alike, one can hope that the growing debates will bring positive change, and that the debates themselves will be conducted in the full light of public scrutiny.

Seek understanding, speak your mind

Muslims and non-Muslims alike are crying out for Islam to be understood. There has to be a sharp increase in Islam-literacy. However, for this to happen it is essential for non-Muslims and Muslims alike to shake off the restrictions which *Sharia* law and Islamic tradition would place upon the dissemination of knowledge about Islam. For example, Ibn Naqib, in the *Reliance of the Traveller*, cites a *hadith* 'Whoever speaks of the Book of Allah from his own opinion is in error.'[1] Whatever sense this may make within the restraints imposed by *Sharia* law, non-Muslims should not be intimidated by claims that they have no right to express opinions about Islam, the Quran and the *Sunna* of Muhammad. In this age when primary source material is available on these subjects as never before, Christians, Jews, atheists and Muslims should take every opportunity to inform themselves, and speak out their views on these matters which affect us all.

I have described some of the difficulties which Muslims are facing in coming to terms with the practice of female circumcision, and holding up the *Sunna* of Muhammad against the standards of modern medical science and contemporary ethics.

An even greater challenge faces the Muslim world in rethinking Islam's teachings concerning the treatment of non-Muslims, especially the doctrines of *jihad* and the *dhimma*. This will be the subject of the following chapters.

---

1 Nuh Ha Mim Keller, ed. and trans., *Reliance of the Traveller*, p.751.

CHAPTER 5

Muhammad against the Unbelievers

The spread of Islam has gone through several phases,
secret and then public, in Mecca and Medina.
God then authorized the faithful to defend themselves
and to fight against those fighting them,
which amounts to a right legitimized by God.
This ... is quite reasonable, and God will not hate it.
Grand Mufti of Saudi Arabia, Sheikh 'Abdul Aziz al-Sheikh,
in response to Pope Benedict's Regensburg lecture[1]

The principal concern of this book is the treatment of non-Muslims under the *Sharia*. As the life and teaching of Muhammad – the *Sunna* – is, together with the Quran, considered to be the bedrock of Islamic law, it is appropriate to consider carefully the progress of Muhammad's interactions with disbelievers. These interactions begin and end with rejection. At the start there was the rejection of Muhammad by his fellow tribes people, the pagan Arabs of Mecca, for, as the Iranian intellectual Ali Dashti put it, 'Mohammad made his way into history with empty hands and in a hostile society',[2] but by the end of the story, the tables had been turned, and it was Muhammad who became the rejecter, imposing defeat upon all who refused to accept his message.

During the twenty-three years which elapsed between the first tentative beginnings of Islam and Muhammad's death, his attitude to Christians and Jews went through a striking transformation. This was what Dashti called his 'metamorphosis':[3]

> Amicable behavior toward possessors of scriptures is recommended in several ... Meccan and early Medinan scriptures ... In the course of the Madinan decade, however ... changes occurred, and finally *sura 9* ... came down like a thunderbolt onto the heads of the scripture-possessors. These people ... were ordered ... to choose between the alternatives of conversion, payment of tribute and acceptance of inferior status, or condemnation to

---

1 'Saudi mufti defends spirit of jihad'. *Middle East Times*, September 18, 2006, viewed 20 September 2006, <http://www.metimes.com/print.php?StoryID=20060918-110403-1970r>.
2 'Ali Dashti, *Twenty Three Years*, p.8.
3 Ibid., p.82.

death. ... With the passage of years, these scripture-possessors had become the 'worst creatures' (*sura* 98, verse 5).[1]

It is the purpose of this chapter to describe this metamorphosis, and attempt to explain its inner logic. It will be suggested that out of Muhammad's bitter experiences of rejection was forged an ideology which validates dominating others and pouring rejection upon them. This will prepare the way for a consideration of the theory and practice of the treatment of Christians and Jews under Islamic law.

Historical reliability and balance

It must be acknowledged that many scholars have raised concerns about the historicity of the *hadiths* and *sira* as sources for Muhammad. One reason for this concern is that there are no surviving literary sources on Muhammad's life until more than a century after his death in 632 AD. Indeed, apart from some coins and inscriptions, the existing sources are from the ninth century or later.[2]

What is important for this study is that Islam itself has built its spiritual worldview on the foundation laid by these existing resources, late though they are, and unreliable as they may be. Muslim theologians and jurists have relied upon the historical soundness of the Islamic canon of Quran, *sira* and *hadiths* for over a thousand years. Our focus is not upon the historical Muhammad – an as yet shadowy figure – but upon the Muhammad of faith and sacred law, a theological construct whose biography has been documented in remarkable and vibrant detail. Such a focus is appropriate, because it is this figure, as defined by the canon of Islam, whose example and witness has, root and branch, grounded the whole *Sharia* system.

In introducing this chapter it may be helpful to stress that it does not attempt to be a balanced biography. Rather, it focuses upon Muhammad's experiences of, and responses to rejection. It is a series of reflections on how Muhammad dealt with those who rejected him and his message. For more information the reader may consult any one of a number of biographies.[3]

---

1 Ibid., p.84-85.

2 See the essays in Ibn Warraq, *The Quest for the Historical Muhammad*, and Ohlig and Puin's *The Hidden Origins of Islam: New Research into Its Early History*.

3 The reader can, for example, consult Dashti's *Twenty Three Years*; Lings' *Muhammad* or John Glubb's *Life and Times of Muhammad*. All biographies of Muhammad have their distinctive biases, and most are polemical to some degree, so the use of secondary sources cannot substitute for reading Ibn Ishaq's biography.

A painful start

Orphaned

Muhammad was born in c. 570 AD, into an Arab tribe in Mecca. It is recorded that his father, 'Abdullah bin 'Abd al-Muttalib, died while his wife was pregnant with Muhammad, their first born.[1] Muhammad was then fostered out to another family to be cared for in his early years. His mother died when he was six, and his powerful grandfather looked after him for a while, but then also passed away when Muhammad was eight years old. So Muhammad went to live with his father's full brother Abu Talib.

Abu Talib was not the wealthiest of the sons of 'Abd al-Muttalib, and he already had a large family of his own, so Muhammad was given the humble task of looking after his uncle's camels and sheep. From this time in his life Muhammad gained a strong sense of compassion for the poor and for orphans, and later he was to state: 'There is no prophet but has shepherded a flock', turning his lowly role into a mark of distinction.[2]

Although some of Muhammad's other uncles were wealthy, it seems they did nothing to help him. Later Muhammad would have bitter things to say about some of them. Q111 expresses contempt for one uncle, Abu Lahab. He would burn in hell, because of his contemptuous bearing. Indeed Muhammad nicknamed his uncle *Abu Lahab* 'father of flame' to indicate his intended fate.

> Perish the hands of Abu Lahab, and perish he;
> his wealth avails him not, neither what he has earned;
> he shall roast at a flaming fire
> and his wife, the carrier of the firewood,
> upon her neck a rope of palm-fibre.

When Abu Lahab's wife, Muhammad's aunt, heard these words, she retorted that she too could recite poetry:

> We reject the reprobate,
> His words we repudiate,
> His religion we loathe and hate.[3]

---

1 Guillaume, *The Life of Muhammad*, p.68-69. Ibn Kathir reports traditions that Muhammad was born before 'Abdullah's death, but gives no weight to them. (*The Life of the Prophet Muhammad*, vol.1:146-47).

2 Ibid., p.72.

3 Ibid., p.161.

An unequal marriage

As a young man, Muhammad was twenty-five, and in Khadijah's employ, when she proposed marriage to him. She was older than the future prophet, but it is unclear by how much. Varying reports say she was forty, thirty-five, twenty-eight, and even twenty-five.[1]

According to some accounts, Khadijah had her father marry them while he was drunk, lest he should refuse, and when he came to his senses he was furious to discover what had been done.[2]

In Arabian culture, a man had to pay a bride price for a bride, after which she was considered a chattel, even to the extent that a wife formed part of a man's estate, and his male heir could marry her if he wished. In contrast to the usual situation, Khadijah was powerful and wealthy and Muhammad poor with few prospects. Ibn Ishaq calls her a woman 'of dignity and wealth'[3] among the Quraysh. Khadijah had also been married twice before. The contrast between the usual understanding of marriage and the arrangement between Khadijah and Muhammad was striking.

A bereaved parent

Khadijah and Muhammad were to have six (by some accounts seven) children together. Muhammad had three (or by some accounts, four) sons, but they all died young, leaving him no male heirs. This was no doubt another source of disappointment in Muhammad's family arrangements.

In conclusion, in Muhammad's family circumstances there are several potentially painful features including being orphaned and losing his grandfather, becoming a poor dependent relation, having to be married by a drunk father-in-law, and becoming the target of hostility from powerful relatives. The great exceptions to the pattern of rejection in Muhammad's story were the care shown to him by his uncle Abu Talib, and Khadijah's choice of him for a marriage partner, which rescued him from poverty.

---

1 Ibn Kathir in his *Life of the Prophet Muhammad* vol.1, p.191, reports that Khadijah was 35, and 'it is also said that she was 25'. Glubb (*The Life and Times of Muhammad*, p.75) reports a tradition that she was 28. Khadijah's age when she died is also unclear: Ibn Kathir reports a tradition that she was 65 or 50, 'the latter being more likely'. An age at death of 50 would imply that Khadijah was about 26 at the time of their marriage. The younger age is also consistent with Ibn Ishaq's report that she bore seven children to Muhammad (Guillaume, *The Life of Muhammad*, p.83).

2 Ibn Kathir, *Life of the Prophet Muhammad*, vol.1, p.192.

3 Guillaume, *The Life of Muhammad*, p.82.

A new religion is founded

When Muhammad was around forty years old, he began to experience visitations from a spirit he identified as the angel Jibril (Gabriel of the Bible).

Self-rejection

Muhammad became extremely distressed at these visitations, and wondered whether he was possessed. He even contemplated suicide: 'I will go to the top of the mountain and throw myself down that I may kill myself and gain rest.'[1] His wife Khadijah comforted him in his great anxiety and took him to her cousin, Waraqa, a Christian, who pronounced that he was a prophet, and no madman.

Later, when the revelations ceased for a time, Muhammad was again beset with suicidal thoughts, but each time he was about to throw himself off a mountain, Jibril would appear and reassure him: 'O Muhammad! You are indeed Allah's Messenger in truth.'[2] It seems Muhammad feared being rejected as a fraud, for in one of the early *suras* Allah assures Muhammad that he had not and would not disown him:

> The Lord has neither forsaken thee nor hates thee and the Last shall be better for thee than the First.
> Thy Lord shall give thee, and thou shalt be satisfied.
> Did He not find thee an orphan and shelter thee? (Q93:3-6)

The Muslim community grew slowly at first, Khadijah becoming the first convert. The next was Muhammad's young cousin 'Ali, who had been brought up in Muhammad's own house. Others followed, mainly from among the poor, slaves or freed slaves. They were attracted to Muhammad's message of justice, care for the poor and orphans, and divine punishment of arrogant rich oppressors.

Muhammad's own tribe

At first the new religion was kept secret by its followers, but after three years Muhammad received word from Allah to make it public. He did this by convening a family conference at which he invited his relatives into Islam. His cousin 'Ali declared his hand, saying 'O prophet of God, I will be your helper in this matter.'[3]

---

1 Ibid., p.106.
2 *Sahih al-Bukhari*. The Book of the Interpretation of Dreams. 9:91:6982; Guillaume, *The Life of Muhammad*, p.106.
3 Guillaume, *The Life of Muhammad*, p.118.

His fellow Quraysh tribespeople of Mecca were at first disposed to listen to Muhammad, but only until he began to disparage their gods. After this the Muslims became what Ibn Ishaq called 'a despised minority'.[1] Tensions were high, and some of Muhammad's followers came to blows with the idol worshippers.

As opposition mounted, Muhammad's uncle Abu Talib protected him. When others in Mecca approached saying 'O Abu Talib, your nephew has cursed our gods, insulted our religion, mocked our way of life … either you must stop him or you must let us get at him …', Abu Talib put them off.[2]

The disbelieving Arabs began to attack Muslims, beating them and 'seducing them from their religion'.[3] They also instituted an economic and social boycott against Muhammad's clan, forbidding commerce and intermarriage with them. There was resentment against Muhammad because of the division he had brought to the Quraysh tribe, and this became widely known and talked about throughout Arabia. Although Muhammad was protected by his uncle, the Quraysh would mock him, playing upon his name by calling him *mudhammam* 'reprobate', as his aunt had done in her ditty.

Despite all these measures, Islam continued to grow, although slowly and mainly among the poor. Only a few people of influence believed in Muhammad, including 'Umar, his uncle Hamza, and the merchant Abu Bakr.

Because the Muslims were mostly poor people, they were especially vulnerable. Ibn Ishaq summarizes their treatment at the hands of the Quraysh:

> Then the Quraysh showed their enmity to all those who followed the apostle; every clan which contained Muslims attacked them, imprisoning them, and beating them, allowing them no food or drink, and exposing them to the burning heat of Mecca, so as to seduce them from their religion. Some gave way under pressure of persecution, and others resisted them, being protected by God.[4]

Muhammad's person did not escape the dangers and insults: he had dirt thrown over him, and even animal intestines when he was praying.

---

1 Ibid., p.118.
2 Ibid., p.119.
3 Ibid., p.120.
4 Ibid., p.143.

Muhammad's influential supporters did what they could. Bilal, a slave, became a Muslim, and was being tortured by his owner, in order to make him leave Islam. Bilal was crying out 'One! One! [god]' When Abu Bakr saw what was happening he persuaded Bilal's owner to exchange Bilal for a heathen slave. Abu Bakr freed a number of other Muslim slaves as well.

When the persecutions did not let up, eighty-three Muslim men and their families emigrated to Christian Abyssinia for refuge, where they found protection.

Self-doubt

At one point Muhammad appeared to waver from his monotheism, under pressure from the Quraysh. They had offered to him a deal whereby they would worship Allah if he worshipped their gods. This he would not accept, receiving the verses of Q109:6 'To you your religion, to me my religion!' However Muhammad must have hesitated, for al-Tabari records that as he was receiving Q53, there were 'revealed' to him what came to be known as the 'Satanic verses' in reference to the goddesses al-Lat, al-Uzza and Manat: 'these are the exalted *gharaniq* (cranes) whose intercession is approved'.

When they heard this verse, the heathen Quraysh were delighted and began to worship with the Muslims. However the angel Jibril came and rebuked Muhammad, and the verse from Satan was abrogated. Muhammad made it known that the verse had been withdrawn, which attracted even more scorn from the Quraysh, so 'they became more violently hostile to the Muslims and the apostle's followers'.[1]

After this, Muhammad received the following verse:

> We sent not ever any Messenger or Prophet before thee, but that Satan cast into his fancy, when he was fancying; but Allah annuls what Satan casts, then Allah confirms His signs – surely Allah is all-knowing, All-wise. (Q22:52).

Here again we see Muhammad taking a potential cause for shame, and turning it into a mark of distinction: all the prophets, he had said, were shepherds before him, and now he announced that all the prophets had also been led astray by Satan at some point. So this lapse was not an embarrassment, but a sign of his authenticity!

---

1 Ibid., p.167.

In the face of mockery and charges that he was a faker, which stung him deeply, Muhammad received verses from Allah, validating him, and stating that his character was remarkable, he was not in error, but a man of integrity:

> ... thou art not, by the blessing of the Lord, a man possessed. ... surely thou art upon a mighty morality ... (Q68:1-4)

> By the Star when it plunges, your comrade is not astray, neither errs, nor speaks he out of caprice. (Q53:1-3)

Also, a variety of traditions report that Muhammad came to believe in the superiority of his race, tribe, clan and parentage. This was apparently in reference to claims which criticized his ancestry:

> I am Muhammad ... And whenever people divided off into two groups God placed me in the better. I was born from my own parents and was tainted by none of the debauchery of the era before Islam. I was the product of true marriage, not fornication, right down from Adam to my father and my mother. I am the best of you in spirit and the best of you in parentage.[1]

> I was sent on through the best of generations of humankind, age after age, until I received my mission in the century in which I lived.[2]

> From mankind he chose the Arabs and from them Mudar. From Mudar he chose Quraysh [Muhammad's tribe] and from them the Banu Hashim [Muhammad's clan]. From Banu Hashim he chose me. I am the choicest of the chosen; so whoever loves the Arabs, it is through loving me that he loves them.[3]

> Gabriel said to me, 'I searched the earth from east to west but found no man superior to Muhammad; and I searched the earth from east to west but found no tribe superior to the Banu Hashim.'[4]

At this point the focus was on validating Muhammad's call and character in the face of denigration from the Quraysh. The doctrine of the perfection of Muhammad's example for all Muslims to follow was to be revealed later, in the verses from the Medina period.

More experiences of rejection

Things had not been going well for some time when Muhammad lost both his wife Khadijah and his uncle Abu Talib in the same year. These

---

1 Ibn Kathir, *The Life of the Prophet Muhammad*, vol.1:135.
2 Ibid., vol.1:136.
3 Ibid., vol.1:138.
4 Ibid., vol.1:138.

were huge blows. He had depended upon the comfort and support of Khadijah, and the protection of his uncle. After this the Quraysh were emboldened to be even more hostile against him.

Arab society was based around alliances and client relationships. The way to find security was to come under the protection of someone more powerful than yourself. With dangers to him and his followers increasing, and having been rejected by his own tribe, the Quraysh, Muhammad went out to seek alternative protectors elsewhere.

Muhammad's method of recruiting support was to attend fairs, and to invite the visiting tribes into Islam. He would declare that he was a prophet, and call them to become believers and provide protection for him until Allah was ready to make his message clear.[1] He approached one tribe, offering them the prospect of future victory and success over other Arab tribes, but they replied: 'I suppose you want us to protect you from the Arabs with our breasts and then if God gives you victory someone else will reap the benefit! Thank you, No!'[2]

Muhammad also went alone to Ta'if to seek protection against his own tribe, the Quraysh. The people of Ta'if mocked him cruelly. One of their leaders replied with contempt, 'Could not God have found someone better than you to send?' Another added, 'By God, don't let me ever speak to you. If you are an apostle from God as you say you are, you are far too important for me to reply to, and if you are lying against God it is not right that I should speak to you.'[3] Muhammad asked them not to tell anyone else what they had said to him, but they ignored this request, and he was chased away by a mob.

Things were not looking good for Muhammad. Yet eventually he did manage to find a community who was willing to protect him. These were Arabs from Medina, a city where many Jews also lived.

New allies and flight from Mecca

During an annual fair at Mecca, a representative group of visitors from Medina pledged loyalty and obedience to Muhammad, agreeing to live by his message of monotheism. On going back to Medina they established weekly Friday prayers there. They also foreswore theft, fornication, infanticide and slander, but they did not yet promise the protection Muhammad had been seeking.

---

1 Guillaume, *The Life of Muhammad*, p.194.
2 Ibid., p.195.
3 Ibid., p.192.

This first pledge came to be known as the 'Pledge of Women' because no commitment to fight was made. However at the next year's fair a larger group of Medinans pledged the protection which Muhammad had been seeking so urgently. The Medinans, who came to be known as *Ansar*, or 'helpers', undertook to wage 'war in complete obedience to the apostle':[1]

> When God gave permission to his apostle to fight, the second 'Aqaba (pledge) contained conditions involving war which were not in the first act of fealty. **Now they bound themselves to war against all and sundry for God and his apostle,** while he promised them for faithful service thus the reward of paradise.[2]

After this, a decision was taken for the Muslims to migrate to Medina to form a political safe-haven, under the protection of the Ansar of Medina. Muhammad was the last to leave Mecca, together with Abu Bakr, escaping from his would-be assassins in the middle of the night through a back window of Abu Bakr's house. When they arrived in Medina Muhammad was able to proclaim his message unhindered, and virtually all the Medina Arabs converted to Islam within the first year. Muhammad was by this time just over fifty-two years old.

During the Meccan years, we find that Muhammad was rejected by his own family, and by his own tribe, the Quraysh. With few exceptions, only the humble poor believed in him, and he was mocked, threatened, humiliated and attacked by the rest.

Muhammad had been very unsure of himself at first, fearing rejection of his sense of prophetic calling. He even wavered at one point, seeming to accept the Quraysh's gods in the Satanic Verses episode. He needed (and received) Allah's repeated reassurance that he would not be rejected. Gradually, despite the rejections of his own and other tribes, Muhammad acted with determined perseverance and acquired a group of dedicated followers.

Rejection and the Meccan revelations

Peaceful witness?

Many writers have claimed that Muhammad's decade of witness in Mecca was peaceful. In one sense this was true. There was as yet no doctrine of violent striving, the call to war had not yet been revealed,

---

1 Ibid., p.208.
2 Ibid., p.208.

and the lives and property of unbelievers had not yet been declared to be *halal*, or 'licit' for Muslims to take.

However it would be wrong to conclude that Muhammad's message in Mecca was simply one of love and peace. Although no physical violence is commanded, it was certainly contemplated, and the early revelations denounce the Quraysh tribespeople in terrifying language, announcing dire torments for rejecters in the hereafter.

The Meccan message in essence was that those who did not heed Muhammad's warnings would be made to pay dearly for their mistake. For example, concerning Umayya bin Khalaf, who reviled Muhammad whenever he saw him:[1]

> Woe unto every backbiter, slanderer,
> who has gathered riches and counted them over
> thinking his riches have made him immortal!
> No indeed; he shall be thrust into the Crusher;
> and what shall teach thee what is the Crusher?
> The Fire of Allah kindled roaring over the hearts
> covered down upon them, in columns outstretched. (Q104)

In one of the earliest *suras* to be revealed, Muhammad berates a wealthy 'miser' who was calling his warnings 'lies':

> … as for him who is a miser, and self-sufficient,
> and cries 'lies' to the reward most fair,
> We shall surely ease him to the Hardship;
> his wealth shall not avail him when he perishes. …
> Now I have warned you of a Fire that flames,
> whereat none but the most wretched shall be roasted,
> even he who cried 'lies', and turned away … (Q92:8-18)

Concerning those who alleged that Muhammad was inventing his revelations:

> Upon the day when the heaven spins dizzily
> and the mountains are in motion,
> woe that day unto those that cry 'lies',
> such as play at plunging,
> the day when they shall be pitched into the fire of hell:
> 'This is the fire that you cried 'lies' to!
> What, is this magic, [i.e. fake] or is it you that do not see?
> Roast in it! And bear you patiently, or bear not patiently,

---

1 Ibid., p.162.

equal it is to you: you are only being recompensed for that you were
working.' (Q52:9-16)

Concerning those who accused Muhammad of sorcery and rejected his
signs (Q54:2, 42):

Nay, but the Hour is their tryst,
and the Hour is very calamitous and bitter.
Surely the sinners are in error and insanity!
The day when they are dragged on their faces into the Fire:
'Taste now the touch of Hell.' (Q54:46-48)

Concerning those who refused to accept that Muhammad was a 'warner'
sent from Allah:

And for those who disbelieve in their Lord
there awaits the chastisement of Hell – an evil homecoming!
When they are cast into it they will hear it sighing,
the while it boils and wellnigh bursts asunder with rage.
As often as a troop is cast into it, its keepers ask them,
'Came there no warner to you?'
They say, 'Yes indeed, a warner came to us;
but we cried lies, saying,
"Allah as not sent down anything; you are only in great error."'
They also say, 'If we had only heard, or had understood,
we would not have been of the inhabitants of the Blaze.'
So they confess their sins.
Curse the inhabitants of the Blaze! (Q67:6-11).

The Meccan al-Nadr bin Harith used to mock Muhammad by
following up his preaching to assemblies with legend-telling. He called
Muhammad's message plagiarized fairy-tales, but Allah had this to say
about him:[1]

When our signs are recited to him, he says,
'Fairy-tales of the ancients!' ...
No indeed; but upon that day they shall be veiled from their Lord,
then they shall roast in Hell.
Then it shall be said to them, 'This is that you cried "lies" to.' (Q83:13-
17)

Concerning others who had accused Muhammad of being mad,
possessed or a conveyer of fairy tales:

[Allah speaking to Muhammad:]
... thou are not ... a man possessed.

---

1 Ibid., p.162.

… thou shalt see, and they will see,
which of you is the demented. …
So obey thou not those who cry 'lies'.
They wish that thou shouldst compromise, then they would compromise.
And obey thou not every mean swearer, backbiter,
going about with slander, hindered of good,
guilty aggressor, coarse-grained, moreover ignoble,
because he has wealth and sons.
When Our signs are recited to him,
he says 'Fairy-tales of the ancients!'
We shall brand him upon the snout![1] (Q68:2-16)

Here the Quran speaks against those who were wealthy and had sons (in contrast to Muhammad himself), and were calling Muhammad a liar. Allah will brand such a person on the nose, and then all will see who the liar really is!

One of the essential functions of the Meccan judgment verses in the Quran was to vindicate Muhammad in the face of rejection from the Quraysh Arabs. This comes into stark focus when Muhammad says that those who laughed at the Muslims will get their comeuppance. The believers, sitting back drinking wine in luxury on their couches in paradise will laugh when they gaze down at the unbelievers roasting in hellfire:

Behold, the sinners were laughing at the believers,
when they passed them by winking at one another,
and when they returned to their people they returned blithely,
and when they saw them they said, 'Lo, these men are astray!'
So today [i.e. sometime in the future in paradise] the believers are
laughing at the unbelievers, upon couches gazing.
Have the unbelievers been rewarded what they were doing? (Q83:29-36)

Already a characteristic of the Meccan period, the judgment theme was continued by Muhammad into Medina, where he announced a day of reckoning, and contrasts the torments of the wicked with the joys of those who 'strive':

Faces on that day humbled, labouring, toilworn,
roasting at a scorching fire, watered at a boiling fountain,
no food for them but cactus thorn unfattening, unappeasing hunger.

Faces on that day jocund, with their striving well-pleased,
in a sublime Garden … (Q88:2-7)

---

1 Arberry has 'muzzle'.

Such messages undoubtedly stoked the fires of division and conflict in Mecca. Muhammad's announcements of hellfire were not merely general warnings to unjust people: they rejected and specifically damned identifiable individuals in Muhammad's community. The pagans did not like what they were hearing.

Forewarned in Mecca

Not only did Muhammad preach eternal judgment, Ibn Ishaq records that it was early in the Meccan period that Muhammad first foreshadowed his future use of violence. The men of Mecca were insulting him when Muhammad turned and rebuked them: 'Will you listen to me, O Quraysh? By Him who holds my life in His hand, I bring you slaughter.' Ibn Ishaq reports that the mockers were intimidated by this response, and began to speak more kindly to him, saying 'you are not so violent'.[1]

Later, just before Muhammad fled to Medina, a group of Quraysh came to him and confronted him with the charge that he was threatening to kill those who rejected him: 'Muhammad alleges that … if you do not follow him you will be slaughtered, and when you are raised from the dead you will be burned in the fire of hell.' Muhammad confessed this was correct: 'I do say that. You are one of them,' and threw dust on their heads.[2]

These two traditions indicate that even before migrating to Medina, Muhammad was contemplating taking up the sword. Ibn Ishaq said of the Meccans at this time: 'they knew that he had decided to fight them'.[3] However Muhammad as yet had found no allies to support him. He was too weak to move to the next phase of his program.

The first verses of the Quran sent down about fighting were received as Muhammad was being driven out of Mecca:[4]

> **Leave is given to those who fight because
> they were wronged** – surely Allah is able to help them –
> who were expelled from their habitations without right,

---

1 Guillaume, *The Life of Muhammad*, p.131.

2 Ibid., p.222.

3 Ibid., p.221.

4 According to Ibn Kathir (*Tafsir*, vol.6, p.582) this verse was sent down when Muhammad was driven out of Mecca. However Ibn Ishaq locates the sending down of this verse to before the migration (Guillaume, *The Life of Muhammad*, pp.212-13), stating that the migration only took place after the permission to fight was given.

except to say 'Our Lord is Allah.' ...
Assuredly Allah will help him who helps Him ... (Q22:39-40)

For the battles ahead, Muhammad would rely on the forces which began to gather about him in Medina. Ibn Kathir's commentary on these verses reflects a widely held view that Allah was wise to withhold the command to fight until the security of Medina was established:

> **Allah prescribed *Jihad* at an appropriate time,** because when they were in Makkah [Mecca], the idolaters outnumbered them by more than ten to one. Were they to engage in fighting at that time, the results would have been disastrous. ... [but] when they settled at al-Madinah and the Messenger of Allah joined them there, and they gathered around him and lent him their support, and they had a place where Islam prevailed, and a stronghold to which they could retreat; then Allah prescribed *jihad* against the enemy, and this was the first ayah [verse] to be revealed for it.[1]

Out of the crucible of rejection and persecution in Medina came the Muslim community's resolve – confirmed by divine mandate – to go to war against their opponents. Ibn Ishaq sums up this change:

> When Quraysh became insolent towards God and rejected His gracious purpose, accused His prophet of lying, and ill treated and exiled those who served Him and proclaimed His unity, believed in His prophet, and held fast to His religion, He gave permission to His apostle to fight and to protect himself against those who wronged them and treated them badly.[2]

Winners and losers

The Islamic concept of success and the language of winners and losers, first begin to emerge as themes in the *suras* of the Quran in the middle of Muhammad's thirteen years in Mecca. For example, the Quran warns that those who care for their relatives and the vulnerable will do well, receiving Allah's favor:

> And give the kinsman his right, and the needy, and the traveller; that is better for those who desire Allah's Face: those – they are the prosperers. (Q30:38)

Around this time, in repeated references to the conflicts between Moses and the Egyptian idolaters, the Quran describes the outcomes in terms of winners and losers (e.g. Q20:64,69; Q26:40-44; Q29:39).

However it is only towards the end of the Meccan period that Muhammad applies the terminology of success to the struggle between

---

1 Ibn Kathir, *Tafsir*, vol.6, p.584.
2 Guillaume, *The Life of Muhammad*, p.212.

himself and his opponents. In the tenth *sura*, from the period just before the migration to Medina, Muhammad declares that those who reject Allah's revelations will be losers:

> The truth has come to thee from thy Lord; so be not of the doubters, nor be of those who cry lies to Allah's signs so as to be of the losers. (Q10:95)

Muhammad's *fitna* worldview

The Arabic word *fitna* 'trial, persecution, temptation' is of crucial importance in understanding Muhammad's metamorphosis, which was one of the spiritual fruits of the formative Meccan period. The word is derived from *fatana* 'to turn away from, to tempt, seduce or subject to trials'.[1] The base meaning is to prove a metal by fire. *Fitna* can include either temptation or trial, including both positive and negative inducements, up to and including torture. It could encompass seducing someone, or tearing them limb from limb.

Fitna became a key concept in theological reflection upon the early Muslim community's experiences with unbelievers. The charge of Muhammad against the Quraysh was that they had subjected him and the rest of the Muslims to *fitna* – including insult, slander, torture, exclusion, economic pressures, and other temptations – in order to get them to leave Islam or to dilute its claims.

Ibn Kathir reports that after the migration to Medina, the first verses revealed concerning fighting made clear that **the whole purpose** of fighting and killing was to eliminate *fitna*, because it could cause Muslims to turn away from their faith:[2]

> And fight in the way of Allah with those who fight with you,
> but aggress not: Allah loves not the aggressors.
> And slay them wherever you come upon them,
> and expel them from where they expelled you;
> **persecution (*fitna*) is more grievous than slaying**
> ....
> **Fight them, til there is no persecution (*fitna*)**;
> and the religion is Allah's;
> then if they give over [i.e. cease their disbelief and opposition to Islam],
> there shall be no enmity save for evildoers.' (Q2:190-93)

---

1 E.W. Lane, *An Arabic-English Lexicon*. Book 6, p.2334ff.
2 Ibn Kathir, *Tafsir*, vol. 1, p.527. Ibn Ishaq (Guillaume, *The Life of Muhammad*, p.213) links this verse to the second pledge in Mecca, the first time fighting was endorsed by Muhammad.

The idea that *fitna* of Muslims was 'more grievous than slaying' proved to be a significant one. The same phrase would be revealed again after an attack on a Meccan caravan (Q2:217) during the sacred month (a period during which Arab tribal traditions prohibited raiding). It implied, at the very least, that shedding the blood of infidels is a lesser thing than a Muslim being led astray from their faith.

The other significant phrase in this passage from Q2 is 'fight them until there is no *fitna*'. This too was revealed more than once, the second time being after the battle of Badr, during the second year in Medina (Q8:39).

These *fitna* phrases, each revealed twice in the Quran, established the principle that *jihad* was justified by the existence of an obstacle to people entering Islam, or of inducements to Muslims to abandon their faith. However grievous it might be to fight others and shed their blood, undermining or obstructing Islam was worse.

Some Islamic jurists maintained a more limited and narrower interpretation, namely that '*fitna* is worse than slaughter' simply meant fighting should continue 'until no Muslim is persecuted so that he abandons his religion'.[1] However most extended the concept of *fitna* to include even the mere existence of unbelief, so the phrase could be interpreted as 'unbelief is worse than killing'.[2] Thus Ibn Kathir equated *fitna* with what he called 'committing disbelief' and 'associating' (i.e. polytheism), alongside hindering people from following Islam:

> Since *jihad* involves killing and shedding of blood of men, Allah indicated that these men [i.e. polytheists] are **committing disbelief** in Allah, associating with Him (in the worship) and hindering from His path, and this is a much greater evil and more disastrous than killing.[3]

Understood this way, the phrase '*fitna* is worse than killing' became a universal mandate to fight and kill all infidels who rejected Muhammad's message, whether they were interfering with Muslims or not. Merely for unbelievers to 'commit disbelief' – to use Ibn Kathir's phrase – was a greater evil than their being killed.

On this understanding the concept of *jihad* warfare to extend the dominance of Islam was based. Thus Ibn Kathir, when commenting on Q2 and Q8, said that the command to *fight* means to go to war 'so that

---

1 Ibn Kathir, *Tafsir*, vol. 4, p.314.

2 Ibid., vol. 1, p.529.

3 Ibid., vol. 1, p.528.

there is no more *Kufr* (disbelief)'[1] and the Quranic statements 'and the religion is Allah's' (Q2:193) or 'the religion is Allah's entirely' (Q8:39) mean 'So that the religion of Allah [i.e. Islam] becomes dominant above all other religions.'[2]

The renowned modern jurist Muhammad Taqi Usmani (b. 1943) reports that religious authorities have universally accepted that *jihad* is warfare to make Islam dominant:

> ... the purpose of **Jehad ... aims at breaking the grandeur of unbelievers and establish that of Muslims**. As a result no one will dare to show any evil designs against Muslim on one side and on the other side, people subdued from the grandeur of Islam will have an open mind to think over the blessings of Islam. ... **I think that all Ulema (religious scholars) have established the same concept about the purpose of Jehad**.[3]

It is significant that Islamic sacred history traces the beginning of the Islamic calendar from the migration to Medina, the point at which Allah declared an end to tolerance of opposition. This was a defining moment in the establishment of Islam, after which forbearance of *fitna* would no longer be an option: *jihad* had been declared.

Implications for non-Muslims

For our purposes, what is important is that the key theological features of the treatment of non-Muslims under Islam came to be grounded in events in Muhammad's story, which took place around the migration of the *Umma*, the Muslim community, to Medina. The root for the rejection of non-believers in the *Sharia* can be found in Muhammad's own emotional worldview, demonstrated by his responses to rejection.

However as yet the People of the Book were hardly in Muhammad's focus. Repeatedly Christians he met would affirm and support his prophetic calling.[4] Nevertheless, in Medina, where both Judaism and Christianity came to be forcefully identified as forms of 'association' or 'polytheism' (*shirk*), they too were subjected to the destructive and retributive force of these anti-*fitna* verses. The doctrine of subjugating the People of the Book through *jihad* became an outworking of the

---

1 Ibid., vol. 4, p.315. See also Q48:28.

2 Ibid., vol. 1, p.531.

3 M. Taqi Usmani, *Islam and Modernism*, pp.133–34. Usmani is deputy chair of the Islamic Fiqh (Jurisprudence) Academy of the Organization of the Islamic Conference, and presided for 20 years as a *Sharia* judge on Pakistan's Supreme Court.

4 In addition to Waraqa, his wife Khadijah's cousin, other Christians who believed in Muhammad included a deputation of Ethiopian Christians said to have come from Najran, and the Christian slave 'Addas in Ta'if. (Guillaume, *The Life of Muhammad*, pp.83, 179, 193).

command that Islam should, in the words of Ibn Kathir, become 'dominant above all other religions' (Q48:48), so that the success of Islam would be clearly manifest in the world.

We can observe a trend in Muhammad's treatment of the pagan Arabs whereby a sense of offense at the trials they heaped upon the Muslims is used to justify the doctrine that the very existence of disbelief constitutes *fitna*. The same trend comes to be applied to the People of the Book. As rejecters of Islam, they become permanently marked as guilty, and deserving to be treated as inferior.

Other rejection reactions

In the story of Muhammad's prophetic career, we have observed a range of responses to rejection. Early on Muhammad shows self-rejecting reactions, including suicidal thoughts, fear that he was possessed, and despair.

There are also self-validating reactions as if to counter the fear of rejection, such as the very claim that he was a prophet; assertions that Allah would punish his enemies in hell; claims to cover points of potential embarrassment, such as Muhammad's reports that all prophets had been shepherds and had all been led astray at some point by Satan; verses sent down from Allah which declared that Muhammad had an excellent character; and other verses which declared that those who followed Muhammad's revelations would be winners in this life and the next.

Finally however, aggressive responses came to dominate. These represent the right to pursue *jihad* as retribution, and the elimination of *fitna* and the continued rejection it represented.

Muir aptly summarized the use made by Muhammad of the Muslims' early experiences of rejection:

> Persecution, though it may sometimes have deterred the timid from joining his ranks, was eventually of unquestionable service to Mahomet. It furnished a plausible excuse for casting aside the garb of toleration; for opposing force to force against those who 'obstructed the ways of the Lord;' and at last for the compulsory conversion of unbelievers.[1]

---

1 William Muir, *The Life of Mahomet*, p.115.

Retribution from Medina

The story of Muhammad's military ascendancy in Medina has been told in many places, and I do not propose to focus on it here. In essence, Muhammad engaged in a series of campaigns and battles against the Quraysh, which ultimately led to his triumphant return to Mecca, and then against other neighboring Arab tribes. Eventually it became obligatory for every pagan Arab to accept Islam or face the sword.

In pursuing his campaign against the Meccans, Muhammad progressively set aside all restraints which stood in the way of total victory. Restrictions on fighting in certain months were abandoned. Muhammad also set aside treaties which had been contracted with the Meccans, and verses from Allah were produced to justify this. An early principle that fighting should only be against those who had fought against Muslims[1] was revised: Allah revealed other verses which allowed Muslims to initiate fighting against polytheists, and evidence of hostility or oppression was no longer needed.[2]

A doctrine was announced promising eternal rewards in paradise for Muslim *jihad* fighters who died in battle, along with regulations for dividing up the booty (Muhammad's share was a fifth). Old family ties were discounted, as the Muslim community was trained to accept that their only allegiance was to Allah, to Allah's prophet and the *Umma*.

Before we tackle the subject of Muhammad's evolving relationship with the Jews, there are some events from this period to consider which contribute to the evolving understanding of *jihad*.

Striving against the Arabs

Fighting in the sacred month

Muhammad's cousin 'Abdullah ibn Jahsh had gone out from Medina on an expedition to find out what the Quraysh were up to. He reported back, saying that, although it was the sacred month, he had taken it upon himself to attack the Quraysh's caravan, killing some of them, capturing others, and taking merchandise as booty. Although 'Abdullah ibn Jahsh had been anxious about how Muhammad would receive this news, the following verse was received:

---

1 'And fight in the way of Allah with those who fight with you, but aggress not: Allah loves not the aggressors.' (Q2:190)

2 See Q9:5, 29; Mark Durie, 'The Creed of the Sword', p.119.

They will question thee concerning the holy month, and fighting in it.
Say: 'Fighting in it is a heinous thing,
but to bar from Allah's way, and disbelief in Him,
and the Holy Mosque, and to expel its people from it –
that is more heinous in Allah's sight;
and persecution (*fitna*) is more heinous than slaying.' (Q2:217)

What this says is that, however bad it was to violate the traditional truce of the sacred month, the persecutions which the Meccans had directed against the Muslims were worse, and killing the Meccans was not as bad as what the Meccans had done to the Muslims.

Consider also the collective nature of this perspective: while many individuals had participated in abusing Muhammad in Mecca, the principle of retribution was enacted against all Meccans collectively. From this point on, raids against the Meccans' trading routes provided a lucrative source of wealth for the Muslims in Medina.

Victory at Badr

Another key moment comes when Muhammad reacts to the victory after the first major confrontation between the Muslims and the Meccans, at the battle of Badr. The Muslims had gone out in overwhelming force to attack a Meccan caravan, but the Meccans had brought in reinforcements. Nevertheless the Muslims won a great victory. This was the first time that Muhammad got to wreak revenge on his former adversaries from the Quraysh.

A telling incident was Muhammad's treatment of 'Uqba, who had earlier thrown camel dung and intestines on him. 'Uqba was captured at Badr, and pleaded for his life saying 'But who will look after my children, O Muhammad?' The answer was 'Hell!', and then Muhammad had 'Uqba killed.[1]

The bodies of the killed Meccans were thrown into a pit, and Muhammad went to the pit in the middle of the night to mock them, calling them 'people of the pit'. In the Meccan *suras* Allah had warned the Quraysh that in the afterlife Muhammad would be vindicated, so Muhammad called out to the bodies: 'O people of the pit … You called me a liar when others believed me; you cast me out when others took me in; you fought against me when others fought on my side.' Then he asked them: 'Have you found what Allah threatened is true? For I have found that what my Lord promised me is true.' His companions, overhearing

---

1 Guillaume, *The Life of Muhammad*, p.308.

Muhammad, asked him: 'Are you calling to dead bodies?' He replied that the slain Quraysh now knew that what Allah had warned them had come true, and 'You cannot hear what I say better than they, but they cannot answer me.'[1]

These incidents show that Muhammad was savoring retribution against those who had rejected him. He insisted on having the last word.

The conquest of Mecca

When Muhammad conquered Mecca he discouraged slaughter, saying that his followers should fight only if they were resisted. However there was a small hit-list of people to be killed under all circumstances. Three were apostates, two (one a woman) were people who had insulted Muhammad in Mecca, and two were slave girls who used to sing satirical songs about him. (A few of these targeted individuals later managed to escape execution by converting and obtaining immunity.)[2]

What is striking about the Meccan hit-list is that it reflects Muhammad's revulsion for *fitna*, enticement of Muslims from their faith. The apostates embodied the threat of *fitna*, for they were witness to the possibility of leaving Islam, while those who mocked or insulted Muhammad were dangerous because they had the power to undermine the faith of others. Not only in Mecca, but also Medina, those who mocked Muhammad seemed to be at the top of his assassination list.

Apostates mutilated and killed

Some Arab shepherds had become Muslims, but later they renounced Islam and killed the Muslim who was with them. Muhammad had them captured and brought to him. Their eyes were put out with heated iron, and their hands and feet were cut off. Muhammad commanded that they be left in the sun until they died.[3] This was in accordance with the Quran:

> This is the recompense of those who fight against Allah and His
> Messenger, and hasten about the earth, to do corruption there:
> they shall be slaughtered, or crucified, or their hands and feet shall
> alternately be struck off [i.e. right hand, left foot],
> or they shall be banished from the land. (Q5:33-34)

---

1 Ibid., p.305-6.

2 Ibid., p.550-1.

3 *Sahih al-Bukhari*. The Book of Medicine, 7:76:5727, and The Book of Commentary, 6:65:4610; *Sahih Muslim* The Book Pertaining to the Oath, for Establishing the Responsibility of Murders, Fighting, Requital and Blood-Wit (*Kitab al-Qasama*). 3:14:4130-37.

This incident is striking for the extent of the mutilations imposed upon the apostates before they were killed. The purpose was not merely to execute the perpetrators, but to degrade them, as retribution for opposing 'Allah and His Messenger.'

Both *Sahih al-Bukhari* and Ibn Kathir's Tafsir link Q5:33 to this violent execution. Al-Bukhari, in his Book of Commentary, states in relation to this verse that 'To wage war against Allah [trans. above as 'fight against Allah'] means to reject faith in Him.'[1] Ibn Kathir explains the phrase in similar terms:

> 'Wage war' mentioned here means **oppose and contradict, and it includes disbelief**, blocking roads and spreading fear in the fairways. Mischief in the land refers to various kinds of evil.[2]

What is striking about Ibn Kathir's definition of 'fight against Allah' is its extreme breadth. Just as *fitna* came to include mere disbelief in Muhammad, so also 'fight against Allah' could be something as simple as to 'contradict' Muhammad. By this logic, whoever speaks a word against Muhammad, or confesses disbelief in his prophethood, could be regarded as being at war with Allah, and by implication with Muslims.

The treaty of Hudaybiyyah

Before the conquest of Mecca, Muhammad had a vision in which he performed a pilgrimage to Mecca. This was impossible at the time, as the Muslims were in a state of war with the Meccans. After his vision, Muhammad approached Mecca with a large force, and negotiated a treaty which allowed him to make his pilgrimage. The treaty was to be for ten years, and one of its stipulations was that Muhammad would return to the Meccans anyone who came to him without the permission of their guardian. This would include slaves and women. The treaty also allowed people from either side to enter into alliances with each other.

Muhammad, for his part, did not keep his side of the treaty, because when people came to him from Mecca to reclaim their wives or slaves, he would refuse to return the fugitives, citing the authority of Allah. The first case was a woman, Umm Kulthum, whose brothers came to retrieve her. Muhammad refused, for, as Ibn Ishaq put it, 'Allah forbade it':[3]

---

1 *Sahih al-Bukhari*. The Book of Commentary. Vol. 6, p.108. Introduction to the Chapter 'The recompense of those who wage war against Allah ...[Q5:33].'

2 Ibn Kathir, *Tafsir* vol.3, p.161.

3 Guillaume, *The Life of Muhammad*, p.509.

> O believers, when believing women come to you as emigrants, test them.
> Allah knows very well their belief.
> Then, if you know them to be believers,
> return them not to the unbelievers.
> They are not permitted to the unbelievers,
> nor are the unbelievers permitted to them. (Q60:10).

This *sura* instructs the Muslims not to take unbelievers as their friends. It says that if any Muslims secretly love the Meccans, they have gone astray: in any case, the unbelievers' desire is only to cause the Muslims to disbelieve. Ibrahim (Abraham) is cited as a good example: he is reported in the Quran as saying to his own relatives 'We disbelieve in you, and between us and you enmity has shown itself, and hatred for ever, until you believe in Allah alone.' (Q60:4)

The whole message of this *sura* is in conflict with the spirit of the treaty of Hudaybiyyah, which had stated 'We will not show enmity one to another and there shall be no secret reservation or bad faith.'[1]

Robert Spencer, in his discussion of this incident, points out an inconsistency in the Islamic understanding of these events:

> Although Muslim apologists have claimed throughout history that the Quraysh broke it first [the treaty of Hudaybiyyah], this incident came before all those by the Quraysh that Muslims point to as treaty violations. ... The breaking of the treaty in this way would reinforce the principle that nothing was good except what was advantageous to Islam, and nothing evil except what hindered Islam.[2]

Later, the Muslims attacked and conquered Mecca, on the basis that the Quraysh had violated the treaty, and Allah would declare in Q9 no more treaties could be initiated with idolaters:

> A proclamation from Allah and His Messenger, unto mankind on the day of the Greater Pilgrimage: 'Allah is quit, and His Messenger, of the idolaters.' ...
>
> With them fulfil your covenant till their term; surely Allah loves the godfearing. Then, when the sacred months are drawn away, slay the idolaters wherever you find them, and take them, and confine them, and lie in wait for them at every place of ambush. ... (Q9:3-5)

This sequence of events illustrates what became an entrenched Islamic perspective, that non-Muslim disbelievers were by nature pact breakers, unable to keep covenants:

---

1 Ibid., p.504.

2 Robert Spencer, *The Truth about Muhammad*, pp.138-39.

> How should the idolaters have a covenant with Allah and His
> Messenger? ... How? If they get the better of you, **they will not observe
> towards you any bond or treaty**, giving you satisfaction with their
> mouths but in their hearts refusing; and the most of them are ungodly.
> (Q9:7-8)

At the same time, Muhammad, under instruction from Allah, claimed
the right to break pacts with infidels. When Muhammad, claiming
the authority of a higher power, violated his agreements, this was not
regarded as unrighteous by Islamic tradition.

Such incidents as these reveal that Muhammad, by consigning
unbelievers to the category of those who would seduce Muslims from
their faith (i.e. they would commit *fitna*) made it impossible to have
normal relationships with them, as long as they refuse to accept Islam.

Striving against the Jews

Muhammad's interactions with the Jews of Medina and Khaybar form
the foundation for the later development of the *dhimma* pact system for
'People of the Book'.[1] We will now consider the main elements of these
initial Muslim-Jewish encounters.

Muhammad's initial views on the Jews

During the Meccan period, the primary interest which Muhammad
had with Jews concerned his claim that he was a prophet in a long line
which included many Jewish prophets. It is striking that in the Meccan
suras, and the revelations from the first months in Medina, there are no
general denunciations of Jews, and indeed comparatively few references
to Jews at all. When the Quran did refer to the Jews in Mecca, it was to
make the point that although some of them were believing, and some
were not, Muhammad's message would come as a blessing to them.
One of the very earliest *suras* expresses this clearly:

> The unbelievers of the People of the Book and the idolaters would never
> leave off, till the Clear Sign came to them,
> a Messenger from Allah, reciting pages purified, therein true Books. ...
> They were commanded only to serve Allah,
> making the religion His sincerely,

---

1 Bostom's study *The Legacy of Islamic Antisemitism* details the progress of Muhammad's dealings
   with the Jews, as well as the legacy of his actions. Mark Gabriel, former Al-Azhar professor, has
   also covered the same subject from a Christian perspective in his *Islam and the Jews*. See also:
   Haggai Ben-Shammai, 'Jew-hatred in the Islamic tradition and Qur'anic exegesis,' in Shmuel
   Almog, *Antisemitism through the Ages*; and Saul S. Friedman, 'The myth of Islamic toleration,' in
   Without Future: the Plight of Syrian Jewry.

Men of pure faith, and to perform the prayer,
and pay the alms (zakat) – that is the religion of the True.

The unbelievers of the People of the Book
and the idolaters shall be in the Fire of Hell,
therein dwelling forever; those are the worst of creatures.

But those who believe, and do righteous deeds, those are the best of
creatures; their recompense is with their Lord – Gardens of Eden,
underneath which rivers flow,
therein dwelling for ever and ever. (Q98:1-8)

Muhammad had encountered some Christians in his time in Mecca,
and these contacts had been encouraging. Khadijah's Christian cousin,
Waraqa had identified Muhammad as a prophet, and Abyssinian
Christians who met him in Mecca had believed. Perhaps he hoped
that Jews would also respond positively to his message, discerning in
him a 'Clear Sign' from Allah. (Q98) Indeed Muhammad believed that
what he was teaching was the same as the Jewish religion, including
'performing the prayer' and paying *zakat*. (Q98:5) He even directed his
followers to pray facing 'Syria', which is interpreted to mean towards
Jerusalem, copying the Jewish custom.[1]

When Muhammad arrived in Medina, Islamic tradition records that he
implemented a covenant to which the Jews were a party. This covenant
recognized the Jewish religion 'the Jews have their religion and the
Muslims have theirs' and it commanded loyalty from the Jews to the
Muslim *Umma*. Each group would help the other against external
attacks. The document three times states 'loyalty is a protection against
treachery'. According to Islamic sources, the covenant also stated that
'Muhammad is the prophet of Allah' and would be the final arbiter of
any disputes.[2]

Opposition in Medina

Muhammad began to present his message to the Jewish residents
of Medina, but met with unexpected resistance. Islamic tradition
attributes this to envy: '… the Jewish rabbis showed hostility to the
apostle in envy, hatred, and malice, because God had chosen His apostle
from the Arabs.'[3] They 'used to annoy the apostle with questions and

---

1 Dudley Woodberry, in 'Contextualization among Muslims: reusing common pillars' argues that
   many Islamic religious practices were based upon Jewish models, including the ritual prayers,
   fasting, and the form of the *shahada*.
2 Guillaume, *The Life of Muhammad*, p.233.
3 Ibid., p.239.

introduce confusion, so as to confound the truth with falsity.'[1] Some of Muhammad's revelations included Biblical references, and no doubt the rabbis contested this material, pointing out contradictions with the Bible.

The prophet of Islam found the rabbis' questions troublesome, and at times more of the Quran would be sent down to him, furnishing him with replies. A long list of such conversations, and the Quran's responses, can be found in Ibn Ishaq's *sira*, relating to the first hundred or so verses of Q2 'The Cow'.[2] Again and again, when Muhammad would be challenged by a question, he would turn the incident into an opportunity for self-validation, bringing forth a fresh verse of the Quran.

One of his simplest strategies was to assert that the Jews were deceivers, quoting passages that suited them, but concealing others which would not have helped their cause:

> … do not let their saying grieve thee; assuredly We know what they keep secret and what they publish. (Q36:76; see also Q2:77)

Another answer from Allah was that the Jews had deliberately falsified their scriptures:

> … there is a party of them that heard Allah's word, and then tampered with it, and that after they had comprehended it, wittingly? (Q2:75)

Ibn Ishaq called the rabbis the 'men who asked questions', who 'stirred up trouble against Islam to try to extinguish it'.[3] This equivalence of 'asking questions' with 'trying to extinguish Islam' indicates that the rabbis' questions were not regarded as reasoned responses to Muhammad's invitation to accept Islam, but as *fitna*, an attempt to destroy Islam and the faith of Muslims, and as we have seen, Muhammad had already committed himself to the proposition that *fitna* was 'worse than slaughter'.

A hostile theology of the rejecters

Muhammad's frustrating conversations with Jews led him to adopt a more hostile attitude to them. Whereas in the past, verses had said some Jews were believers, and others not, now the Quran declared that the whole race was cursed and only very few were true believers:

---

1 Ibid., p.239.
2 Ibid., pp.247-70.
3 Ibid., p.240.

> Some of the Jews pervert words from their meanings saying
> 'We have heard and we disobey' ... Allah has cursed them for their
> unbelief, so they believe not **except a few**. (Q4:46)

The Quran announced that in the past some Jews were transformed into monkeys and pigs for their sins. (Q7:166; Q5:60; Q2:65) Allah also stated that they were prophet-killers. (Q5:70) Allah had renounced his relationship with the covenant-breaking Jews, hardening their hearts, so Muslims can always expect to find them treacherous (except for a few):

> So for their breaking their compact We cursed them and made their
> hearts hard, they perverting words from their meanings;
> and they have forgotten a portion of that they were reminded of;
> and thou wilt never cease to light upon some act of treachery on their
> part, except a few of them. (Q5:13)

Having broken their covenant, the Jews are declared to be 'losers' who have forsaken their true guidance:

> Thereby He guides many astray, and thereby He guides many;
> and thereby He leads none astray save the ungodly such as break the
> covenant of Allah after its solemn binding,
> and such as cut what Allah has commanded should be joined,
> and such as do corruption in the land they shall be the losers. (Q2:27)

Muhammad began to announce hellfire against the Jews, just as he had against the Meccans who had earlier rejected him.

Before he came to Medina, Muhammad had thought Judaism was valid:

> Surely they that believe, and those of Jewry, and the Sabeans,
> whoso believes in Allah and the Last Day, and works righteousness –
> their wage awaits them with their Lord, and no fear shall be on them,
> neither shall they sorrow. (Q2:62: cf also Q5:44)

However Ibn Kathir, in his commentary on this verse (Q2:62), points out that it was superseded by:

> Whoso desires another religion than Islam,
> it shall not be accepted of him;
> in the next world he shall be among the losers. (Q3:85)

Ibn Kathir also reports the comments of Ibn 'Abbas (d. 687), one of Muhammad's companions, and a key figure in the early development of Quranic interpretation:

> Allah does not accept any deed or work from anyone, unless it conforms to
> the Law of Muhammad, that is, after Allah sent Muhammad. Before that

every person who followed the guidance of his own Prophet was on the correct path, following the correct guidance and was saved.[1]

In Medina, Muhammad came to the view that he had been sent to correct the errors of the Jews:

People of the Book, now there has come to you Our Messenger,
making clear to you many things you have been concealing of the book,
and effacing many things. (Q5:115)

Muhammad thus concluded that his coming had abrogated Judaism, that the Islam he brought was the final religion, and the Quran the last revelation. All who rejected this message would be 'losers' (Q3:85). It would no longer be acceptable for Jews – or Christians – to follow their old religion: they had to acknowledge Muhammad, and become Muslims too, like everyone else.

Muhammad took this a step further. Not only was Islam the final religion, it was in fact the first! He announced that Abraham had in fact been a Muslim, and not a Jew (Q3:67). Jesus also was a Muslim, and his disciples had confessed 'we are Muslims' (Q3:52; Q5:111). Muhammad also began to use the expression 'the religion of Abraham' (from which the contemporary phrase 'Abrahamic faith' is derived) to refer to Islam **in contrast to** Judaism and Christianity:

And they say, 'Be Jews or Christians and you shall be guided.' Say thou:
'Nay, rather the creed of Ibrahim, a man of pure faith ...' (Q2:135)

Not only Muhammad but both Dawud (David) and Isa (Jesus) had allegedly also cursed the Jews:

Cursed were the unbelievers of the Children of Israel by the tongue of
Dawud, and Isa, Mariam's [Mary's] son; that, for their rebelling and their
transgressions. (Q5:78)

Further accusations which the Medinan *suras* lay against the Jews included:[2]

- The Jews are the greatest enemies of Islam. (Q5:82)
- Jewish people do not love Muslims and will not love a Muslim until he converts to Judaism. (Q2:120)
- Jews start wars and cause trouble in the earth. (Q5:64)
- Jews say Allah has a son, and they call 'Uzair'[3] the son of Allah. (Q9:30)

---

1 Ibn Kathir, *Tafsir*, vol.1, p.249.
2 Mark Gabriel, *Islam and the Jews*, p.97ff.
3 'Uzair is generally taken to be a reference to Ezra.

- Jews are cursed because they accused Allah of having a weak hand. (Q5:64)
- Jews love the present life of this world and do not care about things of eternity. (Q2:96)
- Jews claim they killed the Messiah. (Q4:157)

This full-frontal theological onslaught upon Judaism reflects the profound offense taken at the Jew's rejection of Muhammad's message. This was a self-validation moment for Muhammad, like those he had resorted to with the Meccan idolaters. However, in this case, Muhammad went further, and implemented aggressive responses as well.

Rejection turns into violence

Muhammad began a campaign to intimidate, and ultimately to eliminate the Jews from Medina. Emboldened by victory over the idolaters at Badr, he visited the Qaynuqa' Jewish tribe and announced in their market place:

> O Jews, beware lest God bring upon you the vengeance that He brought upon Quraysh [at Badr] and become Muslims. You know that I am a prophet who has been sent – you will find that in your scriptures and God's covenant with you.[1]

On a pretext, Muhammad besieged the Qaynuqa' Jews and they surrendered unconditionally. Their fate hung in the balance, but one of the Muslims who had an alliance with the tribe interceded with Muhammad and secured the Qaynuqa' Jews' freedom. Muhammad was unhappy with this, and a verse was revealed saying that Muslims were not to befriend Jews (Q5:51,57).[2]

Then Muhammad commenced a series of targeted assassinations of Jews. At first people were killed who had composed mocking, rejecting poems against him: Asma bint Marwan, killed while she lay sleeping with her children; an extremely old man Abu Afak, killed in his sleep; and Ka'b ibn al-Ashraf, killed by use of subterfuge.[3] Then Muhammad issued a command to his followers 'Kill any Jew that falls into your power',[4] and more Jews lost their lives.

---

1 Guillaume, *The Life of Muhammad*, p.363.

2 It is a repeated theme of the Quran that Muslims should not make unbelievers their friends (or protectors). See, e.g. Q3:28,118; Q4:89,144; Q9:16,23; Q58:14; Q60:1.

3 *Sahih al-Bukhari.* Book of *Jihad* (Fighting for Allah's Cause). 4:56:3031.

4 Guillaume, *The Life of Muhammad*, p.369.

A profound shift had taken place in Muhammad's understanding. Non-Muslims had rights to their property and lives only if they had supported and honored Islam and Muslims. Anything else was *fitna*, and a pretext for fighting.

The renowned *hadith* compiler known as Muslim recorded a tradition which lays out Muhammad's warning to the Jews in Medina, combined with an invitation to become Muslims:

> ... the Messenger of Allah ... came to us and said: '(Let us) go to the Jews'... The Messenger of Allah ... stood up and called out to them (saying): 'O ye assembly of Jews, accept Islam (and) you will be safe [*aslim taslam*].' [And after repeating this another two times, he said]: 'You should know that the earth belongs to Allah and His Apostle, and I wish that I should expel you from this land. Those of you who have any property with them should sell it, otherwise they should know that the earth belongs to Allah and His Apostle' (and they may have to go away leaving everything behind).[1]

It is interesting that this is the earliest record of the invitation *aslim taslam* 'accept Islam and you will be safe' which Muhammad and his followers were later to use as part of their formal declarations of war on Christian nations.[2]

The remarkable announcement that 'the earth belongs to Allah and His Apostle' expressed a principle that became foundational for theologies of *jihad*. If all earthly authority not submitted to Islam is usurped authority, then all warfare which seeks to wrest control from un-godly authorities is defensive in nature, taking property which rightfully belongs to Islam. All Islamic warfare against unbelievers is thus defensive, and land and booty taken in *jihad* is liberated rather than conquered. The caliph 'Umar, according to al-Tabari's history, repeatedly refers to the capture of land and booty in such terms. The conquered territories of Syria and Palestine were, 'Umar said, addressing the Muslims, 'property which God has restored to you'.[3]

---

1 *Sahih Muslim*. The Book of *Jihad* and Expedition. 3:17:4363. See also *Sahih al-Bukhari*. The Book of *al-Jizya* and the Stoppage of War. 4:58:3167. Tradition reports that a few Jews did accept this invitation: 'they went and became Muslims and saved their lives, their property, and their families' (Guillaume, *The Life of Muhammad*, pp.94-95).

2 This call is found, for example, in the famous letter to Heraclius, the Byzantine Emperor (*Sahih al-Bukhari* 4: pp.120ff. The Book of *Jihad*. 4:56:2940) and also in an attack ordered by Muhammad on the people of Najran (Guillaume, *The Life of Muhammad*, p.645).

3 al-Tabari, *The Battle of al-Qadisiyyah and the Conquest of Syria and Palestine. The History of al-Tabari*, vol. 12, p.154.

Muhammad's task of dealing with the Jews was not yet complete. The Banu Nadir were next. Some Nadir Jews were alleged to be plotting to kill Muhammad. Muhammad was warned, and the whole Nadir tribe was accused of breaking their covenant, so they were attacked, and after an extended siege were likewise driven out of Medina, abandoning their property as booty for the Muslims.

Islamic tradition accuses the remaining Jews, the tribe of Qurayza, of having allied themselves with the Quraysh of Mecca, in violation of their covenant. The Qurayza had remained neutral when the Meccans had besieged Medina and then withdrawn without a battle. Muhammad besieged the Qurayza on the basis of a command from the angel Gabriel. When the Jews surrendered unconditionally, the men were beheaded in the market place of Medina – six to nine hundred by varying accounts – and the Jewish women and children were distributed as booty (i.e. as slaves) among the Muslims.[1] A very few Jewish men converted to Islam, and in this manner gained their liberty. In this campaign Muhammad gained for himself a wife from among the slaves: Rayhana, a daughter of one of the leading Qurayza Jews.

A *hadith* summarizes the result of Muhammad's campaign of violence:

> … The Messenger of Allah turned out all the Jews of Medina, Banu Qainuqa' (the tribe of 'Abdullah bin Salam) and the Jews of Banu Haritha and every other Jew who was in Medina.[2]

Muhammad was not quite finished with the Jews of Arabia. After clearing Medina of their presence, he attacked Khaybar. On the way to that siege, his cousin 'Ali was made the proud standard bearer for the Muslims, and perhaps it was this which emboldened him to put the following question to Muhammad:['Ali asked:] 'Allah's Messenger, on what issue should I fight with the people?' Back came Muhammad's telling answer:

> 'Fight until they bear testimony to the fact that there is no god but Allah and Muhammad is His Messenger, and when they do that, then their blood and their riches are inviolable [safe] from your hands …'[3]

The Khaybar campaign started out with the two-choice scenario: convert or die. However when the Muslims defeated the Jews of

---

1 Guillaume, *The Life of Muhammad*, p.464.
2 *Sahih Muslim.* The Book of *Jihad* and Expedition. (*Kitab al-Jihad wa'l-Siyar*). 3:17:4364.
3 *Sahih Muslim.* Book Pertaining to the Merits of the Companions of the Holy Prophet (*Kitab Fada'il al-Sahabah*). 4:29:5917.

Khaybar, a third choice was negotiated: conditional surrender. Thus did the Khaybar Jews become the first *dhimmis*.

This concludes our discussion of Muhammad's dealings with the Jews. What is important is that the Quran treats Christians and Jews alike as representatives of a single category, the 'People of the Book'. This meant that the treatment of Jews in the Quran and the life of Muhammad, as 'People of the Book', became a model for the treatment of Christians down the ages as well.

'We are the victims'

One of the themes of Muhammad's program was an emphasis on the victimhood of Muslims. To sustain the theological position that conquest is liberation, it becomes necessary to seek grounds to find the infidel enemy guilty and deserving of attack. Also, the more extreme the punishment, the more necessary it becomes to insist upon the enemy's guilt. Since, by divine decree Muslims' sufferings were 'worse than slaughter', it became obligatory for Muslims to regard their victimhood as greater than whatever they inflicted upon their enemies. The greater victimhood of Muslims became a doctrinal necessity, a feature of the 'compass of faith' for Muslims.

It is this theological root, grounded in the Quran and the *Sunna* of Muhammad, which explains why, again and again, some Muslims have insisted that their victimhood is greater than that of those they have attacked. Islamic commentators on Muhammad's dealings with the Jews emphasize the victimhood of the Muslims, and the treachery of the Jews. A typical perspective is offered by Yahiya Emerick in *The Complete Idiot's Guide to Understanding Islam*:

> Muhammad kept his end of the treaty [with the Jews] at all times, and many Jews converted to Islam of their own free will. He never forced any conversions nor did he act in an unjust manner ... The expulsion of the three organized Jewish tribes was due to their own duplicity and treachery.[1]

A modern example of the 'greater Islamic victimhood' principle is Muslim convert Marmaduke Pickthall's influential 1927 lecture 'Tolerance in Islam'. Pickthall alleged, in an allusion to the genocide of the Armenians, that '... before every massacre of Christians by Muslims

---

1 Yahiya Emerick, *The Complete Idiot's Guide to Understanding Islam*, p.199.

of which you read, there was a more wholesale massacre or attempted massacre of Muslims by Christians.'[1]

The same mentality was displayed by Professor Ahmad bin Muhammad, Algerian Professor of Religious Politics, in a debate with Dr Wafa Sultan on Al-Jazeera TV. Infuriated by Dr Sultan's arguments, he began shouting:

> We are the victims! ... There are millions of innocent people among us [Muslims], while the innocent among you ... number only dozens, hundreds, or thousands, at the most.[2]

This victim mentality continues to plague many Muslim communities to this day, and weakens their capacity to take responsibility for their own actions.

These dynamics were manifested in Muslim reactions to the knighting of Sir Salman Rushdie by Queen Elizabeth in 2007. Lord Ahmed objected to Salman Rushdie being knighted, because he had 'blood on his hands'.[3] But one must ask, 'What blood, and who shed it?' While it is true that translators of Rushdie's books were assassinated, and Muslims died in riots instigated by those who were calling for Rushdie's blood, from Lord Ahmed's perspective, it is not the killers who are to be held accountable for these deaths, but the author whose *fitna* provided a pretext for their aggression.

The Queen, in knighting Rushdie had 'hurt the sentiments of 1.5 billion Muslims' said Pakistan Religious Affairs Minister, Ijaz-ul-Haq, who also proposed that 'If someone exploded a bomb on his body he would be right to do so unless the British Government apologizes and withdraws the "sir" title.' This illustrates the principle that *fitna* – in this case dishonoring Muslims by knighting Rushdie – 'is worse than slaughter' – in the form of suicide bombing targeting British citizens.

Muhammad the rejecter

This concludes our overview of Muhammad's history of rejection, both received and imposed upon others, and his self-vindicating pursuit of success over his enemies.

---

1 Marmaduke Pickthall. 1927. 'Tolerance in Islam'. A lecture, viewed 8 June 2009, <http://www. zaytuna.org/articleDetails.asp?articleID=51>.

2 'LA Psychologist Wafa Sultan Clashes with Algerian Islamist Ahmad bin Muhammad over Islamic Teachings and Terrorism,' Clip #783 Broadcast: July 26, 2005, viewed 8 May 2009, <http://www.memritv.org/clip/en/783.htm>.

3 'Britain In A Tizzy As "Sir" Rushdie Turns 60.' *News Post India*, 19 June, 2007, viewed 8 May 2009, <http://newspostindia.com/report-4013>.

As we have seen, the prophet of Islam experienced rejection at many levels: in his family circumstances, from his own community in Mecca, and from the Jews in Medina. In responding, Muhammad passed through self-rejection, then self-validation, and finally aggression. Muhammad the orphan became the orphan-maker. The self-doubter, who had contemplated suicide because he feared he was being tormented by demons, became the ultimate rejecter, imposing his creed by force of arms to supersede and replace all other faiths.

In Muhammad's emotional worldview, the defeat and degradation of disbelievers would 'heal' his followers' sentiments and quench their rage. This healing 'Islamic peace', won through battle, is described in the Quran:

> Fight them, and Allah will chastise them at your hands
> and degrade them, and He will help you
> against them, and **bring healing to the breasts of a people who believe,
> and he will remove the rage within their hearts**;
> and Allah turns towards whomsoever He will:
> Allah is all-knowing, All-wise. (Q9:14-15)

The *sira* narratives record that at first Muhammad and his followers did experience actual persecution at the hands of the Meccan polytheists, but when he assumed power in Medina Muhammad came to regard even disbelief in his prophethood or jokes at his expense as persecution, and licensed the use of violence to deal with disbelievers and mockers – whether polytheist, Jew or Christian – so they would be silenced, or intimidated into submission. Muhammad instituted an ideological and military program which systematically eliminated all manifestations of rejection expressed towards him and his religious community. He claimed that the success of his program validated his prophethood, because Allah had granted it to him, as one of the distinctive marks of his prophetic office, that he would take booty and be 'victorious through terror'.[1]

In eliminating all forms of spiritual opposition to his program, Muhammad in effect asserted that:

- Non-Muslims were guilty of the penalty of *jihad* waged against them – for they were rejecters of his prophethood, by nature deceivers and pact-breakers.

---

1 *Sahih al-Bukhari*. Book of *Jihad* (Fighting for Allah's Cause). 4:56:2977. Al-Bukhari introduces this hadith with a quotation from Q3:151 'We shall cast terror into the hearts of those who disbelieve ...'

- Non-Muslims whose lives were spared should be grateful, for it was Islam which spared them in the midst of their guilt.
- Non-Muslims were to be treated as inferior, cursed and destined to fuel hell.

Thus non-Muslims were thought to be well suited to live under the humiliations of defeat in this life, lest they thrive, and their success become an offensive source of *fitna* for the Muslim community. In contrast the daily call to prayer invites Muslims to 'come to success' and, through genuine devotion to Allah, to share in the benefits of the superiority of the *Umma*.

The Quran establishes markers along the progress of Muhammad's prophetic career. As such it is revealed as Muhammad's own, intensely personal document, a record of Muhammad's growing sense of hostility and aggression in the face of rejection. The characteristics which – as we shall see – came to be imposed upon non-Muslims, such as silence, guilt and gratitude, can all be grounded in the evolution of Muhammad's own responses to rejection, and his violent and ideologically comprehensive imposition of failure and rejection upon all who refused to confess, 'I believe there is no god but Allah and Muhammad is his prophet.'

CHAPTER 6

The *Dhimma*: Doctrine and History

Khaybar, Khaybar ya Yahud, jaish Muhammad sa ya 'ud
'Remember Khaybar, O Jews, Muhammad's army will return!'
A popular Arabic chant[1]

The alien in the land

In the Torah, the Law of Moses, there are many detailed instructions for how the Israelites should conduct themselves. Among these are rules for how they should relate to 'aliens' – non-believers – living among them:

> When an alien lives with you in your land, do not mistreat him. The alien living with you must be treated as one of your native-born. **Love him as yourself**, for you were aliens in Egypt. I am the Lord your God. (Leviticus 19:33-34; cf Exodus 23:9)

Such instructions establish that outsiders who live in Israel are people to be treated with compassion, not disregard or contempt. As vulnerable people, they are, along with orphans and widows, to be shown justice and a duty of love no different from that showed to fellow Israelites. Indeed positive discrimination is required towards them, to mitigate their vulnerability:

> When you are harvesting in your field and you overlook a sheaf, do not go back to get it. **Leave it for the alien**, the fatherless and the widow, so that the LORD your God may bless you in all the work of your hands. (Deuteronomy 24:19)

The ethical principles underlying these regulations are reciprocity and equality, compassion for the vulnerable, and the fear of the Lord. Just as God had mercy on the Israelites in Egypt when they were themselves aliens subject to arbitrary and cruel treatment, so also should the Israelites show mercy to those who are aliens among them.

The later prophets list mistreatment of aliens as among those sins which were inviting God's judgment upon Israel:

---

1 This chant was one of the cries of protest recorded in the video *Protest rally outside the Danish Embassy in London, February 3 2006*. The NEFA Foundation, viewed 8 June 2009, <http://www.youtube.com/watch?v=YWGbFsy7NjA>.

See how each of the princes of Israel who are in you uses his power to shed blood. In you they have treated father and mother with contempt; in you **they have oppressed the alien** and mistreated the fatherless and the widow. (Ezekiel 2:6-7; cf Malachi 3:5)

The biblical principle of care for one's neighbor, specifically including those of different faiths, was reiterated by Jesus in his parable of the Good Samaritan (Luke 10:25ff), which holds up compassion towards an outsider as the epitome of what it means to 'love your neighbor as yourself'. The principle of equality of treatment for others, of loving one's neighbor as oneself, irrespective of whether they happen to share your faith, should be foundational for all Christian societies.

Three choices and two kinds of surrender

In contrast to the Biblical principle of compassion for the alien, the traditional Islamic attitude to non-believers living under Islamic rule is based on non-reciprocity, the superiority of the *Umma* and the necessity to discriminate accordingly between Muslims and non-Muslims. Non-Muslims are to be tolerated, but only as inferiors to Muslims.

A key term for describing the Islamic treatment of non-believers is *dhimmitude*. Bat Ye'or defines *dhimmitude* as 'the totality of the characteristics developed in the long term' by communities subjected in their own homeland 'to the laws and ideology imported through *jihad*.'[1] This subject relates to the circumstances of peoples conquered by *jihad*.

The word *Islam* means 'submission', and there are two kinds of submission to Islam. One is the submission of the convert, who accepts Islam as his or her way of life, and follows Muhammad. The other is the surrender of the defeated non-believer.

Bassam Tibi, Professor of International Relations at Göttingen University, defines the mission of Islam to wage war until non-Muslims accept conversion or surrender:

At its core, Islam is a religious mission to all humanity. Muslims are religiously obliged to disseminate the Islamic faith throughout the world. 'We have sent you forth to all mankind.' (Q. 34:28) **If non-Muslims**

---

1 Bat Ye'or, *The Decline of Eastern Christianity under Islam*, p.221. The term *dhimmitude* was defined and made known by Bat Ye'or, a pseudonym meaning 'daughter of the Nile', as this author comes from the Egyptian Jewish community. See *The Dhimmi* (1985) and *The Decline of Eastern Christianity under Islam: from Jihad to Dhimmitude* (1996), which include a great many primary materials gathered from Muslim and non-Muslim sources. Bat Ye'or's later books *Islam and Dhimmitude: Where Civilizations Collide* (2002), and *Eurabia* (2005) extend the treatment of this subject into the contemporary world, with a focus on Europe and the Arab-Israeli conflict.

submit to conversion or subjugation, this call (da'wa) **can be pursued peacefully. If they do not, Muslims are obliged to wage war against them.** In Islam, peace requires that non-Muslims submit to the call of Islam, either by converting or by accepting the status of a religious minority [sic] (dhimmi) and paying the imposed poll tax, jizya. World peace, the final stage of the da'wa, is reached only with the conversion or submission of all mankind to Islam.[1]

As Islamic jurists have stated down through the centuries, and numerous scholars of Islam have reported, it was Muhammad and his followers who adopted the mission of fighting against non-believers to extend the power and rule of Islam:

Narrated Ibn 'Umar

Allah's Messenger said: '**I have been ordered** (by Allah) **to fight against the people until they testify** that none has the right to be worshipped but Allah and that Muhammad is the Messenger of Allah, ... so if they perform all that, then they save their lives and property from me ...'[2]

This is the institution of *jihad*, a struggle to impose the supremacy of Islam throughout the world, and to establish the *Dar al-Islam*, or house of Islam, which is the region where Islam rules.

A former Chief Justice of Saudi Arabia, 'Abdullah ibn Humaid (d. 1981), described the traditional view in a widely disseminated essay on the meaning of *jihad* in the Quran. He explained how at first Muhammad adopted a peaceful approach, and then later an increasingly militant position, in which it became mandatory for Muslims to go to war, not only in self-defense, but to extend the authority and power of Islam over all other religions:

So at first 'the fighting' was forbidden, then it was permitted, and after that it was made obligatory – (1) against those who start 'the fighting' against you ... (2) And against all those who worship others along with Allah ...[3]

By those who 'worship others along with Allah', Sheikh 'Abdullah means all who are not Muslims: it is obligatory, he argues, to fight against them until they surrender to the armies of Islam, or convert.

---

1 Bassam Tibi, 'War and Peace in Islam', p.129. Note that of course initially the *dhimmi* populations were the majority: it took centuries for them to be reduced to minority status. (See Griffith, *The Church in the Shadow of the Mosque*, p.11.)

2 *Sahih al-Bukhari*. Book of Belief (i.e. Faith) (*Kitab al-Iman*) 1:2:25. See also *Sahih Muslim*. The Book of Faith (*Kitab al-Iman*). 1:10:29-35.

3 'Abdullah bin Muhammad bin Hamid, 'The call to Jihad (holy fighting for Allah's cause) in the Holy Quran.'

The historian al-Tabari (d. 923) describes a series of pronouncements by the caliph 'Umar at the time of the conquest of Syria and Palestine. These related to the division of booty, and the treatment of the conquered peoples. Al-Tabari reports that 'Umar's instructions concerning the conquered peoples were to give them these two alternatives to the sword: conversion or surrender.

> Summon the people to God; those who respond unto your call, accept it [i.e. their conversion] from them, but those who refuse must pay the poll tax [*jizya*] out of humiliation and lowliness [i.e. they must surrender]. **If they refuse this, it is the sword without leniency.**[1]

In such a fashion the soldiers of Islam spread their faith. The *Sahih al-Bukhari* records the words of a declaration of war delivered by 'Umar's troops to the Persians, in which these alternatives were offered:

> Our Prophet, the Messenger of our Lord, has ordered us to fight you till you worship Allah Alone or give *Jizya* (i.e. tribute)…[2]

'Umar's call to convert or surrender was entirely consistent with Muhammad's teachings, as shown by the following authentic *hadith*, in which Muhammad lays out the three options for non-believers:

> Fight in the name of Allah and in the way of Allah.
> Fight against those who disbelieve in Allah. Make a holy war …
> When you meet your enemies who are polytheists,
> invite them to three courses of action.
> If they respond to any one of these, you also accept it and withhold yourself from doing them any harm.
> Invite them to (accept) Islam;
> if they respond to you, accept it from them
> and desist from fighting against them ….
> If they refuse to accept Islam, demand from them the *Jizya*.
> If they agree to pay, accept it from them and hold off your hands.
> If they refuse to pay the tax, seek Allah's help and fight them.[3]

After Pope Benedict delivered a lecture in Regensburg, referring to the claim that Islam was spread by the sword, the Grand Mufti of Saudi Arabia, Sheikh 'Abdul Aziz al-Sheikh, issued a protest on the official Saudi news service. The Grand Mufti's objection was that the sword was only a last resort, if the non-Muslims refused to convert or surrender to the armies of Islam:

---

1 al-Tabari, *The Battle of al-Qadisiyyah and the Conquest of Syria and Palestine. The History of al-Tabari*, vol. 12, p.167.

2 *Sahih al-Bukhari*. The Book of *al-Jizya* and the Stoppage of War. 4:58:3159.

3 *Sahih Muslim*. The Book of Jihad and Expedition. (*Kitab al-Jihad wa'l-Siyar*). 3:27:4294.

[Muhammad] gave three options: either accept Islam, or surrender and pay tax, and they will be allowed to remain in their land, observing their religion under the protection of Muslims.[1]

The first two options are clear: Islam or the sword. But what does the third choice mean? What does it mean to be 'allowed to remain in their land'? What follows after surrender, apart from taxes? What does it mean to live as a non-Muslim under Islamic rule?

Almost from the very beginning, the *Dar al-Islam* included non-Muslim peoples. Sometimes they were minorities, but more often, especially at first, they were majority populations under Islamic occupation. Whatever the numbers, their role in the Islamic state was strictly defined by *Sharia* law. We will now turn to a consideration of how the *Sharia* came to make provision for non-Muslims.

Remembering Khaybar

As we have seen, the Islamic *Sharia*, or 'way', is based upon the example of Muhammad, the *Sunna*. The *Sunna* also forms the basis for Islam's treatment of conquered but yet unconverted peoples. Through what might be regarded as an accident of history, the fate of millions of Jews, Christians, Zoroastrians, and later Hindus under Islam was determined by how Muhammad treated conquered peoples, and in particular his conquest of the Jewish farming community at Khaybar.[2]

Some Muslims are asking for the name Khaybar to be better known.

- During a Muslim demonstration outside the Danish embassy on February 3, 2006, one of the protestors shouted to the embassy: 'You have declared war against Allah and his prophet. Take lesson of Theo Van Gogh! Take lesson of the Jews of Khaybar! Take lessons from the examples that you can see! For you will pay with your blood!'[3]
- When Amrozi, the smiling Bali bomber, entered the courtroom on August 7, 2003, the day of his sentencing, he cried out 'Jews,

---

1 P.K. Abdul Ghafour, 'Learn about Islam, Mufti tells Benedict'. *Arab News*, September 18, 2006, viewed 8 June 2009, <http://www.arabnews.com/services/print/print.asp?artid=86719&d=18 &m=9&y=2006&hl=Learn%20About%20Islam,%20Mufti%20Tells%20Benedict>. See also 'Saudi mufti defends spirit of jihad'. *Middle East Times*, September 18, 2006, viewed 8 June 2009, <http://www.metimes.com/print.php?StoryID=20060918-110403-1970r>. Downloaded 20 September, 2006.

2 Bat Ye'or points out this link in *The Dhimmi*, pp.44-46 and *The Decline of Eastern Christianity under Islam*, p.38: 'Muslim jurisconsults subsequently derived the status of the tributaries from the treaty concluded between Muhammad and the Jews who farmed the Khaybar oasis.'

3 Evan F. Kohlman, *Protest rally* (video).

remember Khaybar. The armies of Muhammad are coming back to defeat you.'[1]

▪ Hizbullah, during its attacks on Israel in 2006, named one of its missiles the 'Khaybar' rocket.

Why should the Danes or the Jews remember or learn from Khaybar?

Before his attack on Khaybar, as we have seen, Muhammad had made war against Jewish tribes in Medina. Some tribes he expelled from Medina. Others, the Qurayza Jews, he destroyed after they had surrendered unconditionally to him. He did this by putting their men to the sword and enslaving their women and children (the story has been told in chapter 5). This established the principle that in Islamic law adult males who surrender unconditionally can be put to death, and women and children are to be enslaved.[2]

The outcome was different in Khaybar. The Khaybar Oasis was fertile, and mainly inhabited by Jews. Muhammad attacked and after a siege was victorious. At the end the remaining Jewish combatants negotiated a surrender. They pointed out that only they had the skill of cultivating the land to maintain its productivity and they asked to be allowed to remain on the land – which henceforth belonged to the Muslims – tending it, and paying a tax of half their harvest to Muhammad:

> When the people of Khaybar surrendered on these conditions they asked the apostle to employ them on the property with half share in the produce, saying, 'We know more about it than you and we are better farmers.'[3]

In return for these privileges, the remaining Jews of Khaybar would be spared future *jihad* attack from the Muslims – giving them 'protected' status – and, what is most important, they would be allowed to keep their Jewish faith.

The dhimma pact

This pact of surrender came to be known as a *dhimma* or 'covenant of liability'.

---

1 Mark Durie, 'Remembering Khaibar'. The original report of Amrozi's cry was by Martin Chulov 'I wanted the smile wiped off his face', published on p.1 of *The Australian* newspaper on August 8, 2003.

2 See, for example, 'Battle Procedures' in *Kitab al-Kharadj*. Trans. Bat Ye'or, *The Decline of Eastern Christianity under Islam*, p.302. (Excerpted from Henri Fagnan, French trans. *Le Livre de l'impôt foncier (Kitâb el-Kharâdj)*).

3 Guillaume, *The Life of Muhammad*, p.515.

The word *dhimma* is derived from an Arabic verb *dhamma* 'to blame, dispraise, find fault with, censure, in respect of evil conduct:'[1] it is the opposite of 'praise' or 'commend'. The noun *dhimma* implies a liability arising from fault or blame, and was used as the term for a covenant or treaty, the non-observance of which would attract blame and liability,[2] so the word *dhimma* could be translated 'pact of liability'.

Based on the precedent of Khaybar, and also on the way Muhammad treated conquered Jewish farmers of Fadak, Tayma and Wadi-l Qura, the institution of the *dhimma* was developed in *Sharia* law to provide for those of the conquered 'People of the Book' who refused to convert to Islam. The *dhimma* pact established the legal status for all communities incorporated into the *Dar al-Islam* as a result of *jihad*.

According to the laws of *jihad*, the alternatives to the *dhimma* were conversion, slavery or death. Any community of 'People of the Book' which negotiated a surrender to Islamic armies and became incorporated into the *Dar al-Islam*, was subject to a *dhimma*. The *dhimma* pact fixed the legal, social and economic place of non-Muslims in the Islamic state. In return, the people of the pact, known as *dhimmi*s, were required to pay tribute (*jizya*) and other taxes, including a land tax (*kharaj*), in perpetuity to the Muslim Community (the *Umma*), and to adopt a position of humble and grateful servitude to it.

This was enshrined in verse 9:29 of the Quran:

> Fight against those who do not believe in Allah ... of those who have been given the Book [i.e. Jews and Christians], until they pay the *jizya* [tribute] out of hand and are humbled.

The *dhimma* pact assured the defeated Jewish and Christian communities of a place under Islamic law: it granted them a degree of religious freedom and promised to spare them from further attacks, subject to certain conditions.

The *jizya* tax was administered as a head tax, levied on each adult non-Muslim male, and paid for the benefit of the Muslim community. It was often used to fund further military campaigns. Until the modern period, every non-Muslim living under Islam was required to pay this annual tribute in recognition of their defeated status.

---

1 E.W. Lane, *An Arabic-English Lexicon*. Book 1, p.975. See also Griffith, *The Church in the Shadow of the Mosque*, p.16.

2 Ibid., p.976.

It is important that the 'divine' revelation of Q9:29 defines an inseparable link between fighting (*jihad*) and the *dhimma* pact. *Jihad* warfare is designed to extend Islam, and make all peoples subject to its power. They became subject, if not by conversion or slavery, then by the *dhimma* pact and ongoing payment of tribute, the *jizya*.

According to Q9:29, the *dhimma* was intended to apply to 'People of the Book' – Jews and Christians. In contrast, Abu Yusuf (d. 798) ruled that pagan Arabs had to choose between Islam and the sword (Q9:5):

> The land of the Arabs is different from the land of the non-Arab in this respect that the Arabs are only fought against to make them accept Islam. … nothing but acceptance of Islam was accepted of them. … either they should become Muslims or they should be killed.[1]

On this principle Arabia was forcibly Islamized during the *Ridda* (apostasy) Wars, in an act of religious cleansing after Muhammad's death.

It was a matter of dispute between the schools of Sunni law as to whether non-Arab pagans could be included in a *dhimma* pact. The disagreement was due to a discrepancy between the Quran and the *Sunna*: the Quran only allowed for the People of the Book to pay *jizya*, but Muhammad's example established a precedent for accepting *jizya* from the pagan Zoroastrians.[2] When India was conquered, the *dhimma* was extended even to Hindus, a concession which was consistent with the Hanafi school of Islam that became established there.

In summary, within the Islamic state all non-Muslims who are not objects of war are considered to be *dhimmis,* people who are allowed to exist within the *Dar al-Islam* by virtue of their community's surrender under the conditions of a *dhimma* pact at some time in the past. These are the conquered peoples of Islam.

Paying the *jizya*

The phrase 'until they pay the *jizya* out of hand and are humbled' in Q9:29 is of crucial importance for understanding the whole *dhimmi* condition, and we will devote some care to unpacking it. Although this is but one verse in the whole Quran, it is rich with meaning, and forms the foundation of the whole treatment of *dhimmis* in Islamic law.

---

1 Abu Yusuf Ya'qub, *Kitab al-Kharadj*. Trans. by Browne, *The Eclipse of Christianity in Asia*, p.29.

2 Browne, *The Eclipse of Christianity in Asia*, pp.30-31. The Shafa'i school resolves the discrepancy by declaring Zoroastrians to be 'People of the Book'.

The pivotal role of this verse in determining the status of *dhimmis* is often poorly understood, denied or concealed. The concept of a tribute paid in perpetuity by people dwelling in their own ancestral lands can seem so strange to the modern mind that special care is taken here to draw out the implications of these words for the reader, using the interpretations of Muslim scholars themselves down the centuries.

There are three key elements to consider in Q9:29: the *jizya* tribute itself, the phrase 'out of hand' (*'an yadin*), and the concept of being 'humbled' (*saghirun*).

Jizya as compensation

The renowned Andalusian jurist Averroes (Ibn Rushd, d. 1198) explained that, according to established consensus of jurists, exacting *jizya* from Jews and Christians is one of the two purposes for making war against them, the other being their conversion to Islam:

> Why wage war? The **Muslim jurists agree** that the purpose of fighting the People of the Book ... is one of two things: it is either for the conversion to Islam or the payment of the *jizya*. The payment of the *jizya* is because of the words of the Exalted, 'Fight against such as those who have been given the Scripture as believe not in Allah or the Last Day, and forbid not that which Allah and His Messenger hath forbidden, and follow not the religion of truth, until they pay the tribute readily being brought low.' [Q9:29][1]

What was the significance of the *jizya* as a form of revenue for Muslims? Averroes explains that *jizya* is a broader concept than the head-tax on *dhimmis*. It includes resources exacted in times of war from enemies in order to compensate the Muslims for discontinuing their attack – what is more usually understood in English by the word *tribute* – as well as taxes on infidel merchants who are trading inside the *Dar al-Islam*, the region where Islamic rule applies, to afford them protection from *jihad*.

Ibn Taymiyya (d. 1328) classified the revenues of the Islamic state into three categories, making clear that *jizya* is a payment to save *dhimmis* from slaughter. These categories of revenues are:

1. booty looted from enemies by force, under war conditions (*ghanima*),

2. contributions paid by Muslims as a religious duty (*sadaqa*), and

---

1 Imran Ahsan Khan Nyazee, trans., *The Distinguished Jurist's Primer* (*Bidayat al-Mujtahid wa Nihayat al-Muqtsid*). Vol. 2, p.464.

3. *fay* income – including the *jizya* – which consists of resources released by the infidels without having to be taken by force.[1]

Derived from a root meaning to 'return to a good state' or 'restore', Lane reports that Muslim scholars defined *fay* as 'such, of the possessions of the unbelievers, as accrues to the Muslims without war ... or such as is obtained from the believers in a plurality of gods after the laying-down of arms'.[2] This bloodless booty is what Allah has:

> '... restored [as though it were theirs of right – Lane] to the people of his religion, of the possessions of those who have opposed them, without fighting, either by the latter's quitting their homes and leaving them vacant to the Muslims, or **by their making peace on the condition of paying a poll-tax [*jizya*] or other money or property to save themselves from slaughter.**'[3]

According to Ibn Taymiyya, as a part of the *fay*, the *jizya* was a restitution of an 'inheritance', of which the Muslim 'was deprived' because it had been unlawfully held by infidels. Through victory in warfare Allah has 'restored' these resources to benefit the Muslim community and thus the service of Allah:

> These possessions received the name of *fay* since Allah had taken them away from the infidels in order to **restore** them to the Muslims. In principle, Allah has created the things of this world only in order that they may contribute to serving Him, since He created man only in order [for Allah] to be ministered to. Consequently, the infidels forfeit their persons and their belongings which they do not use in Allah's service to the faithful believers who serve Allah and unto whom Allah restitutes what is theirs; thus is **restored to a man the inheritance of which he was deprived, even if he had never before gained possession.**[4]

From this perspective, taking *jizya* from *dhimmis* is an act of liberation, in which Muslims receive back compensation for what was rightfully theirs as Allah's servants. Indeed, the Arabic word *jizya* means 'compensation' or 'reparations'. Lane's dictionary of Arabic derives the word from the Arabic root *j-z-y*. This root refers to something given as a compensation, acquittal or satisfaction, which stands instead of something else. Thus *jizya*, according to the definitions of Arabic

---

1 Henri Laoust, French trans., *Le traité de droit public d'Ibn Taymiya*, p.27. English trans. in Bat Ye'or, *The Decline of Eastern Christianity under Islam*, p.296.

2 E.W. Lane, *An Arabic-English Lexicon*. Book 1, p.2468.

3 Ibid, Book 1, p.2468, citing Abu `Ubayd al-Qasim b. Sallam al-Baghdadi (d. 837), the *Mughrib* of al-Mutarrizi (d. 1213) and *al-Misbah al-Munir* of Ahmad b. Ali al-Fayyumi (d. 1364).

4 Henri Laoust, French trans., *Le traité de droit public d'Ibn Taymiya*, p.36. English trans. in Bat Ye'or, *The Decline of Eastern Christianity under Islam*, p.297.

lexicographers, is 'the tax that is taken from the free non-Muslim of a Muslim government whereby they ratify the compact [the *dhimma* pact] that ensures them protection, **as though it were a compensation for their not being slain.**'[1]

The medieval Andalusian commentator Abu Hayyan (d. 1344), known for his linguistic expertise, confirms this definition:

> It was called *jizya* because it is taken from the root *j-z-y*, which means to return compensation for what has been given, as if they are rewarding those who gave them the security [of life and property].[2]

As does the Baghdadi commentator al-Alusi (d. 1854):

> [*jizya*] comes from the root *j-z-y* i.e. 'pay off one's debts' or 'I reward him for what he has done to me'. For they pay it as a reward to those who gave them a pardon from death.[3]

And the Algerian commentator Muhammad ibn Yusuf at-Fayyish (d. 1914):

> It was said: it [*jizya*] is a satisfaction for their blood. It is said 'X' has sufficed ... to compensate for their not being slain. Its purpose is to substitute for the duties (*wajib*) of killing and of slavery ... It is for the benefit of Muslims.[4]

Writing in 1799, William Eton, referring to the *jizya* payment ritual as administered under Ottoman rule, reported that:

> The very words of their formulary, given to the Christian subjects on their paying the capitation tax [*jizya*], import, that the sum of money received, is taken as compensation for being permitted to *wear their heads that year*.[5] [Eton's emphasis]

The *jizya* is money paid by a defeated foe, which compensates or rewards an attacker for forgoing the right to take the defeated person's life and to resume rightful possession (according to Ibn Taymiyya) of his God-given property.

The link between the *jizya* head-tax and military defeat was explained by Abu Yusuf Ya'qub, an eighth century Hanafi jurist, who said that no-one could be exempted from the *jizya*, because it is a redemption

---

1 E.W. Lane, *An Arabic-English Lexicon*. Book 1, p.422, citing *al-Nihaya fi Gharib al-Hadith* by Majd al-Din ibn Athir (d. 1210), and others.

2 *Tafsir Bahr al-Muhit*. Commentary on Q9:29, viewed 21 February 2008, <http://altafsir.com>.

3 *Ruh al-Ma'ani*. Commentary on Q9:29, viewed 21 February 2008, <http://altafsir.com>.

4 *Taysir al-Tafsir*. Commentary on Q9:29, viewed 21 February 2008, <http://altafsir.com>.

5 William Eton, *A Survey of the Turkish Empire*, p.104.

or compensation paid in lieu of the *dhimmi*'s blood and the rightful looting of their possessions:

> The wali [governor of a province] is not allowed to exempt any Christian, Jew, Magian, Sabean, or Samaritan from paying the tax, and no one can obtain a partial reduction. It is illegal for one to be exempted and another not, because **their lives and possessions are spared only on account of the payment of the poll tax [*jizya*]** ...[1]

The origins of the concept of tribute-as-compensation lie in the culture of pre-Islamic Arabic tribal warfare. Bravmann has shown that the 'law of the ancient Arabs considers it self-evident that the prisoner taken captive in a fight reward his captor who spared his life and released him (instead of killing him, as he could actually have done).'[2] In other words the captive owed his life to the captor, and could redeem this debt by paying a reward. However *al-Hidayah*, a highly regarded Hanafi legal manual (al-Marghinani, d. 1197) explains that the *jizya* is not merely compensation for being spared in the past – and thus satisfaction for a past debt – but redemption against **future** *jihad* attack:

> ... [*jizya*] is a substitute for destruction in respect of the infidels ... but it is a substitute for destruction with regard to the future, not with regard to the past, because infidels are liable to be put to death only in future, **in consequence of future war** ...[3]

In the Islamic laws of war, enemy males who have reached puberty can lawfully be put to death if captured. There are some exceptions – such as hermits, the blind, the destitute and the insane. What is noteworthy about these is that the same exceptions apply to paying the *jizya*.[4] Thus the noted Hanbali authority Ibn Qudama (d. 1223) said 'not to enforce it except upon those over whose heads blades have passed', (i.e. the tax is payable only if their lives would otherwise have been forfeit).[5] He also states, citing Shafi'i, that '*jizya* is to be taken from them on the basis of whether they are to be killed. We have previously said that (if) they are

---

1 Abu Yusuf Ya'qub, *Kitab al-Kharadj*. Trans. Bat Ye'or, *The Decline of Eastern Christianity under Islam*, p.322. (Excerpted from Henri Fagnan, French trans. *Le Livre de l'impôt foncier (Kitâb el-Kharâdj)*).

2 Meïr Bravmann, 'The ancient background of the Qur'anic concept *al-gizyatu 'an yadin*,' p.352.

3 Walter Short, 'The jizya tax: equality and dignity under Islamic law?' p.87.

4 Compare, for example, Ibn Rushd's list of men who should not be killed (*Bidayat al-Mudjtahid*, in Andrew Bostom, *The Legacy of Jihad*, p.151), and Ibn Qudama's list of men who need not pay *jizya* ('Legal War,' in Andrew Bostom, *The Legacy of Jihad*, p.163).

5 Ibn Qudama. *al-Mughni, Bab al-Jizya*, vol.10, pp.581-82.

not to be killed, they are not to pay the *jizya*, like the women and the young.'[1]

The granting of these exemptions was controversial, and often more a matter of theory than practice.[2] Goitein introduces his study of the *jizya* by stating:

> There is no subject of Islamic social history on which the present writer had to modify his views so radically while passing from literary to documentary sources, i.e. from the study of Muslim books to that of the records of the Cairo Geniza as ... the poll tax to be paid by non-Muslims.[3]

He considers that the letters of *dhimmi* Jews 'prove that poverty, old age, and illness did not provide any excuse for exemption'.[4]

The link between the *jizya* and the idea of paying compensation for one's life is also seen in the principle of Islamic law that if the *jizya* is not paid, the *jihad* must be restarted, as the Shafi'i jurist of Baghdad al-Mawardi (d. 1058) makes clear:

> They make a payment every year in which case it constitutes an ongoing tribute by which their security is established. ... It is not permitted to resume the *jihad* against them as long as they make the payments. ... If they refuse to make payment, however, the reconciliation ceases, their security is no longer guaranteed and war must be waged on them – like any other persons from the enemy camp.[5]

In accordance with the rules of *jihad*, Ibn Qudama explains that in case of non-compliance with the *dhimma* pact, the *dhimmi*'s life and possessions are forfeit:

> A protected person who violates his protection agreement, whether by refusing to pay the head tax [*jizya*] or to submit to the laws of the community ... makes his person and his goods 'licit' [*halal* – freely available to be killed or captured by Muslims].[6]

---

1 Ibid., p.586.
2 Bat Ye'or reports that 'Armenian, Syriac, and Jewish sources provide abundant proof that the *jizya* was exacted from children, widows, orphans, and even the dead.' (*The Decline of Eastern Christianity under Islam*, p.78).
3 Goitein, 'Evidence on the Muslim poll tax from non-Muslim sources: a *geniza* study,' p.278.
4 Ibid., p.281.
5 Asadulah Yate, *The Laws of Islamic Governance* [*al-Ahkam al-Sultaniyyah*], pp.70-78.
6 Ibn Qudama, 'Legal War.' In Andrew Bostom, *The Legacy of Jihad*, p.163. English trans. Michael J. Miller. (Excerpted from Henri Laoust, trans., *Le Précis de droit d'Ibn Qudama*).

'Out of hand'

Muslim jurists have interpreted the expression 'out of hand' (Q9:29) in various ways. The word *yad* 'hand' can be used in Arabic with many different senses, including 'power', 'control', 'authority' and 'assistance'. This allows for a great variety of meanings, and typically commentators will acknowledge multiple available interpretations. There are three main ways in which the expression *'an yadin* has been explained.

Bravmann has argued that 'hand' here originally meant a benefaction or boon granted. The non-Muslims had been given 'a hand'– the gift of not being killed – so the phrase means in consideration for being allowed to live.[1] This meaning is proposed in the commentary of al-Baydawi (d. 1280): 'It is a favor (or a blessing) for them, as sparing their lives in exchange for the recompense of *jizya* is doing them a great favor (or blessing)',[2] and also by al-Khazin (d. 1340): 'they pay it with gratitude confessing the graciousness of Muslims in accepting *jizya* from them'.[3]

A second interpretation, supported by many jurists, is that the expression 'out of hand' in Q9:29 means in a forthcoming, obedient manner. The *jizya* is not so much taken, as given submissively. Al-Zamakhshari (d. 1143) compares this with a sheep which has a leash tied round its neck. Refusing to pay is like taking off the leash:

> (*'an yadin*): does this refer to the hand of the giver or the receiver? It refers to the giver, i.e. from a forthcoming rather than a withholding hand, because he who refuses and withholds … [is] like the proverb 'He took the leash of obedience off his neck.' (al-Zamakhshari)[4]

The submissive manner of giving the *jizya* signifies the *dhimmi's* agreement to accept all conditions imposed upon them by the *dhimma*.

A third line of interpretation requires that the *dhimmi* should pay the *jizya* in person, with his very own hand, and not by an intermediary:

> 'by hand': i.e. he does the giving with his physical hand – he should not send it (Ibn 'Ajibah d. 1809).[5]

---

1 Meïr Bravmann, 'The ancient background of the Qur'anic concept *al-gizyatu 'an yadin,*' p.350.

2 al-Baydawi, *Anwat al-tanzil wa-asar al-ta'wil*. Commentary on Q9:29, viewed 21 February 2008, <http://altafsir.com>. See also Helmut Gätje, *The Qur'an and its Exegesis*, p.139; Bravmann and Claude Cahen 'A propos de Qur'an IX.29: hatta yu'tu l-Gizyata wa-hum sagiruna,' p.349.

3 *Tafsir Lubab al-Ta'wil*. Commentary on Q9:29, viewed 21 February 2008, <http://altafsir.com>.

4 *al-Kashshaf,* Commentary on Q9:29, viewed 21 February 2008, <http://altafsir.com>. Also M. Ahmad, ed., *al-Kashshaf…*, pp.262-63. Partially trans. in Andrew Bostom, *The Legacy of Jihad*, p.127.

5 *Tafsir al-Bahr al-Madid fi Tafsir al-Quran al-Magid* by Ibn 'Ajibah. Commentary on Q9:29, viewed 21 February 2008, <http://altafsir.com>.

'Belittled' – ritual humiliation

The expression 'belittled' (or 'humbled') translates the Arabic *saghir* of Q9:29 meaning 'small'. Citing this expression, Islamic legal thought strongly identified the *jizya* with the concept of belittlement.

The commentator al-Baghawi (d. 1122) stated that being 'small' can refer to the way the payment of *jizya* is enforced upon *dhimmis*, but also (citing Shafi'i) to 'the application of the Islamic laws upon them'.[1] Thus 'small' refers to the whole manner of life of the *dhimmi* under the Islamic *Sharia*, as well as specifically to the manner of paying the *jizya*. We will shortly consider the conditions imposed upon *dhimmis* living under Islamic law, but for the moment we will consider the 'belittling' aspects of the *jizya* payment ritual itself.

For the *dhimmi*, the annual *jizya* payment was a powerful and public symbolic expression of the *jihad*-dhimmitude nexus, which fixed the horizon of the *dhimmi*'s world. Although the ritual varied in its specific features, its essential character was an enactment of a beheading, in which one of the recurrent features was a blow to the neck of the *dhimmi*, at the very point when he makes his payment.

To understand the significance of neck striking, let us turn to the Quran:

> When thy Lord inspired the angels, (saying): I am with you. So make those who believe stand firm. I will throw fear into the hearts of those who disbelieve. Then **smite the necks** and smite of them each finger. That is because they opposed Allah and His messenger. (Q8:12-13: see also Q47:4)

To 'smite the necks' of the enemies of Allah means, in the Quran, to kill them, either through decapitation or cutting their throats. This was a favored method of putting non-Muslim enemies to death in Muhammad's time, and it remains popular among Islamic militants today. The *jizya* payment was thus a ritualized decapitation, symbolizing the very penalty which the payment was designed to avoid.

A sign of the deep cultural resonance of this ritual is that striking someone on the neck remains a highly insulting action in Arabic cultures even to this day.

---

1 *Ma'alam al-tanzil.* Commentary on Q9:29, viewed 21 February 2008, <http://altafsir.com>. Similar observations are also made by al-Tha'labi in his commentary Q9:29, viewed 21 February 2008, <http://altafsir.com>.

Cutting the forelock

Imposing a symbolic representation of decapitation upon captives was apparently a pre-Islamic custom, and striking the neck was not the only form it took. Bravmann explains that, in pre-Islamic Arabia, someone whose life was spared could have his forelock cut off.[1] Instead of cutting off the head, only the hair would be severed. Ibn al-Qayyim al-Jawziyya (d. 1351) reported that:

> ... the cutting of the hair is said to mean enslavement and humiliation. It was the practice of the Arabs, if they trusted a war prisoner, to cut off the front of his hair and allow him to go around displaying his enslavement, humiliation and subjugation.[2]

There is a reference to this practice in Ibn Ishaq's *Life of Muhammad*, in connection with the Qurayza massacre. A Muslim named Thabit had owed his life to al-Zabir, a Qurayza Jew, who some time earlier had captured him, cut off his forelock, and set him free. Consequently, Thabit gained Muhammad's permission to spare the Jew's life in return.[3]

In keeping with the Arab custom, after Islamic conquest *dhimmis* were required, as a sign of their subjugation, to cut their forelocks. The 'Pact of 'Umar', an early instance of a *dhimma* pact reportedly agreed to by the Christians of Syria, refers to *dhimmis* as agreeing that 'We shall clip the fronts of our heads',[4] and Ibn Qudama states '... they [the *dhimmis*] are to remove the hair from the front of their heads'.[5]

Neck-seals

Another early symbolic representation of ritual decapitation was the use of lead or iron neck-seals, worn around the neck by *dhimmis* as a

---

1 Bravmann, 'The ancient background of the Qur'anic concept *al-gizyatu 'an yadin*,' pp.351-55.

2 Subhi al-Salih, ed., *Ahkam Ahl al-Dhimmah*, vol 2: 749-50.

3 Yet in the end, al-Zabir preferred to die, as he had lost all his companions: 'my life holds no joy now that they are dead and I cannot bear to wait another moment'. Guillaume, *The Life of Muhammad*, p.465.

4 Cited from the *Siraj al-Muluk* of al-Tartushi (an Andalusian jurist of the 11th century) in the *Internet Medieval Sourcebook*, viewed 8 June, 2009 <http://www.fordham.edu/halsall/source/pact-umar.html>. The reference to cutting the forelock is also included in the version of the Pact of 'Umar cited in *Tafsir Ibn Kathir*, commentary on Q9:29, found on <http://altafsir.com>, (viewed 21 February 2009) but omitted in the (abridged) English translation of *Ibn Kathir*. The Umayyad period poet Jarir (ca 650-728) lampooned his rival Farazdaq, a notorious prodigal, by alleging that he spent his nights 'drinking at [the tavern of] everyone whose forelock has been cut off, whose finger-tips are moist, and whose wine-press is dripping', to which an ancient commentator has added 'forelock: i.e. *dhimmi* whose forelock has been cut off'. It was only *dhimmis* who produced and sold wine. (Meïr Bravmann, 'The ancient background of the Qur'anic concept *al-gizyatu 'an yadin*,' p.355.)

5 Ibn Qudama, *al-Mughni*, vol.10, p.620.

visible sign that they had paid the *jizya* tax.[1] The commentary of al-
Tha'labi (d. 1035) reports a tradition in which Ibn 'Abbas refers to this
practice, and commenting on Q9:29, calls what appears to be a neck
seal the 'belittling' or 'abasement' (*al-sughar*): 'You are told to put the
"abasement" around the neck of one of them: would you take it off their
necks and put it around your own?'[2]

Neck-striking

In respect of neck-striking, the great Persian commentator al-Baydawi
(d. 1316) attributed this ritual to the authority of Ibn 'Abbas:

> According to Ibn 'Abbas, the *dhimmi* is struck on the neck (with the hand)
> when the tribute is collected from him ...[3]

Seven centuries after al-Baydawi, the Egyptian jurist al-Adawi (d.
1787) gave the following account:

> Following this [the handing over of the *jizya* payment] the emir will
> strike the *dhimmi* on the neck with his fist; a man will stand near the emir
> to chase away the *dhimmi* in haste; then a second and a third will come
> forward to suffer the same treatment as well as all those to follow. All
> [Muslims] will be admitted to enjoy this spectacle. None will be allowed
> to delegate a third party to pay the *jizya* in his stead, for they must suffer
> this degradation personally.[4]

A more detailed fifteenth century description of this event is provided
by the Moroccan jurist al-Maghili (d. 1504):

> On the day of payment they [the *dhimmis*] shall be assembled in a public
> place like the *suq*. They should be standing there waiting in the lowest and
> dirtiest place. The acting officials representing the Law shall be placed
> above them and shall adopt a threatening attitude so that it seems to them,
> as well as to the others, that our object is to degrade them by pretending
> to take their possessions. They will realize that we are doing them a favor
> (again) in accepting from them the *jizya* and letting them (thus) go free.
> They then shall be dragged one by one (to the officer responsible) for the
> exacting of payment. When paying, the *dhimmi* will receive a blow and
> will be thrown aside so that he will think that he has escaped the sword

---

1 Bat Ye'or, *The Dhimmi*, pp.169, 205; Chase Robinson 'Neck-sealing in early Islam'. Ibn Qudama
states that the *dhimmi* 'is to have a lead or an iron seal upon his neck or a bell to differentiate
between him and the Muslims when in the bath.' (*al-Mughni*, vol.10, p.619).

2 *Tafsir al-Tha'labi*, Commentary on Q9:29, viewed 21 February 2008, <http://altafsir.com>.

3 Helmut Gätje, *The Qur'an and its Exegesis*, p.139. However Abu Hayyan attributes the blow on
the neck to al-Kalbi. (*Tafsir Bahr al-Muhit*. Commentary on Q9:29, viewed 21 February 2008,
<http://altafsir.com>.)

4 François-Alphonse Belin, French trans., *Fetoua* by Ahmad ad-Dardi el-Adaoui. English trans.
in Bat Ye'or, *The Decline of Eastern Christianity under Islam*, p.362.

through this (insult). This is the way that the friends of the Lord [*sayyid*: Muhammad], of the first and last generations will act toward their infidel enemies, for might belongs to Allah, to His Prophet, and to the believers.[1]

Historical sources from the nineteenth century – four centuries after al-Maghili – show that this ritual of defeat continued to be practiced in Morocco right up to the beginning of the modern era. James Riley, an American captain, who was shipwrecked off the coast of North Africa, captured and enslaved, and escaped to tell the tale, described a *jizya* ceremony which took place at Mogodore in 1815. He relates how each Jew, on paying the *jizya*, was struck a 'smart blow' to the head.[2] Eighty years later, in 1894, an Italian-protected Jew describes being required to pay the tax in Marrakesh, and taking as his receipt two blows to the neck. When he addressed the Muslim authorities, saying 'Know that I am an Italian-protected subject', he was given a third, more violent blow for good measure![3]

Muslim commentators provide various elaborations of features of the ritual, all designed to degrade the *dhimmi* and represent his vulnerability under the Muslims' hand. Lewis reports that 'A piece of symbolism prescribed in many law books is that the *dhimmi*'s head must be below, the tax collector's hand above, when the money changes hands.'[4] This relative positioning reflects the presentation of the head of the *dhimmi* under the hand (symbolically the sword) of the Muslim.

Other reported elements of the ritual include:

- the *dhimmi* comes to the place of payment walking, not riding (or he approaches on his hands and knees);
- he makes the payment standing, while the receiver is seated;
- he is shaken violently and made to become agitated;
- the Muslim has a whip in his hand;
- the *dhimmi* is ordered to pay the *jizya*, even though this is what he is already doing;
- he is beaten up;

---

1 George Vajda, French trans. 'Adversos Judaeos', p.811. English trans. by Paul Fenton in Bat Ye'or, *The Dhimmi*, p.201.

2 James Riley, *An Authentic Narrative of the Loss of the American Brig Commerce*, p.333. Riley also related that the poorest class of Jews, if unable to pay, were beaten and arrested, and, if not ransomed, forced to convert to Islam.

3 Letter from a Marrakesh Jew, 25 February 1894, in *Bulletin, Alliance Israélite d'Études Universelle* (January-February 1894). Trans. in Bat Ye'or, *The Dhimmi*, p.327.

4 Bernard Lewis, *The Jews of Islam*, p.15.

- he is dragged forward by the throat, using clothes pulled together at the throat, or by a rope tied around the neck (*labbaba*);
- he is struck on the back of the neck;
- he is struck under the ear (or on the jaw under the ear);
- he is pulled by the beard;
- the Muslim places a foot on the *dhimmi*'s neck;
- he is thrown aside.

Several of these indignities involve interfering with the *dhimmi*'s neck or head, which is consistent with a ritualized representation of a beheading. The two different kinds of blows to the neck (on the back of the neck and under the ear) are execution gestures, corresponding to different methods of decapitation, as is taking hold of the beard.[1]

The verb *labbaba*, used in the commentaries on Q9:29 to describe dragging by the throat, also symbolizes killing, but in a different way. The related noun *labbat* refers to the pit of the throat, the soft spot just above the center of the chest. Lane refers to this as 'the stabbing place in an animal',[2] and Wehr as 'throat of an animal; spot where its throat is cut in slaughtering'.[3] In Arabic, to 'take' someone's *labbat* means to throttle him. The verb *labbaba* is an intensive form meaning to drag someone along by the throat, either by pulling their clothes together at the front (as in a fight), or by a rope placed around their neck.[4] According to Lane, the non-intensive form *labba* simply means 'strike upon the *labbat*',[5] i.e. to punch in the throat, so the intensive *labbaba* involves a more comprehensive violation of this sensitive and vulnerable vital point.

A typical collection of *jizya* ritual features is provided by the Persian Hanafi jurist Nasafi (d. 1310):

> 'belittled' i.e. they have to be degraded and belittled by making him [the *dhimmi*] come in person, walking and not riding. He should hand [the *jizya*] over while standing and the receiver should be seated down, and

---

1 On this last point, see Riley's account of a beheading in Mogodore in 1815, in which the executioner took hold of the beard of the victim by the left hand, and 'very leisurely' cut through the neck. (*An Authentic Narrative of the Loss of the American Brig Commerce*, p.335.)

2 E.W. Lane, *An Arabic-English Lexicon*. Book 1, p.2643.

3 Hans Wehr, *A Dictionary of Modern Written Arabic*, p.854.

4 E.W. Lane reports the meaning of the stem II intensive derivative *labbaba* as 'He drew together his garments at his bosom and breast, in altercation, or contention, and then dragged him along,' or 'He put round his neck a rope, or a garment, and held him with it.' (*An Arabic-English Lexicon*. Book 1, p.2642.)

5 E.W. Lane, *An Arabic-English Lexicon*. Book 1, p.2641. In Arabic an intensive verb form implies a more complete or damaging effect. For example, *qatala* 'kill' has an intensive *qattala* 'massacre' and *kasara* 'break' has an intensive *kassara* 'break into pieces'.

he should be shaken violently, agitated and in turmoil. He should be dragged by the throat (*labbaba*), and told 'Perform *jizya* you *dhimmi!*' This is followed by a strong blow to the back of the neck.[1]

A similar list is found in the account of the Persian Shafi'i commentator al-Razi (d. 1210):

> About 'belittled'; this means *jizya* is to be taken from them in disgrace, humiliation and degradation. This is shown in the way the *dhimmi* has to bring it in person, walking and not riding. He must hand it over standing up while the receiver is seated. He should be yanked forward by his beard and told 'Pay *jizya!*' even though he is already doing it. Then he should be struck on the back of his neck. This is the meaning of 'belittled'. It has been said that the meaning of 'belittled' can be defined by the *jizya* payment. There are many doctrinal writings regarding the rules of what follows the disgrace or degradation and belittling.[2]

The eleventh century prescription of the Persian jurist al-Ghazali (d. 1111) describes a blow to the jaw under the ear rather than on the back of the neck:

> Jews, Christians, and Majians must pay the *jizya* ... on offering up the *jizya*, the *dhimmi* must hang his head while the official takes hold of his beard and hits [the *dhimmi*] on the protuberant bone beneath his ear [i.e. the mandible]...[3]

Al-Baghawi describes a different combination of humiliations, including a blow on the neck, a foot or heel placed on the neck, tugging of the beard, a blow to the jaws, and dragging by the throat.[4]

Al-Suyuti (d. 1505) describes other variations: the *dhimmi*'s head has dirt on it (although this might be a metaphor for humiliation) and the receiver of the *jizya* stands with a whip in his hand:

> [*Saghiruna* means] submissively ... by coercion ... ['*an yadin* means] directly, not trusting the trickery of an intermediary ... by force ... without resistance ... in an unpraiseworthy manner ... while you stand [and the *dhimmi*] sits with the whip in front of you [you take] the money while he has dirt on his head. (al-Suyuti)[5]

---

1 *Madarik al-Tanzil.* Commentary on Q9:29, viewed 21 February 2008, <http://altafsir.com>. Bostom appears to be mistaken when he reports that Hanafi jurisprudence did not sanction the blow on the neck (*The Legacy of Islamic Antisemitism*, note 580, p.195).

2 *Mafatih al-Ghayb.* Commentary on Q9:29, viewed 21 February 2008, <http://altafsir.com>.

3 al-Ghazali, *Kitab al-wagiz fi fiqh adhab al-imam al-Shafi'i.* Andrew Bostom, *The Legacy of Jihad*, p.199, trans. Michael Schub.

4 *Ma'alam al-Tanzil.* Commentary on Q9:29, viewed 21 February 2008, <http://altafsir.com>.

5 al-Suyuti, *Dur al-manthur*, vol.3, p.228. Trans. in Andrew Bostom, *The Legacy of Jihad*, p.127. The phrase translated as 'dirt on his head' appears to be an idiom meaning humiliation.

Al-Tabari (d. 923) describes the *dhimmi* handing over payment on his hands and knees:

> The *dhimmis'* posture during the collection of the *jizya* – [lowering themselves] by walking on their hands, reluctantly; on the authority of Ibn 'Abbas (al-Tabari).[1]

The great majority of Quranic commentaries include a reference to a blow in their explanation of Q9:29. A notable exception is Ibn Kathir, whose focus is upon interpreting the Quran in the light of the *Sunna*, which does not appear to contain any direct precedents for this aspect of the *jizya* ritual.

Below is a table which reports distinct accounts of the *jizya* payment from both Muslim and non-Muslim sources up until the end of the 19th century – including those already mentioned. All of these refer to some kind of blow to or interference with the neck or head.

What is noteworthy about this list is the constancy of the ritual's description across vast stretches of time and space.

Century	Source	Place
10th -11th	al-Tha'labi[2]	Persia
11th	al-Baghawi[3]	Persia
11th	al-Ghazali[4]	Persia
12th	al-Zamakhshari[5]	Syria
12th	al-Razi[6]	Persia
12th	al-Shayzari[7]	Syria
13th	Ibn al-Arabi[8]	Anatolia & Syria

---

1 M. Shair, ed., *Jami' al-bayan* … vol. 10, pp.125-26. Trans. in Andrew Bostom, *The Legacy of Jihad*, p.128.
2 *Tafsir al-Tha'labi*. Commentary on Q9:29, viewed 21 February 2008, <http://altafsir.com>.
3 *Ma'alam al-Tanzil*. Commentary on Q9:29, viewed 21 February 2008, <http://altafsir.com>.
4 al-Ghazali, *Kitab al-wagiz fi fiqh adhab al-imam al-Shafi'i*. Andrew Bostom, *The Legacy of Jihad*, p.199, trans. Michael Schub.
5 Bernard Lewis, *The Jews of Islam*, p.14-15. Also *al-Kashshaf*, Commentary on Q9:29, viewed 21 February 2008, <http://altafsir.com>.
6 *Mafatih al-Ghayb*. Commentary on Q9:29, viewed 21 February 2008, <http://altafsir.com>.
7 al-Shayzari, *Nihayat al-tutba fi talab al-hisba*. Cited in James E. Lindsay *Daily Life in the Medieval Islamic World*, p.121.
8 Ibn al-Arabi, *Ahkam al-Qur'an*. Cairo, 1331 AH. Vol. 1:378. Cited in Kister 2002: 366.

13th	Ibn al-Fuwati[1]	Persia
13th	al-Nawawi[2]	Syria
13th	Nasafi[3]	Persia
13th	al-Baydawi[4]	Persia
13th-14th	Nizam al-Nisaburi[5]	Persia
13th-14th	Isaac ben Samuel of Acre[6]	Syria
14th	Abu Hayyan[7]	Andalusia and Syria
14th	al-Khazin[8]	Persia
15th	al-Maghili[9]	Morocco
15th	Ibn 'Adil al-Dimashqi[10]	Syria
15th	Molla Khosrew[11]	Ottoman Turkey
17th	al-Majlisi[12]	Persia
18th	al-Adawi[13]	Egypt
18th	Ibn 'Ajibah[14]	Morocco

---

1 Bat Ye'or, *The Decline of Eastern Christianity under Islam*, p.348; *The Dhimmi*, p.192.

2 Bat Ye'or, *Islam and Dhimmitude*, p.70.

3 *Madarik al-Tanzil.* Commentary on Q9:29, viewed 21 February 2008, <http://altafsir.com>.

4 Helmut Gätje, *The Qur'an and its Exegesis* [*Anwat al-tanzil wa-asar al-ta'wil.* Commentary on Q9:29, by al-Baydawi.], p.139.

5 *Ghara'ib al-Qur'an wa ragha'ib al-furqan.* Commentary on Q9:29, viewed 21 February 2008, <http://altafsir.com>.

6 Bat Ye'or, *The Dhimmi*, p.353.

7 *Tafsir Bahr al-Muhit.* Commentary on Q9:29, viewed 21 February 2008, <http://altafsir.com>.

8 *Tafsir Lubab al-Ta'wil.* Commentary on Q9:29, viewed 21 February 2008, <http://altafsir.com>.

9 George Vajda, French trans. 'Adversos Judaeos', p.811. English trans. by Paul Fenton in Bat Ye'or, *The Dhimmi*, p.201.

10 *Tafsir al-Lubab fi 'ulum al-kitab.* Commentary on Q9:29, viewed 21 February 2008, <http://altafsir.com>.

11 Andrew Bostom, 'Islamic antisemitism – Jew hatred in Islam.' In *The Legacy of Islamic Antisemitism*, p.113. Concerning Ottoman Turkey, see also William Denton, *The Christians of Turkey*, p.116, who refers to seizing the *dhimmi* by the collar during the *jizya* ritual, citing the *Multka*, a 'digest of Ottoman canon law'.

12 *Risala-yi sawa'iq al-yahud* ['The treatise lighting bolts against the Jews']. Trans. Vera Basch Moreen. Andrew Bostom, *The Legacy of Jihad*, p.219.

13 François-Alphonse Belin. *Fetoua* by Ahmad ad-Dardir el-Adaoui. Trans. in Bat Ye'or, *The Decline of Eastern Christianity under Islam*, p.362, and in *The Dhimmi*, pp.201-2.

14 *Tafsir al-Bahr al-Madid fi Tafsir al-Quran al-Magid* by Ibn 'Ajibah. Commentary on Q9:29, viewed 21 February 2008, <http://altafsir.com>.

18th-19th	al-Shawkani[1]	Yemen
1815	James Riley (American)[2]	Morocco
1863	Jewish and other sources[3]	Bukhara
1888	Jewish sources[4]	Morocco
1894	an Italian Jew[5]	Morocco
19th	al-Alusi[6]	Baghdad
19th	at-Fayyish[7]	Algeria

In addition there are published references to twentieth century *jizya* payments from Morocco (1903),[8] Tunisia (1908),[9] Yemen (prior to the exodus of Yemeni Jews in 1948),[10] Iran (1949),[11] and as late as 1950 in Afghanistan, where Landshut describes the payment being 'accompanied by humiliating ceremonies as laid down in Sura IX, 29 of the Koran'.[12]

These references indicate that for more than a millennium after initial Islamic conquest, and in widely spread localities throughout the Islamic world, there continued to be humiliating rituals, involving ritual enactment of a decapitation, to show that the *jizya* was a compensation for the *dhimmi*'s head. The procedure thus stands for fourteen centuries of ritualized defeat.

The significance of this length of time is hard for us to grasp today. Imagine if, after the Norman invasion in 1066, the Normans had

---

1 *Tafsir Fatih al-Qadir.* Commentary on Q9:29, viewed 21 February 2008, <http://altafsir.com>.

2 James Riley, *An Authentic Narrative of the Loss of the American Brig Commerce*, p.333.

3 Robert Bertram Serjeant, 'A Judeo-Arab House-Deed,' pp.118-19; Michael Zand, 'The inner structure of the Jewish community of the city of Bukhar'; Arminius Vambery, *Travels in Central Asia*, pp.372-73, cited in Bat Ye'or, *Islam and Dhimmitude*, p.71.

4 Tudor Parfitt, *The Road to Redemption*, p.159.

5 Letter from a Marrakesh Jew, an Italian protégé, 25 February 1894, in *Bulletin, Alliance Israélite d'Études Universelle* (January-February 1894). Trans. in Bat Ye'or, *The Dhimmi*, p.327.

6 *Ruh al-Ma'ani*, Commentary on Q9:29, viewed 21 February 2008, <http://altafsir.com>.

7 *Himyan al-zad ila dar al-ma'ad.* And also *Taysir al-tafsir.* Commentary on Q9:29, viewed 21 February 2008, <http://altafsir.com>.

8 Littman, David G., 'Jews under Muslim Rule – II: Morocco 1903-1912.' In Bostom *The Legacy of Islamic Antisemitism*, p.536.

9 Jacques Chalom, *Les Israelites de la Tunisie*, p.193.

10 Tudor Parfitt, *The Road to Redemption*, p.105; S. Landshut, *Jewish Communities in the Muslim Countries of the Middle East*, p.73; Andrew Bostom, 'Islamic antisemitism – Jew hatred in Islam.' In *The Legacy of Islamic Antisemitism*, p.45.

11 Andrew Bostom, 'Islamic antisemitism – Jew hatred in Islam.' In *The Legacy of Islamic Antisemitism*, p.138.

12 S. Landshut, Jewish Communities in the Muslim Countries of the Middle East, p.67.

required Anglo-Saxons to line up once a year on every village green of England to pay war reparations and be ritually stabbed in the heart. Imagine too that this practice is still current today, it has been endorsed by every Archbishop of Canterbury since 1066, it will continue in England more than four centuries hence, and when it finally stops, this will only be due to the military intervention of a foreign power.

Such was the plight of the Jews of Morocco – and of non-Muslims all over the Islamic world – for more than a thousand years until emigration or European occupation brought an end to it. For the Jews of Yemen and Afghanistan it was only the exodus to Israel after 1948 that finally released them from the humiliations of the *jizya* ritual.

A blood pact

As a ritualized enactment of one's own decapitation, the *jizya* payment can be considered to be a 'blood pact' or 'blood oath', in which the participant invokes death against themselves by simulating the manner of their execution, should they ever fail to keep the conditions of their pact. Such oaths have been used for centuries in initiation ceremonies by secret societies and occult groups, for they are recognized to have psycho-spiritual power to bind initiates to submission and obedience.

The *jizya* ritual symbolically offers the consent of the *dhimmi* who participates in it to forfeit his very head if he violates any of the terms of the *dhimma* covenant, which has spared his life. It is an act of self-cursing, which says in effect 'You can rightfully have my head if I break any of the conditions of my covenant.' Later, if a *dhimmi* violates his covenant, he has already pronounced the death penalty against himself, by virtue of undergoing this public ritual, and if he is killed, it would be by his own prior permission.

The *jizya* ritual was hated by *dhimmis*; no doubt it was psychologically very damaging. The 18th century Moroccan commentator Ibn 'Ajibah said that it represented the death of the 'soul', through the *dhimmi*'s execution of their own humanity:

> [The *dhimmi*] is commanded to put his soul, good fortune and desires to death. Above all he should kill the love of life, leadership and honor. ... [He] is to invert the longings of his soul, he is to load it down more heavily than it can bear until it is completely submissive. Thereafter nothing will be unbearable for him. He will be indifferent to subjugation or might. Poverty and wealth will be the same to him; praise and insult will be the

same; preventing and yielding will be the same; lost and found will be the same. Then, when all things are the same, it [the soul] will be submissive and yield willingly what it should give.[1]

The intended result of the *jizya* ritual is for the *dhimmi* to lose all sense of his own personhood. In return for this loss, the *dhimmi* was supposed to feel humility and gratitude towards his Muslim masters. Al-Mawardi said that the *jizya* head tax was either a sign of contempt, because of the *dhimmis'* unbelief, or a sign of the mildness of Muslims, who granted them quarter (instead of killing or enslaving them): so humble gratitude was the intended response:

> The *jizya*, or poll tax, which is to be levied on the head of each subject, is derived from the verb *jaza*, either because it is a remuneration due by reason of their unbelief, for it is exacted from them with contempt, or because it amounts to a remuneration because we granted them quarter, for it is exacted from them with mildness. This origin of this impost is the divine text: 'Fight those who believe not in God … [Q9:29][2]

Although some today falsely claim that the *jizya* tax was simply a tax like any other tax, or merely a payment to exempt *dhimmis* from 'military service',[3] the remarks of al-Mawardi and Ibn 'Ajibah make clear that its true meaning is to be found in psychological attitudes of inferiority and indebtedness imposed upon non-Muslims living under Islam, as they willingly and gratefully handed over the *jizya* in service to the Muslim community.

The conditions: *dhimmi* laws

The *Sharia* did not leave this sense of humiliation to chance. As al-Baghawi pointed out, the belittling of *dhimmis* was achieved, not only through the *jizya* ritual, but also through the whole system of *Sharia* law as it applied to the *dhimmi* community.

Historians have documented the social, political, economic and religious conditions of *dhimmi* communities – especially Jews and Christians – in the Middle East. It is a sad history of dispossession and decline,

---

1 *Tafsir al-Bahr al-Madid fi Tafsir al-Quran al-Magid* by Ibn 'Ajibah. Commentary on Q9:29, viewed 21 February 2008, <http://altafsir.com>.

2 Edmond Fagnan, trans., *Al-ahkam as-Sultaniyya (Les statuts gouvernementaux)*, p.300. English trans. in Bat Ye'or, *The Decline of Eastern Christianity under Islam*, p.324.

3 See, for example, Bassam Zawadi, 'Is the Jizya Tax Oppressive?', viewed June 8 2009, <http://www.answering-christianity.com/bassam_zawadi/is_jizya_tax_oppressive.htm>. In addition to claiming that *zakat* was 'in lieu of military service,' Zawadi argues that the *jizya* is just, because it is equivalent to modern taxes: 'In America if someone does not pay their taxes they can go to jail. Does that make America unjust?'

which Griffith has referred to as a 'long slide into demographic ... insignificance'.[1] This was the intended outcome of the institution of the *dhimma*, which was designed to attract conversions to Islam.

In addition to the reality that the taxes, allocated to support the Muslim community, were often severely crippling and caused extreme impoverishment,[2] further legal provisions were applied to *dhimmis* ensuring their humiliation and inferiority.[3]

The famous Pact of 'Umar[4] lists some of the conditions which were to be imposed upon *dhimmi* communities. Ibn Kathir explained the meaning of these conditions:

> Paying *Jizya* is a sign of *Kufr* and disgrace
>
> Allah said,
> '*until they pay the Jizyah*', if they do not choose to embrace Islam,
> '*with willing submission*', in defeat and subservience,
> '*and feel themselves subdued.*' disgraced, humiliated and belittled.
>
> Therefore, Muslims are not allowed to honor the people of *Dhimmah* or elevate them above Muslims, for they are miserable, disgraced and humiliated.
>
> Muslima recorded from Abu Hurayrah that the Prophet said, 'Do not initiate the Salam [pronouncing a blessing as a greeting] to the Jews and Christians, and if you meet any of them in a road, force them to its narrowest alley.'
>
> This is why the leader of the faithful 'Umar bin Al-Khattab, may Allah be pleased with him, demanded his well-known conditions be met by the Christians, **these conditions that ensured their continued humiliation, degradation and disgrace.**[5]

The conditions imposed by *Sharia* law upon *dhimmis* were many and varied. Although not all laws were enforced to the same extent everywhere, nevertheless, across vast expanses of geography and time, the regulations had a consistency and constancy which imposed similar conditions upon *dhimmis* communities everywhere.

---

1 Griffith, *The Church in the Shadow of the Mosque*, p.13.
2 Shlomo Dov Goitein, 'Evidence on the Muslim poll tax from non-Muslim sources.'
3 The landmark study of the legal status of non-Muslims under the Shariah is Antoine Fattal's *Le statut légal des non-musulmans en pays d' Islam* (1958).
4 *Tafsir Ibn Kathir*, vol. 4:406-7.
5 Ibid., vol. 4:405-6.

The regulations are well known, and have been discussed by many scholars. *Sharia* law manuals typically include long lists of them.[1]

An Islamic treatise which deals with this subject in exhaustive detail is the as yet untranslated *Ahkam Ahl al-Dhimmah* 'Commandments of the *dhimmis*', a voluminous compendium of laws pertaining to *dhimmis* written by the Hanbali scholar Ibn al-Qayyim al-Jawziyya (d. 1350).[2]

The *dhimma* regulations characteristically included:

Restrictions relating to conversion

- Under Islam any Muslim who converts to Christianity or Judaism is subject to the death penalty.
- Conversions between faiths are forbidden: if anyone changes religion, it must be to Islam.
- It is forbidden to try to convert a Muslim from their faith.
- It is forbidden to hinder a fellow *dhimmi* from converting to Islam.
- Anyone who converted to Islam gained preferential inheritance rights within their family – they could become the inheritor of the family's property – and a spouse who converted would gain sole guardianship of any children.

Restrictions on marriage

- A Muslim man may marry a Christian or Jewish woman, but their home is a Muslim household, and their children become Muslims under law.
- It is forbidden for a Muslim woman to marry or to have any kind of liaison with a Christian or Jewish man.

Restrictions on worship and practice of faith

- No new churches could be built after conquest.
- Any damaged churches could not be repaired.
- *Dhimmis* were forbidden from any public display of their religion: no crosses, funeral processions, bells, no loud singing etc.
- *Dhimmis* were forbidden from printing or selling Christian books.

Restrictions on opposition to Muslims

- It was forbidden, on pain of death, for a *dhimmi* to raise a hand against a Muslim.

---

1 Those who wish to explore this subject further can consult the books of Bat Ye'or (*The Dhimmi, The Decline of Eastern Christianity under Islam* and *Islam and Dhimmitude*) and Andrew Bostom (*The Legacy of Islamic Antisemitism*), who provide illustrative citations from Islamic authorities.

2 Subhi al-Salih, ed., *Ahkam Ahl al-Dhimmah*.

- Also forbidden was cursing a Muslim, on pain of death.

Vulnerability and legal disability

- *Dhimmi* testimony was not valid against a Muslim. This principle applied throughout the whole Islamic world in one form or another before the colonial period. If a Muslim accused a Christian of a capital offense, such as trying to convert a Muslim, the Christian's own testimony was not valid in their defense. This also entrenched a principle that non-Muslim versions of events are regarded as suspect and unreliable.
- *Dhimmis* were forbidden from striking a Muslim, for whatever reason.
- The blood of a Muslim was not equal to the blood of a *dhimmi*. So, for example, although murder of a Muslim is punished by death, *Sharia* law said that no Muslim could be put to death for killing a non-Muslim.
- If a *dhimmi* kills another *dhimmi*, and then converts to Islam, he can escape punishment: anyone who converts to Islam is let off from a potential death sentence.

Rendering assistance and loyalty to Muslims

- *Dhimmis* had to house and feed Muslim soldiers whenever told to do so.
- *Dhimmis* were forbidden from assisting, forming an alliance with, or receiving protection from the enemies of Muslims.
- *Dhimmis* were forbidden from trying to leave territory under Islamic control.

Prohibition on critiquing Islam

- *Dhimmis* were forbidden from teaching their children the Quran, or teaching them about Islam.
- *Dhimmis* were forbidden from criticizing Muhammad, Islam or the *dhimma* pact itself.

Restrictions on the exercise of authority

- *Dhimmis* were not to hold public office or to exercise authority over Muslims.
- A *dhimmi* could not act as guardian for a Muslim. Thus if a Christian or Jewish child or as yet unmarried woman converts to Islam, the parents lose all rights of oversight for them.

- A *dhimmi* could not own a Muslim slave or buy slaves from Muslims.

Restrictions on housing, public appearance, status and behavior

- *Dhimmi* houses had to be smaller and lower than Muslim houses.
- A *dhimmi* had to vacate his seat for a Muslim.
- A *dhimmi* had to get out of the way of Muslims in the street, moving to the more cramped side of the way.
- *Dhimmis* were not allowed to ride horses or camels because it would raise them in status above Muslims.
- *Dhimmis* had to ride their donkeys side-saddle, with both legs on one side of the animal.[1]
- *Dhimmis* had to adopt a humble demeanor in public.
- A wide range of restrictions is reported on the appearance – clothing, footwear and hairstyles – of *dhimmis*, to ensure that they did not look like Muslims. There were two reasons given for this. One was to belittle the *dhimmis*. Ibn al-Qayyim cites a *hadith* of Muhammad in support of this principle

  > ... I have been sent with a sword in my hand to command people to worship Allah and associate no partners with him. I command you to **belittle and subjugate those who disobey me, for those who look alike are of the same**.[2]

  The other reason was that *dhimmis* had to be instantly recognizable as infidels: 'Muslims are to look like Muslims ... and the infidel is to look like an infidel so as to be identified as an infidel.'[3] According to Islamic scholars, this helped ensure that *dhimmis* would not be treated, by mistake, with the respect due to Muslims. Muhammad had said that it was forbidden to greet *dhimmis* with the *salam* (the greeting of peace), and this could only be consistently achieved if *dhimmis* were instantly identifiable as non-Muslims, even at a distance.

- There were many and varied rules for the clothing of *dhimmis*. A widely reported rule was that *dhimmis*, in contrast to Muslims, had to wear distinctive belts; this was regarded as a special humiliation.[4] Another was that people of each *dhimmi* religion had to wear a

---

1 Ibid., vol 2: 742.
2 Ibid., vol 2: 736.
3 Ibid., vol 2: 736.
4 Ibid., vol 2: 744.

clothing of a particular color. Also, *dhimmis* could only wear certain kinds of shoes or they had to wear a distinctive kind of turban.

- In many areas *dhimmis* were not allowed to wear matching shoes.
- In some periods *dhimmis* were required to wear iron or lead neck seals.
- Another rule was that *dhimmis* were required to cut off the hair at the front of their heads, and there were quite specific requirements about how they could arrange the rest of their hair,[1] for example, they could not part their hair (because Muhammad used to part his hair).[2]
- When attending public baths *dhimmis* were required to wear neck rings or bells so they could be easily distinguished from Muslims, even when naked.[3]
- In many areas, *dhimmis* had to wear colored patches: the yellow patch for Jews was invented under Islamic rule.[4] A report from Andalusia under the Moors describes one local expression of this policy:

> 'The *Qadi*, Ahmad b. Talib, [ninth century] compelled the *dhimmis* [Jews & Christians] to wear upon their shoulder a patch of white cloth that bore the image of an ape [for the Jews] and a pig [for the Christians], and to nail onto their doors a board bearing the sign of a monkey [Q5:65].' (Abu Bakr al-Maliki, d.1148, a Tunisian historian.[5])

- A diverse variety of local laws were devised, according to local custom, to ensure the humiliation of *dhimmis*. For example, in Morocco in the nineteenth century, Jews were required to perform humiliating professions, such as cleaning sewers, removing dead animals, and salting the heads of executed criminals; they had to walk bare-footed outside the ghetto; they had to work for the public authorities for low pay whenever this was demanded of them; they could not drink from public water fountains; and a Jew subjected to a flogging had to pay the fees of the person implementing the punishment.[6]

---

1 Ibid., vol 2: 749ff.

2 Ibn Qudama stated that *dhimmis* were 'not to part their hair because the prophet parted his hair' (*al-Mughni*, vol. 10, p.620).

3 Bat Ye'or, *Islam and Dhimmitude*, pp.191-92.

4 Bernard Lewis, *The Jews of Islam*, p.25.

5 al-Maliki, *Riyad a-Nufus*, Trans. Bat Ye'or, *The Decline of Eastern Christianity under Islam*, p.340.

6 Tudor Parfitt, *The Road to Redemption*, pp.158-59.

*Shi'ite **najis** regulations*

- In addition to other regulations, Shi'ites elaborated a series of restrictions on *dhimmis* related to their supposed uncleanliness (*najis*: Q9:28). In accordance with this belief, Jews were forbidden in Hamadan in the late 19th century to leave their homes during snow or rain, lest moisture which had come into contact with their bodies might later touch a Muslim's feet.[1]

Concerning the origins of the *dhimma* regulations

The historical evidence suggests that the *dhimma* regulations took centuries to be elaborated, but how did all these regulations come into existence? Many questions about their development remain unresolved.

The initial origins of the *jizya* taxation system seem clear. They derived, as we have seen, from the pre-existing Arab ethical code regulating tribal conflict and client-protégé relationships, from which Islam inherited key concepts of warfare[2] and tribute, and the idea that a defeated foe owed a blood debt of servitude to his vanquisher.

But what accounts for the detailed legal provisions which can be found in *Sharia* manuals, and confirmed by many observers down the centuries?

Bat Ye'or observes that some *dhimma* regulations appear to have been adopted from the Byzantine Code of Justinian (534).[3] It must have been non-Muslim administrators of the conquered territories (and converts) who introduced the Arabs conquerors to these laws. It is one of history's bitter ironies that a legal system designed to oppress Jews and heretics came to be turned back against Christians by their Muslim conquerors.

A similar process applied later in reverse in Sicily, when, after conquering the island, the Normans retained the Islamic system of *jizya* taxation, imposing it back upon the conquered Muslim population.[4] Likewise the Spanish imposed a '*jizya*' on Muslim subjects in reconquered Spain, calling it *tributo*, and later carried over this system to their territories in the New World.[5]

---

1 David G. Littman, 'Jews under Muslim rule: the case of Persia,' p.7; Bat Ye'or. *The Dhimmi*, p.333.

2 See the analysis of the origin of *jihad* in Reuven Firestone, *Jihad: The Origin of Holy War in Islam*.

3 Bat Ye'or, *The Decline of Eastern Christianity under Islam*, p.94.

4 Jeremy Johns, *Arabic Administration in Norman Sicily*.

5 Patricia Seed, *Ceremonies of Possession in Europe's Conquest of the New World, 1492-1640*, p.80.

The Pact of 'Umar is an important early source on the *dhimma* regulations, but Muslim scholars have disagreed over whether it should be attributed to 'Umar ibn al-Khattab who ruled from 634-44, or 'Umar ibn Abd al-Aziz, who ruled from 717-20.[1] The time difference between these two rulers is not insignificant.

Apart from the pivotal Q9:29, which authorizes the *jizya* and humbling of non-Muslims, the requirement that non-Muslims be abased under Islamic dominance is found in many passages of the Quran, and gave a theological justification for the humiliating character of the *dhimma* regulations, for example:

> You [the *Umma*] are the best nation ever brought forth to men, bidding to honour, and forbidding dishonour, and believing in Allah. Had the People of the Book believed, it were better for them; some of them are believers, but the most of them are ungodly.

> Abasement shall be pitched on them, wherever they are come upon, except they be in a bond of Allah, and a bond of the people [i.e. they should be under a *dhimma* pact]; they will be laden with the burden of Allah's anger, and poverty shall be pitched on them; that because they disbelieved in Allah's signs, and slew the Prophets without right; that, for that they acted rebelliously and were transgressors. (Q3:110,112)

Other verses of the Quran were also influential, such as the prohibitions against Muslims befriending unbelievers (Q3:118-20) and against non-Muslims exercising authority over Muslims. (Q3:100; Q5:56)

Yet another factor was the *hadiths*. Of tens of thousands of *hadiths* only a comparatively small handful, apart from the traditions about *jihad* conquest, proved to be significant for the *dhimma* regulations. These dealt with issues such as the prohibition on Muslims greeting *dhimmis*, the instruction that 'those who look alike are of the same' (discussed in chapter 6), warnings against killing or torturing *dhimmis*, restrictions on non-Muslims being placed in authority over Muslims, and limitations on non-Muslims' capacity to bear witness in courts.

There is however a chicken-and-egg question about these *hadiths*. Was the *dhimma* developed partly in response to these *hadiths*, or were the *hadiths* developed to provide a theological rationale for the emerging *dhimma* system? It is well known that thousands of *hadiths* were fabricated during the first two Islamic centuries and Islamic orthodoxy came to reject many of these as forgeries, while classifying many others as of dubious reliability. Yet many contemporary scholars would go

---

1 Bat Ye'or, *The Decline of Eastern Christianity under Islam*, p.61.

much further, and reject just about the whole corpus of *hadith* and *sira* literature as being of late origin.

Undoubtedly a significant influence upon the implementation of the *dhimma* laws was simply the quest for power and wealth. During the first few Islamic centuries Muslims were greatly outnumbered by the conquered *dhimmi* populations, and the conquerors derived enormous wealth from the *jizya* taxation system. The *dhimma*, by allowing non-Muslims to keep their religion, yet retain a position of inferiority and absolute distinctness under Islamic rule, ensured a ready and continuing source of revenue for the *Umma*.[1] The *dhimma* laws were vital to maintaining this whole system.

Although there are many questions which may be asked about the emergence of the *dhimma* system,[2] our concern is with its impact on the conquered peoples.

Vulnerable to violence

It must be acknowledged that Islamic law demanded that *dhimmis* be protected. Muhammad had stated that whoever kills a *dhimmi* would not 'smell the smell of Paradise'.[3] Also the caliph 'Umar had advised Muslims to keep their covenant with the *dhimmis* because of self-interest, *dhimmis* being a source of financial support for the Muslims.

> … fulfill Allah's *Dhimma* as it is the *Dhimma* of your Prophet and the source of the livelihood of your dependents (i.e., the taxes from the *Dhimmi*).[4]

Despite 'Umar's advice, the combined impact of the *dhimma* principles proved most pernicious and destructive for the non-Muslim communities. Violence or theft against *dhimmi* populations was extremely hard to defend against: since the *dhimmi*'s witness was invalid in court, they could not bear weapons – even in very dangerous times – and they were forbidden from raising a hand against a Muslim.

---

1 As Abu Yusuf Ya'qub stated, implementing the *jizya* – rather than execution of the males and enslavement of women and children – could be 'preferable in order to increase the *fay*, which enhances the resources of the Muslims against them and the other polytheists'. See 'Battle Procedures' in *Kitab al-Kharadj*. Trans. Bat Ye'or, *The Decline of Eastern Christianity under Islam*, p.302. (Excerpted from Henri Fagnan, French trans. *Le Livre de l'impôt foncier (Kitâb el-Kharâdj)*).

2 One of the puzzles to be resolved is the discrepancies between statements of Muslim jurists on the one hand, and non-Muslim accounts of the impact of conquest on the indigenous *dhimmi* populations. See Bat Ye'or, *The Decline of Eastern Christianity under Islam*, pp.73-74.

3 *Sahih al-Bukhari*. The Book of *al-Jizya* and the Stoppage of War. 4:58:3166.

4 Ibid. 4:58:3162.

A particularly perilous circumstance for *dhimmi* communities was when Muslims were fighting against Muslims. Under such circumstances, the defenseless *dhimmis* became an easy target for both sides.

An example of Muslim conflict resulting in anti-*dhimmi* attacks was a series of pogroms against Jewish communities in Jerusalem, Safed, Tiberius and Hebron in 1834, described by E. R. Malachi.[1] Ibrahim Pasha of Egypt had conquered Turkish Palestine in the late 1820's. When Ibrahim introduced conscription, the Arab peasants and Bedouins rose up in rebellion against his rule, incited by declarations of *jihad* against him. A revolt in Safed commenced on June 14, where the rebels turned their anger against the Jews for thirty-three days. The traditional *jihad* pattern of killings, rapes and looting ensued. Some Jews fled naked to surrounding villages. Jacob Safir described the condition of the refugees in one of these villages:

> For three days we did not eat a thing. Afterwards they gave us a small cake for a whole day's sustenance. We stayed there for forty days in fear of death by the robbers. Our property was taken by strangers and we were not certain that we would survive. We appeared naked, for they had stripped us of our clothing and emptied our homes of everything we owned. They did not leave small items, a door or a window.[2]

Others fled to synagogues in Safed, where 'They fasted, blew the shofar, and awaited their death.'[3]

A month later, on July 24 Ibrahim Pasha's soldiers put down the rebels in Hebron, and in that city they looted and raped the Jews, who had already suffered at the hands of the rebels.[4] Thus did both sides in the conflict target the *dhimmis*.

Another dangerous circumstance for *dhimmis* was when there were hostilities between Muslims and external enemies. For example, the Turkish genocide of the Armenians during World War I was spurred on by the Allied attack on the Dardanelles. When the British and their allies – whom the Turks considered to be Christian – attacked Turkey, this was taken as a further cause to justify attacks against the Christian Armenians, for 'collaborating' with the enemy.[5]

---

1 E.R. Malachi, 'Palestine under the rule of Ibrahim Pasha.' In Andrew Bostom, *The Legacy of Islamic Antisemitism.*
2 Ibid., p.594.
3 Ibid., p.594.
4 Ibid., p.596.
5 'Professor outlines Armenian connection to Gallipoli.' *PM* interview with Robert Manne, ABC. 12 February, 2007.

This pattern has been repeated many times in history, and is being replayed in Iraq today, where Shi'ite-Sunni conflict, combined with US-European military occupation, is associated with appalling attacks by Muslims from both sides against the local Christian population, who pose absolutely no threat to the Muslims of Iraq.

The CBS news program *60 Minutes* broadcast a segment on June 29, 2008 on the Christians of Iraq. Anglican minister Canon Andrew White, known as the 'vicar of Baghdad', was ministering to an underground congregation composed mainly of women and children. The interviewer, Scott Pelley, asked: 'The room is full of children, it's full of women, but I don't see the men. Where are they?' To this White answered, 'They are mainly killed. Some are kidnapped. Some are killed. … Here in this church, all of my leadership were originally taken and killed.'[1] Later in the same segment, Pelley interviewed Colonel Gibbs, a US army commander in Durah, a municipality with thirteen abandoned and ruined churches. Col. Gibbs explained that the occupation force has a 'hands-off-policy' for all religious sites. Consequently, churches were not protected. Moreover 'The Christians do not want us to guard the churches openly,' because 'they feel that if we are overtly protecting the churches that someone underground covertly will come in and murder the Christians because they're collaborating with the U.S. forces.'

In a tragic unfolding of destruction, we are seeing the motifs of the *dhimma* being played out before the eyes of the world in Iraq today. The selective killing of adult males is consistent with the *Sharia* requirement that men, but not women or children, be put to death in *jihad*. Also the Christians' fear that they would be victimized for receiving US protection is entirely consistent with one of the provisions of the *dhimma*, that non-Muslims must not receive protection from anyone but the *Umma*.

Under *dhimma* conditions violence could be life threatening, but often it was designed to humiliate and demean. Many visitors to Jerusalem and to other parts of the Muslim world in 19th and early 20th centuries reported that it was common for Muslim children to throw stones at Jewish men and women, and to abuse them verbally, without fear of reprisal or correction, much as one might throw stones at a stray dog.[2] I myself have met many Christians from the Middle East who

---

1 'Vicar: dire times for Iraq's Christians.' *60 Minutes*, June 29, 2008, viewed 8 June 2009, <http://www.cbsnews.com/stories/2007/11/29/60minutes/main3553612_page2.shtml>.

2 Bat Ye'or, *The Dhimmi*, p.64, p.76, note 47.

have had stones thrown at them by Muslim children. The throwing of stones at Jewish worshippers and Israeli police at the Temple Mount in September 2002 – the act which started the *intifada* – could be interpreted as a continuation of this centuries-old gesture of contempt for *dhimmis*.

Similar abuse was reported from Morocco in 1888 by Arthur Cohen, President of the London Committee of the Deputies of British Jews. Cohen had written a letter to Lord Salisbury asking for intervention in the interests of Moroccan Jews. One of the long list of grievances was that:

> Moors frequently amuse themselves by throwing live coals, broken glass, old tinware and such things in thoroughfares traversed by Jews and enjoy the fun of seeing the latter smart under the burn or wound inflicted on their bare feet.[1] [Moroccan Jews were not allowed to wear footwear outside the ghetto.]

Subject to curses

Not mentioned in the long list of restrictions on *dhimmis* given above is the additional burden of spiritual hostility, for cursing *dhimmis* has been a widespread aspect of Islamic societies. This practice is the inverse of the *Sharia* prohibition on *dhimmis* from cursing Muslims, and Muhammad's prohibition on blessing Christians and Jews.

In 1836 Edward Lane published his classic work *An Account of the Manners and Customs of the Modern Egyptians*. He reports that cursing of *dhimmis* was taught as part of a Muslim's educational formation:

> I am credibly informed that children in Egypt are often taught at school, a regular set of curses to denounce upon the persons and property of Christians, Jews, and all other unbelievers in the religion of Mohammad.[2]

These curses are recorded by Lane in an Appendix. In essence they describe looting, killing of men and enslavement of women and children, which is the lot of *dhimmis* when they have no protection and are subjected to *jihad*. These curses are in fact a prayer that the *dhimma* will be set aside and as such they served to impart the theological requirements of the *dhimma* to the minds of Muslim children:

> [After praying for the Sultan and his armies:] O God, destroy the infidels and polytheists, thine enemies, the enemies of the religion. O God, make their children orphans and defile their abodes,

---

1 Tudor Parfitt, *The Road to Redemption*, p.158.
2 E.W. Lane, *An Account of the Manners and Customs of the Modern Egyptians*, note 1, p.276.

and cause their feet to slip, and give them and their families and their households and their women and their children and their relations by marriage and their brothers and their friends and their possessions and the race and their wealth and their lands as booty to the Muslims: O Lord of the beings of the whole world.[1]

On March 6, 2009, Al-Rahma TV in Egypt presented a broadcast in which a child calls down curses upon Jews in similar fashion, expressing a wish that the men will be killed, women widowed, and children orphaned:[2]

> Oh Allah, completely destroy and shatter the Jews. Oh Allah, torment them with a disease that has no cure or remedy. Send a thunderbolt down upon them from Heaven. Oh Allah, torment them with every kind of torment. ... Oh Allah, turn their women into widows – just like Muslim women were widowed. Allah, turn their children into orphans – just like Muslim children were orphaned.[3]

It is a crushing psychological and spiritual burden to live from generation to generation under a culture of curses and withholding of blessings.

---

1 Ibid., Appendix E, p.575.
2 Memri TV Clip #2093. Al-Rahma TV, 6 March 2009, 'Egyptian Cleric Teaches a Child to Memorize Antisemitic Messages on Al-Rahma TV and Explains: The Understanding of What He Said Will Come,' downloaded 20 May 2009, <http://www.memritv.org/clip/en/0/0/0/0/0/0/2093.htm>.
3 Ibid: transcript, <http://www.memritv.org/clip_transcript/en/2093.htm>.

CHAPTER 7

The Lived Reality

Islam is peace.
George W. Bush[1]

*I am astonished by President Bush when he claims there is nothing
in the Quran that justifies jihad violence in the name of Islam.
Is he some kind of Islamic scholar?
Has he ever actually read the Quran?*
Abu Qatada, jihadist cleric[2]

The shadow of future war

The *dhimma* pact purchased an escape, not only from *jihad* in the past, but
as al-Marghinani pointed out, from **future** war. If a *dhimmi* community
was considered to have broken any of the *dhimma* conditions, the local
Muslim community had the duty to restart *jihad* against them. This is a
condition that the *dhimmi* community had been required to consent to,
and had to live under.

Ibn Kathir's commentary on Q9:29 describes how the caliph 'Umar
took steps to make sure that this element was included in his famous
Pact. *Dhimmis* were required to agree that:

> These are the conditions that we set against ourselves and followers of
> our religion in return for safety and protection. If we break any of these
> promises that we set for your benefit against ourselves, then our Dhimmah
> is broken and **you are allowed to do with us what you are allowed of
> people of defiance and rebellion.**[3]

The eighteenth century Yemeni scholar al-Shawkani (d. 1834) wrote:

1 '"Islam is Peace", says President.' White House Press Release, September 17, 2001. Remarks
   made by President Bush when visiting the Washington D.C. Islamic Center, viewed 17
   September, 2001, <http://www.whitehouse.gov/news/releases/2001/09/20010917-11.html>.
2 Daniel Pipes, 'What's true Islam? Not for the U.S. to say.' *New York Post*, November 26, 2001,
   viewed 8 June 2009, <http://www.danielpipes.org/article/86>.
3 *Tafsir Ibn Kathir*, vol. 4:407.

If their obligations are not fulfilled, they revert to the situation in which their persons and property are no longer protected by the agreement, namely to the state of affairs prior to the agreement of protection.'[1]

Based on the precedent of Muhammad's *Sunna*, a return to *jihad* conditions would result in a massacre of *dhimmi* men, looting of property, and seizing of wives and children. Under the circumstances of a *dhimma* pact violation, these actions would be regarded as legitimate. Thus the laws of *jihad* gave permission for Muslims to regard the *dhimmis* and their property as *halal*, free to be looted,[2] enslaved, raped and killed. More than this, such actions were not merely permissible or recommended; they were obligatory, what Muhammad ibn Yusuf at-Fayyish referred to as the 'duties [*wajib*] of killing and slavery'.[3]

Relevant here is the distinction in Islamic rules of war between warfare against a non-Muslim state, and warfare against non-Muslims who are in a Muslim country. The first type of *jihad* is a **communal obligation**, which it is the duty of the caliph to pursue, and of the Muslim community to support. The second *jihad*, against the enemy within the borders, is **'personally obligatory** upon the inhabitants of that country'.[4] Under the circumstances of an alleged *dhimma* pact violation, Islamic leaders could invoke the concept of *jihad* as a personal obligation to urge all the Muslims in a community to rise up against the *dhimmis*. This was not simply something to be left to the caliph to deal with.

For *dhimmi* women, enslavement meant rape and concubinage (and for some, eventual marriage) to their captors, while for children it meant forced conversion to Islam. Girls would in due course be assigned to Muslim partners, and boys could be used as slave labor (including as slave soldiers), or be adopted by their owners. If they converted to Islam the slaves might be freed, a practice which the *Sharia* encourages. In this way the victors, having killed the men, could use the children and women to augment their own lineages. Alternatively, the captors could sell the slaves for profit. The precedents for all these actions can be found in the example of Muhammad in his treatment of the Jews of Medina and Khaybar.[5]

---

1 al-Shawkani, *Kitab al-sayl al-jarrar al-mutadafiq 'ala hada'iq al-azhar*, vol. 4, p.574. Yosef Tobi, 'Conversions to Islam among Yemenite Jews under Zaydi Rule', p.582, English translation via the Hebrew by Rivkah Fishman. Orig. publ. in *Pe'amim* 42 (1990): 105-26.

2 Permission to take booty is found in the Quran (Q8:41; Q48:19-20), as well as the *Sunna*.

3 *Taysir al-Tafsir.* Commentary on Q9:29, viewed 21 February 2008, <http://altafsir.com>.

4 Nuh Ha Mim Keller, ed. and trans. *Reliance of the Traveller*, p.600.

5 See, for example, Guillaume, *The Life of Muhammad*, pp.464-66, 510-22.

Legally the only thing that separated *dhimmi* communities from this fate at the hands of their Muslims neighbors, for all time, was their permanent compliance with the *dhimma* pact.

On the other hand, the Quran teaches that if Muslims 'fear treachery' this was a solid basis for revoking their covenant with the non-Muslims. The passage also indicates that non-believers, not fearing Allah, are like beasts, and will be hypocritical pact-breakers 'every time':

> Surely the worst of beasts in Allah's sight are the unbelievers,
> who will not believe [in Islam],
> those of them with whom thou has made compact
> then **they break their compact every time**, not being godfearing ...
> And if thou fearest treachery any way at the hands of a people,
> dissolve it with them equally;
> surely Allah loves not the treacherous. (Q8:55-58)

There have been countless cases down through history when, due to pact violations, whether real, alleged or merely anticipated, *dhimmi* communities have been subjected to massacre, rape, looting and enslavement. In addition to such traumatic events, the constant background threat of lawful slaughter, rape, kidnapping and looting established a culture of abuse in which **extra-judicial** attacks (i.e. contrary to *Sharia* requirements) on *dhimmis* were an accepted fact of life. The disability of *dhimmis* in *Sharia* courts meant that it was virtually impossible for them to obtain legal redress if such things happened.

Communal attacks and massacres

Here we review just a few cases where *dhimmi* communities have been subjected to *jihad* attack.

In 1066, the same year that William the Conqueror was invading England, the Jews of Granada, numbering around 3,000, were massacred. This was after a period of forty years during which the vizier of the city had been a Jew, first Samuel ha-Nagid, and then his son Joseph.[1] The Jews had been too successful and a campaign of religious incitement against them called for their destruction on the authority of the *dhimma* regulations.

The dangers of Muslim patronage were made clear in the teachings of al-Maghili some four centuries later (summarized by George Vajda):

---

1 Moshe Perlmann, 'Eleventh-century Andalusian authors on the Jews of Granada.' See also Bat Ye'or, *The Decline of Eastern Christianity under Islam*, pp.228-29.

The Jews who occupy a position serving a sovereign, a vizier, a *qadi*, or some other important personage thus find themselves in a state of permanent rebellion against their status, which from then on no longer protects them.

In a word, all means of coercion must be used with regard to the Jews to make them observe strictly their status as *dhimmis*. To kill a Jew (who by his own fault has lost his status as a member of a protected people [i.e. by gaining favor from a leader and consequently rising in status]) is more meritorious than an expedition into infidel territory; one must persecute people of this sort, wherever they may be found, slay them, take their wives, children and goods. Those who assist them and become accomplices in their transgressions will experience the same eternal damnation as their favorites.[1]

A historic massacre of Serbian leaders known as the 'Massacre of the Serbian Knights' was conducted by Ottoman janissaries on February 4, 1804. This event triggered off an uprising against Turkish rule, which led to the emancipation of the Serbs.[2]

More than five thousand Christians were massacred in Damascus in 1860, in the aftermath of the Ottomans' official abolition of the *dhimma* laws. The local Muslim sentiment in Damascus, incited by preaching from the mosques, was that since Christians were no longer acting submissively as *dhimmis* should, they had forfeited any rights of protection. What ensued followed classical *jihad* war procedures, with looting, massacre of the men, and rape and abduction of women and children. Many families lost every adult male. Most of the Christian ministers were killed. Some abducted children could never be retrieved, but of those who were, some had been circumcised (i.e. forcibly converted). It was estimated that more women were raped than men were killed. Hundreds escaped with their lives by converting to Islam. Many of these later left the area to be able to revert to Christianity, but a few stayed on as Muslims after the massacre.

This massacre, together with others which occurred around the same time, was officially investigated by the Earl of Dufferin, who included in his report a first-hand report from the Reverend S. Robson, an Irish missionary in Damascus during the killings.[3] After the Damascus massacre, it proved impossible to prosecute any of the murderers

---

1 George Vajda, 'Adversos Judaeos', English trans. by Michael J. Miller in Andrew Bostom, *The Legacy of Islamic Antisemitism*, p.347.

2 Misha Glenny. *The Balkans: Nationalism, War and the Great Powers, 1804-1999.* Excerpted at <http://www.nytimes.com/books/first/g/glenny-balkans.html?_r=2&oref=slogin>, viewed 8 June 2009.

3 Bat Ye'or, *The Dhimmi*, p.259ff.

because no one was willing to act as a witness, due to fear on the part of the Christians, and the view on the Muslims' side that no-one should be prosecuted for killing infidels.[1] Robson explained that the attack was attributed to a breakdown in the *dhimma* status of the Christians:

> The Mahometans of Damascus had come to believe that the Christians, by taking advantage of the privileges and liberties conceded to them during the last thirty years, had placed them[selves] in a state of disobedience and rebellion, and forfeited their right to security and protection; and that it was therefore lawful to kill and rob them and carry off their women and children.[2]

A prophetic anticipation of this state of affairs had been given by the Ottoman Grand Vizier Mustafa Resid, just a few years earlier in opposing the Turkish reforms:

> In his denunciation of the reforms, Resid argued the proposed 'complete emancipation' of the non-Muslim subjects, appropriately destined to be subjugated and ruled, was 'entirely contradictory' to 'the 600 year traditions of the Ottoman Empire'. He openly proclaimed the 'complete emancipation' segment of the initiative as disingenuous, enacted deliberately to mislead the Europeans, who had insisted upon this provision. Sadly prescient, Resid then made the ominous prediction of a 'great massacre' if equality was in fact granted to non-Muslims.[3]

In 1907 an attack on European interests in Casablanca led to a bombardment of the city by a French warship, the *Galilee*. As soon as the first canon shot was fired, 'as if the Arabs were only waiting for this sign',[4] thousands of Muslims began to pillage and destroy the Jewish quarters of the city. This continued for three days until the French soldiers disembarked. A Jewish leader, Isaac Pisa, who conducted an investigation after the incident, reported that thirty Jews were killed, 60 wounded, an 'unlimited number of rapes' took place, and more than 250 young women, girls and children were abducted.[5]

The most heinous anti-*dhimmi* reprisal in recent history was the genocide of the Armenians during the First World War, following massacres of hundreds of thousands in the 1890's. It was the aspirations of the

---

1 The events of the massacre and the impossibility of obtaining legal redress was reported in the dispatches of the British Consul James Brant (Bat Ye'or, *The Decline of Eastern Christianity under Islam*, p.408).

2 Bat Ye'or, *The Dhimmi*, p.269.

3 Andrew Bostom, 'Congress must recognize the Armenian genocide.'

4 David G. Littman, 'Jews under Muslim Rule – II: Morocco 1903-1912.' In Andrew Bostom, *The Legacy of Islamic Antisemitism*, p.538.

5 Ibid., p.539.

Armenians for equal treatment – the ultimate rejection of the *dhimma* – which triggered their wholesale destruction by Muslims under the Ottomans. In this case also, the massacre was especially directed at the men. Another *jihad* feature was the often-reported offer of conversion to Islam as a means of escaping death. Many women and girls were abducted into the homes of Muslims. Bat Ye'or recounts the features of the Armenian genocide which conformed to the classical norms of *jihad*:

> The genocide of the Armenians was a *jihad*. ... Despite the disapproval of many Muslim Turks and Arabs, and their refusal to collaborate in the crime, these massacres were perpetrated solely by Muslims and they alone profited from the booty: the victims' property, houses, and lands granted to the *muhajirun*, and the allocation to them of women and child slaves. The elimination of male children over the age of twelve was in accordance with the commandments of the *jihad* and conformed to the age fixed for the payment of the *jizya*. The four stages of the liquidation – deportation, enslavement, forced conversion, and massacre – reproduced the historic conditions of the *jihad* carried out in the *dar-al-harb* from the seventh century on.[1]

Such events need to be understood in the context of the **communal** or collective nature of the *dhimma* pact. As it was the whole community which made the pact, it is the whole community which must pay the price if the pact is broken. Even a breach by a single individual *dhimmi* could result in *jihad* being enacted against the whole community. Muslim jurists have made this principle explicit, for example, the Yemeni jurist al-Murtada wrote that 'The agreement will be cancelled if all or some of them break it ...'[2] and the Moroccan al-Maghili taught 'The fact that one individual (or one group) among them has broken the statute is enough to invalidate it for all of them.'[3]

As a result *dhimmis* have always lived in a state of perpetual concern for the potential impact of their personal actions on their whole community. Individuals would be very reluctant to take any prominent position in the society. Historical accounts tell of how well-off *dhimmi* families

---

1 Bat Ye'or, *The Decline of Eastern Christianity under Islam*, p.197. See also Andrew Bostom, 'Congress must recognize the Armenian genocide'.

2 Yosef Tobi, 'Conversions to Islam among Yemenite Jews under Zaydi Rule.' In Andrew Bostom, *The Legacy of Islamic Antisemitism*, p.582, English translation (via the Hebrew) by Rivkah Fishman. Orig. publ. in *Pe'amim* 42 (1990): 105-26. See also Hady Roger Idris, 'Les Tributaires', p.191.

3 This passage is from notes on al-Maghili compiled by Ibn 'Askar in the *Da'wat al-nasir*. George Vajda 'Adversos Judaeos.' English trans. by Michael J. Miller in Andrew Bostom, *The Legacy of Islamic Antisemitism*, p.345.

could allow their children to go about in rags, and wealthy merchants would do service sweeping the streets, to avoid attracting hostility from Muslim neighbors.

It must be emphasized that there need not be actual *dhimmi* laws in place for reprisals to be enacted which accord with the pattern of the *dhimma* pact. The *dhimma* is not merely a legal contract: it is a religious institution which informs and influences the culture and behavior of whole societies, whether the political authorities uphold the *dhimma* or not. This was repeatedly demonstrated throughout the Muslim world after the Ottomans officially revoked the *dhimma*, and the principle continues to be shown today in the enforcement of many *dhimma* conditions against non-Muslims in Islamic nations.

The sense that individual 'transgressions' of non-Muslims legitimates a communal reprisal remains an enduring issue in Muslim communities. In September of 2005, a reprisal was directed against the Christian Palestinian village community of Taiba on the basis of the actions of an individual man who had a romance with a Muslim woman. A report entitled 'Muslims ransack Christian village', published in the *Jerusalem Post* of September 5, 2005 described the events:

> Efforts were under way on Sunday to calm the situation in this Christian village east of Ramallah after an attack by hundreds of Muslim men from nearby villages left many houses and vehicles torched. The incident began on Saturday night and lasted until early Sunday, when Palestinian Authority security forces interfered to disperse the attackers. Residents said several houses were looted and many families were forced to flee to Ramallah and other Christian villages, although no one was injured.
>
> ... 'More than 500 Muslim men, chanting Allahu akbar [Allah is greater], attacked us at night', said a Taiba resident. 'They poured kerosene on many buildings and set them on fire. Many of the attackers broke into houses and stole furniture, jewelry and electrical appliances.' ... **'It was like a war**, they arrived in groups, and many of them were holding clubs', said another resident.

Several aspects of this attack points to its character as a *jihad* reprisal under *dhimma* conditions:

- the impression that the attack was 'like a war': it was in fact a manifestation of *jihad*;
- the traditional war cry Allahu Akbar 'Allah is greater', uttered by the attackers, showed that they regarded their deeds as having a religious motivation;

- • the looting of non-Muslim homes; and
- • the communal character of the reprisals, for the transgression of an individual.

That this attack did not entirely follow the classic *dhimma* reprisal pattern can be seen in the absence of reported casualties, and apparently no-one was taken captive or enslaved!

Abduction of children

Again and again the historical sources report that *dhimmi* children have been vulnerable to being abducted and forcibly converted to Islam. It was not a part of the *dhimma* that children could be taken at will, but this practice can be understood as a premature realization of the threat of future *jihad*. This vulnerability is further influenced by the interaction of certain theological principles.

First and foremost is the doctrine that everyone is born a Muslim: for this reason converts to Islam are usually referred to as 'reverts'. It is a core concession of the *dhimma* that *dhimmis* are allowed to bring up their children in the faith of their parents' community, although this is contrary to their 'birth faith' as Muslims. On the other hand, revoking this concession by Islamizing a *dhimmi* child can be regarded as an act of mercy done in the best interests of the child.

Another ideological foundation for this practice was the idea that children were not to be killed in warfare because they could instead be enslaved and eventually converted to Islam, as Ibn Qudama explains:

> '... a child will become a slave ... so to kill him is to destroy (the Muslims') wealth, and **as a captive he will become a Muslim,** so to expose him (to death) is to expose one who can be made into a Muslim.'[1]

From this point of view, to interrupt the *jihad* could disadvantage a non-Muslim *dhimmi* child – conceived of as 'one who can be made into a Muslim' – by cutting him or her off from the opportunity of being enslaved and thereby converted to Islam. Abducting a child, while strictly speaking in conflict with the *dhimma* pact, is actually thought to be in the best interests of the child.

Another contributing factor is the principle that once someone converts to Islam, they are not allowed to convert back to their former faith. If a child can be induced to recite the *shahada* – the confession of faith – this might be taken as an irrevocable conversion. Taken together with

---

1 Ibn Qudama. *al-Mughni*, vol.10, pp.581-82.

the *Sharia* principle that it is not lawful for a Muslim child to be in the custody of a non-Muslim, this would imply that the newly converted child must be taken from their parents.

Many cases of such abductions have been documented. For example, Niven C.B. Moore, British Consul in Aleppo, Beirut, wrote in an official report in 1842 that he had been informed of several cases where young children had been induced to enter Islam. One mother complained to him that her son 'had been decoyed away by a Turk, and made a Mahometan'. The local Turkish administrator (the Pacha) refused to intervene, because to do so would have inflamed the sentiment of the 'whole Mussulman population'.[1]

In certain instances Islamic authorities have instituted regulations to institutionalize the abduction of children. In Yemen any orphaned Jewish child was, by the local *Sharia* law, taken away from the Jewish community and forcibly Islamized.[2] This practice continued up until the 1950's, when the Jewish community escaped to Israel.

Under Ottoman rule the practice of confiscating Christian children was legalized. The strongest and fairest male children of *dhimmis* were taken from their communities in regular collections. They were either sold as slaves, or forcibly converted and used to man the Ottoman army. Less commonly they to served the Sultan as administrators.[3] The slave soldiers produced by this system, known as *janissaries* (from Ottoman *yeniçeri* 'new soldier'), were deployed all over the Ottoman Empire and used to fight against their former co-religionists to extend and defend the Sultan's power.

Rape and abduction of dhimmi women

In a legal sense, *dhimmi* women are doubly vulnerable to rape by Muslim men, not only because as women their testimony would be worth half that of a man, but also as *dhimmis* their testimony was not valid against a Muslim's in any case. In many *dhimmi* communities there has been a deep fear that daughters will be taken, perhaps forcibly married, and they and their future children lost to the community.

There are countless references to actual abduction and rape of non-Muslim women and girls, as well as to the fear of this, in sources documenting the history of *dhimmi* communities. Many similar reports

---

1 Bat Ye'or, *The Dhimmi*, p.241.

2 Ibid., pp.381-82.

3 Artak Shakaryan, *Devshirme: the Blood-Tax in the Ottoman Empire.*

can be found in surveys of human rights abuses in Muslim nations. An entirely typical report was given by Laurence Loeb in 1977, commenting on the sexual harassment of Iranian Jewish women:

Kidnapping and Molestation of Jewish women

The kidnapping of Jewish women, especially young virgins (married women were fair game too!), was frightening to Jews. Lotfali Khan-e Zand took girls from Isfahan and Shiraz for his harem ... but lesser men too seized Jewish women for themselves. ...

Today, when even Muslim women are pinched and handled by Muslim men, Jewish women are singled out for special treatment because they are not protected by their kinsmen. The latter do not intervene for fear they will be beaten or even killed.[1]

The conditions of the *dhimma* motivate this fear. Just as the annual payment of the *jizya* symbolizes for men an escape from future death, for women it stands for an escape from future rape. Through the provisions of the *dhimma*, the threat of *jihad* rape lurks in the background of *dhimmi*-Muslim gender relations. This threat can be realized from the chain of events which can follow if the Muslim community believes that *dhimmis* have breached their pact. In this case, when the *jihad* is restarted, the example of Muhammad and *Sharia* law indicate that non-Muslim women, once abducted, are *halal* for the Muslims, and can be used sexually by those who have captured them.

It was this legal principle of the *Sharia* rules of war which a protestor appealed to at a February 3, 2006 demonstration in London when he cried out against the Danish embassy:

We will take revenge on you! Allahu Akbar! May they [Usama Bin Ladin and Zawahiri] bomb Denmark, so we can invade their country, and take their wives as war booty.[2]

As we have seen, the *Sharia* rules of war are so scrupulous as to make clear that married women, once taken captive in *jihad*, are thereby considered to be divorced, so sexual relations with them is not adultery for Muslim

---

1 Laurence Loeb, '"Outcaste": Shi'a Intolerance.' In Andrew Bostom, *The Legacy of Islamic Antisemitism*, p.564. See also the section 'Kidnapping young girls for the purpose of marriage' in Yosef Tobi, 'Conversions to Islam among Yemenite Jews under Zaydi Rule.' In Andrew Bostom, *The Legacy of Islamic Antisemitism*, p.584, English translation (via the Hebrew) by Rivkah Fishman. Orig. publ. in *Pe'amim* 42 (1990): 105-26. James Riley describes rape of *dhimmi* women by Muslims in Morocco in 1815 'without the smallest restraint' as a fact of every day life in the ghetto (*An Authentic Narrative of the Loss of the American Brig Commerce*, p.346).

2 *Protest rally outside the Danish Embassy in London, February 3 2006.* The NEFA Foundation, viewed June 8 2009, <http://www.youtube.com/watch?v=YWGbFsy7NjA>.

men.[1] If not subsequently ransomed, female captives can continue to be treated as concubines, married or sold. The Islamic institution of the harem was constituted of women enslaved through *jihad*: the women of the harem were captives taken from the *dar al-Harb*, or abductees from *dhimmi* communities.

The penalty of capture and rape of women has been imposed countless times throughout history when *dhimmi* communities have been judged to have overstepped the limits of the *dhimma* pact. In particular, this has invariably accompanied massacres of *dhimmi* men.

A *dhimma* regulation which incites rape and abduction of women is the rule that a Muslim woman cannot be married to a *dhimmi*. If a married *dhimmi* woman can be compelled to convert to Islam, as a Muslim woman she will be considered to be automatically divorced from her *dhimmi* husband. Patrick Sookhdeo explains how this works in Pakistan:

> This rule … allows Muslim abductors and rapists of [married] Christian women to evade conviction by forcing their victim to convert to Islam … in front of two witnesses, who can sign a mullah's certificate confirming her conversion. If this is accomplished, the woman's former marriage is annulled, and her abductor can freely and legally marry her …[2]

Another relevant *dhimma* regulation is that a non-Muslim cannot act as guardian to a Muslim. This has the practical affect that if an unmarried girl is compelled to convert to Islam, her parents lose all rights to intervene on her behalf, including the right to authorize her marriage, or even to see her. Instead she will be assigned a Muslim guardian, and in accordance with the *Sharia* principle that a virgin gives permission to marriage 'by her silence'[3] – in other words no formal permission is required – she can rapidly find herself married to a Muslim man, and her parents will have no say in the matter.

An abduction of this kind was reported to have taken place in Pakistan in June 2007. Two Pakistani Christian girls, Anila and Saba Younas, aged 10 and 13, were kidnapped while traveling to visit their uncle. They were allegedly converted to Islam, and quickly married off to Muslims. After their uncle took legal action to restore custody of the girls to

---

1 See, for example, the hadiths in *Sahih Muslim*, the Book of Marriage (*Kitab al-Nikah*), Chapter 597 (DLXVII) Vol. 2, p.896ff. This Chapter has the title: 'It is permissible to have sexual intercourse with a captive woman … In case she has a husband, her marriage is abrogated after she becomes captive'.

2 Patrick Sookhdeo, *A People Betrayed*, p.210.

3 *Sahih al-Bukhari*. The Book of *an-Nikah* (The Wedlock). 7:67:5137.

their parents, Judge Mian Muhammad Naeem ruled that the two sisters 'converted in a legitimate manner to Islam', and for this reason they cannot be 'restored to their family of origin'. The judge also confirmed the validity of the girls' marriages. The kidnappers refused all requests to produce the girls to the court, so the judge made his findings based upon the testimony of Muslim 'guardians' acting on the girls' behalf.[1]

The severe legal incapacity imposed by the *dhimma* on non-Muslims, against the ever-constant background threat of 'lawful' rape under *dhimma*-breach conditions, means that in many Muslim societies there can develop a culture of tolerance of attacks on *dhimmi* women. This tolerance can endure long after the *dhimma* laws themselves have been set aside, just as racially motivated rape and sexual exploitation of black women continued long after the practice of slavery was abolished in the United States.

Seizure of property

The threat of future *jihad* also places the property of *dhimmis* in a situation where all possessions are in perpetual need of redemption through the annual *jizya* payments. *Dhimmi* property, as part of the *fay*, had been 'restored' to the *Umma* through conquest, and was only retained by the *dhimmis* as a concession. Any breach of the *dhimma* cancels this redemption, so that the property 'reverts' to the Muslims.

Seizure of non-Muslim property by Muslims is thus a perennial issue for *dhimmi* communities, and, as with kidnapping, extra-judicial appropriation of non-Muslim property can be exceedingly difficult to reverse. Samir Qumsiyeh, a Bethlehem Christian leader, reports that this is a serious problem in Bethlehem, and is an important reason for the Christian demographic collapse in the birthplace of Christ:

> It is a regular phenomenon in Bethlehem. They go to a poor Christian person with a forged power of attorney document, then they say we have papers proving you're living on our land. If you confront them, many times the Christian is beaten. You can't do anything about it. The Christian loses and he runs away.[2]

A large-scale instance of appropriation of *dhimmi* property took place during the emigration of Jews from Muslim countries to Israel after

---

1 Qaiser Felix, 'Underage Christian sisters kidnapped and forced to marry Muslims,' June 14, 2008. *AsiaNews*, viewed June 8 2009, <http://www.asianews.it/index.php?l=en&art=12750>. And 'Kidnapped Christian girls, judge ratifies marriage and conversion,' July 16, 2008. *AsiaNews*, viewed June 8 2009, <http://www.asianews.it/index.php?l=en&art=12771>.

2 Aaron Klein, *Schmoozing with Terrorists*, p.137.

1948. In many cases Jews had to sell their houses and lands at vastly deflated prices, or abandon them without recompense because local *dhimma* regulations made it illegal for them to sell them. For example, in Yemen a 1920 law made it illegal for Jews who left Yemen to sell their property: instead it had to be forfeited to the Imam.[1] In a similar fashion, during the 1920's and 1930's the Turkish authorities seized assets of Christians who emigrated to Syria or Lebanon.[2]

Such laws make perfect sense in the light of the theology of *jihad* and the *dhimma*. *Dhimmi* property by rights belongs to the *Umma* as part of the *fay*, and could only be retained by the *dhimmis* as a concession subject to annual compensation. Any such concession would cease when the *dhimmis* left the *Dar al-Islam* and stopped paying compensation, so the property would revert to the *Umma*.

The yoke of *dhimma* taxation

The *jizya* and other taxes imposed under the *dhimma* were not a light burden.

The Syrian chronicle completed in 774 by an author known as Pseudo-Dionysius reported that during the preceding decades the *jizya* was beyond the capacity of many to pay. It had to be extracted by beatings, extortion, torture, rape and killings, and this caused multitudes to flee destitute from town to town after they had sold everything they owned to pay it.[3]

The renowned Persian historian al-Baladhuri (c. 892) relates in his history of the Islamic conquests that when 'Amr conquered Egypt he raised two million gold dinars in *jizya* and other annual taxes from the Christian Copts. When his successor managed to increase this to four million dinars, 'Uthman remarked to 'Amr: 'After you the milk camels have yielded more milk.' To this 'Amr replied 'This is because you have emaciated their young.'[4]

Arthur Tritton has analyzed *jizya* payment records from the early centuries, documented in Egyptian papyri from the period 700-720 AD, as well as data on wages and costs of commodities. While the

1 Andrew Bostom, 'Islamic antisemitism – Jew hatred in Islam.' In *The Legacy of Islamic Antisemitism*, p.45.
2 Vahé Tachjian. 'The expulsion of non-Turkish ethnic and religious groups from Turkey to Syria during the 1920s and early 1930s.' Section F – General and Legal Interpretations.
3 Bat Ye'or, *The Decline of Eastern Christianity under Islam*, pp.74, 78, 305ff.
4 al-Baladhuri, *The Origins of the Islamic State*, p.340.

reported *jizya* rates varied between 2½ to 4 dinars, amounts actually paid averaged 2½ dinars.[1] In this same period a sheep cost ½ dinar, and wages for hired laborers such as carpenters, shipbuilders and sawyers ranged between 8 and 24 dinars a year.[2] Thus, for laborers, the *jizya* normally amounted to the equivalent of 1-3 months wages. This compares with the *zakat* tax rate for Muslims of 2.5% (one 40th) of annual income, or just over one week's wages.

Tritton also reports documentary evidence of other kinds of payments exacted from the Egyptians, including land tax (*kharaj*), requisitions and tribute levied on communities and monasteries, and still other contributions as well:

> At this time many of the Egyptians fled from their holdings. It is safe to assume that one reason for their doing so was the burden of taxation. It is obvious that there are serious discrepancies between the account given by the lawyers [i.e. in *Sharia* rulings] and that of the papyri. The latter prove the existence of taxes which are not even hinted at by the legal system.[3]

Centuries later, Goitein reports that in the worst cases, Egyptian *dhimmis* could have to enslave themselves or their family to pay the *jizya*, or else convert and become a recipient of its benefits. Many, having sold all they had to pay it, took to wandering as beggars. In some cases men had to go into hiding because they had no means to pay the tax, and, as they could no longer earn a living, their wives and children starved.[4]

A Jewish merchant in Muslim Sicily complained about the unbearable burden of the *jizya*: 'They [the Jews] were sorry and preferred death to life. Most of them are poor and destitute. For fear of the rulers, many went bankrupt, and unfortunately some fled overseas.'[5]

The American James Riley reported that in Morocco in the early 19th century, Jews who could not pay the *jizya* were beaten and compelled to convert to Islam.[6]

Muzafer Ferro Mehmedovic, in a study of the Islamization of the Albanians, cites many reports that the unbearable burden of Ottoman taxes upon Albanian Christians compelled them to adopt Islam from the

---

1 Tritton, *The Caliphs and their Non-Muslim subjects*, p.198.

2 Ibid., p.199.

3 Ibid., pp.202-3.

4 Shlomo Dov Goitein, 'Evidence on the Muslim poll tax from non-Muslim sources: a *geniza* study.'

5 Jeremy Johns, *Arabic Administration in Norman Sicily*, p.27.

6 James Riley, *An Authentic Narrative of the Loss of the American Brig Commerce*, pp.333-34.

15th to the 19th centuries. The Ottomans fixed taxation rates, including *jizya* quotas, upon whole communities, so that the more households converted to Islam, the greater the incentive was for the rest to follow their example:

> ... among the means that Turks use to attract Christians to their religion is the practice of releasing those who convert to Islam from all kind of taxes, forcing those that would remain as Christians to pay instead.[1]

This financial burden resulted in mass conversions and gave rise to crypto-Christianity (known as *laramanë* in Albanian, *dipistis* in Greek and *dvovjerstvo* in Serbian):[2]

> Those who have abandoned their faith regret their fall deeply by saying that they have lost the grace of God ... Some declare, and they are many, that in their heart they still are Christian and the reason why they changed their names was only for the purpose of escaping Turkish taxes which they can't pay.[3]

Concealment and denial

There are many voices, not only from the Islamic community, which seek to conceal the objectionable features of the *dhimma* system. False, or at best misleading claims are often heard. Here is a list of some of these claims, followed in each case by a correction:

The jizya was a tax just like any other tax.

> The *jizya* was a discriminatory tax, intentionally administered in a humiliating manner, which was regarded as a payment to redeem one's life and property.

---

1 Letter to Rome from Francesco Leonardi, 1638. In Mehmedovic, *The Islamisation of the Albanians*, p.120, citing Francesco Leonardi, 'Pjesë nga relacioni i misionarit, Francesco Leonardit, mbi Serbinë dhe Shqipninë', in *Relacione mbi gjendjen e Shqipërisë Veriore e të mesme në shekullin XVII, Vëllimi II* (1634 – 1650), Injac Zamputi (editor and translator), Shtypshkronja Mihal Duri, Tiranë, 1965, p.183.

2 Mehmedovic, *The Islamisation of the Albanians*, p.118. For references to crypto-Christianity in 8th century Syria, see Sidney H. Griffith, *The Church in the Shadow of the Mosque*, pp.58-59. It had also been a problem in the early centuries of Islam that conversion deprived the state of revenue and increased the tax burden on the remaining *dhimms*. Daniel Dennett argued in *Conversion and the Poll Tax in Early Islam* that this was solved in the first Islamic centuries by levying land tax (*kharaj*) on *dhimmis* and converts alike.

3 Letter from Gregor Mazreku, 1650. Mehmedovic, *The Islamisation of the Albanians*, p.120, citing Gregor Mazreku, 'Relacion i priftit të Prizrendit, Gregor Mazrekut, mbi gjendjen në famulline e vet', in *Relacione mbi gjendjen e Shqipërisë Veriore e të mesme në shekullin XVII, Vëllimi II* (1634 – 1650), Injac Zamputi (editor and translator), Shtypshkronja Mihal Duri, Tiranë, 1965, pp.441-42.

The jizya merely purchased an exemption from the zakat tax which Muslims had to pay.

This misleading claim relies on the fact that *zakat* was paid by Muslims, and *jizya* by non-Muslims. In reality Muslim jurists never describe *jizya* as an exemption from *zakat*, but rather as an exemption from being looted, enslaved and killed. Also the *jizya* was much heavier than the *zakat* tax on Muslims.

The jizya was a light tax, adjusted to the financial capacity of the dhimmi to pay, and thus no real imposition on non-Muslims.

This misleading claim appeals to the idea that the tax was set in proportion to the *dhimmi's* wealth,[1] and draws the false inference that it was therefore light and not a burden. As we have seen, the *jizya* was a very heavy tax.

The jizya purchased an exemption from military service.

Until modern times, Muslim jurists never described *jizya* in such terms. What is true is that *dhimmis* were forbidden from bearing arms. As such they could not go for *jihad*, misleadingly referred to as 'military service',[2] which was regarded as the duty of Muslims only. Nor did they have any means of defending themselves.

The term dhimma means 'pact of protection', implying that Muslims would protect the dhimmis from external enemies outside the Islamic state, and the jizya was payment in return for this service.

The basic meaning of *dhimma* is 'liability'. It is true that Muslims were meant to protect *dhimmis* from external attack, but the primary function of the *jizya* was to compensate the conquerors for stopping the *jihad*.

Q9:29 had nothing to do with the dhimma pact.

All commentaries agree that Q9:29 was the basis for the *dhimma*.

---

1 See e.g. *Sahih al-Bukhari*. The Book of *al-Jizya* and the Stoppage of War. 4:58, p.241 which relates that Syrian *dhimmis* were charged four dinars, while Yemenis paid only one dinar 'on the basis of the degree of prosperity'.

2 See e.g. *Sahih Muslim*. The Book of Jihad and Expedition. (*Kitab al-Jihad wa'l-Siyar*). 3:27, p.1137, note 2224, and Bassam Zawadi, 'Is the Jizya Tax Oppressive?', viewed June 8 2009, <http://www.answering-christianity.com/bassam_zawadi/is_jizya_tax_oppressive.htm>.

*There is no connection between **jihad** and the **dhimma**.*

Major Islamic theologians and commentators link the *dhimma* with the concept of cessation of *jihad*. Moreover Q9:29 makes clear that paying *jizya* (as part of the *dhimma*) was one of the intended outcomes of *jihad*.

Dhimmi populations entered this state voluntarily.

Their other choices were death or conversion to Islam.

*The institution of the **dhimma** was a later innovation, and not introduced by Muhammad.*

Muhammad introduced a *dhimma* at Khaybar, and also took the *jizya* from other communities in Arabia and Yemen. What is true is that the full *dhimma* regulations only developed later.

Islamic societies were model examples of interfaith harmony and peaceful coexistence.

This belief derives from the dogma of the perfection of the *Sharia*, and is not based upon historical realities.

Islam granted equal rights to all its citizens, and rejected discrimination of all kinds.

The *Sharia* treats slaves, women and *dhimmis* as inferior before the law to free, male Muslims. It is moreover misleading to refer to *dhimmis* as 'citizens'.[1]

*Dhimma regulations were only rarely enforced, and reports of **dhimma** laws are exaggerated.*

Historical accounts of both Muslims and non-Muslims show that they were neither exaggerated nor neglected. Many reports describe situations where conditions were worse than the *Sharia* provided for. The only extended period of reported non-enforcement of *dhimma* conditions has been in the modern era.

Such claims, although beguiling, are false. They have only been developed in the modern era. This revisionist history has been created to protect the *dhimma* from the glare of objective scrutiny. The dogma of Islamic superiority is so intensely and ardently held, and there is so much at

---

1 Referring to *dhimmis* as 'second class citizens', Griffith questions whether 'the term "citizen" can even be meaningfully used of people whose presence in the body politic is merely tolerated.' (*The Church in the Shadow of the Mosque*, p.16).

stake in allowing it to be questioned, that facts and interpretations are massaged and distorted in defense of this ideal.

One example, an internet article 'Refuting Allegations against 9:29 (jizya tax)' argues that Muslims paid 'much higher' taxes than *dhimmis*, while giving *dhimmis* 'all the benefits' of living under Islamic rule. Moreover Christians and Jews were also given 'equal rights' and 'were allowed to build houses of worship'. The article concludes 'If Jizya is unfair on anyone, it would be the Muslims … Still, you never hear them complain.'[1] The whole point of this ahistorical rhetoric is to paint Islam in as noble and generous a light as possible.

Another example is found in the notes to Abdul Hamid Siddiqi's English translation of the *Sahih Muslim*:

> This word *Jizya* is derived from the verb *Jaza*, which means 'he rendered (something) as a satisfaction' or 'as a compensation (in lieu of something else)'. This is a sort of compensation to the Muslim society on the part of unbelievers, living in the protection of the Islamic State for not participating in the military service and enjoying the 'covenant of protection' (*dhimma*). No fixed rate has been set either by the Qur'an or by the Holy Prophet for this tax, but from all available ahadith [*hadiths*], it is evident that it is considerably lower than Zakat to which Muslims are liable. It should also be borne in mind that only such of non-Muslim citizens, who, if they were Muslim, would be expected to serve in the armed forces of the State, are liable to the payment of Jizya, provided they can easily afford it.[2]

Although Muslim commentators and jurists down the ages have always been quite clear that *jizya* is a compensation instead of blood and looting, this modern camouflage of *jizya* would make it appear a trifling recompense for the generous treatment of non-Muslims under Islamic rule. Those who pay *jizya*, instead of being ones whose lives would have been forfeit in *jihad*, become the class of potential recruits exempted from having to 'serve in the armed forces'.

Sadly, Christian leaders have misrepresented the conditions of dhimmitude. An example is Colin Chapman's cursory description of the *dhimmi* condition in his widely-read *Cross and Crescent: Responding to the Challenge of Islam*. Chapman rehearses several revisionist emphases described above, claiming that *dhimmis* were protected, prohibited from military service, and 'not allowed' to pay the Muslim taxes:

---

1 'Refuting Allegations against 9:29 (jizya tax),' viewed June 8 2009, <http://www.guideto salvation.com/Website/jizya.htm>.

2 *Sahih Muslim.* The Book of Jihad and Expedition. (*Kitab al-Jihad wa'l-Siyar*). 3:27, p.1137, note 2224.

> All non-Muslims living under Islamic rule paid a land tax (*kharaj*). Jews and Christians were treated as *dhimmis*, members of a protected community, and paid in addition a poll tax (*jizyah*). They were not allowed to do military service or pay the Muslims' alms tax [*zakat*].[1]

The fantasy is so entrenched that it can come as a shock to some Muslims when they are confronted with their own Islamic sources. Subhi al-Salih, editor of the 1981 edition of Ibn al-Qayyim's detailed study in the laws of dhimmitude, criticizes him for 'exaggeration in the explanation of some topics due to the spirit of his time, influenced by religious rigidity'.[2] He also castigates Ibn al-Qayyim for 'astonishing naïveté' in suggesting that *dhimmis* were required to have neck seals, or to wear bells when bathing:

> Worst and more bitterly than this [i.e. than the statements on neck-sealing] is what our Imam [Ibn al-Qayyim] has related, with astonishing naïveté, about *dhimmis* having to hang bells around their necks every time they enter a bath. Apart from the fact that there is no evidence for this practice, it is not in harmony with the spirit of Islam.[3]

In fact the requirement that *dhimmis* should wear bells in public baths is very well documented.

Al-Salih also is incredulous to discover that Ibn al-Qayyim regarded the *jizya* as punitive, and not some kind of a charge for services rendered to the *dhimmis*:

> We were expecting, in the context of this Islamic goodness, that Ibn al-Qayyim would lean towards explaining *jizya* as a rent for living in *Dar al-Islam*, or payment in return for their protection ... but, **contrary to our expectations, he supported the idea of categorizing *jizya* as a punitive measure (*'uquba*). ...**

> Did he (Ibn al Qayyim) not regard the facts written about our leaders to be correct? The works of the successors? The sayings of the jurists? Or did he not believe that Khalid ibn al-Walid wrote to Saluba ibn Nastuna and his people: **'If we protect you, you pay us jizya, otherwise we do not protect you.'** Or was he influenced by the sectarian rigidity and disagreements of his time, which led him into conclusions we do not believe are strongly supported by Islam?[4]

A crucial flaw in al-Salih's conception of the *jizya* is that the protection offered was not in the first place from third parties, but **from Islam**

---

1 Colin Chapman, *Cross and Crescent*, p.128.
2 Subhi al-Salih, ed., *Ahkam Ahl al-Dhimmah*, vol. 1:15.
3 Ibid., vol 1:31.
4 Ibid., vol 1:8.

itself. The *jizya* was 'protection money', as is demanded by organized crime gangs today. These gangs may stress that they protect those who pay – and they may attack other gangs who encroach on their turf – but it is clearly understood by all parties that if payments cease, the most immediate danger will be an attack from the 'protecting' gang. It is part of the abusive nature of criminal protection rackets that those who buy their right to life and property are supposed to feel indebted to the generosity of their 'protectors'.

Khalid ibn al-Walid's letter to Saluba ibn Nastuna, which was relied upon by al-Salih, is often cited by apologists for the *dhimma*, so it merits careful consideration.

We can first observe that al-Salih misquotes the letter from Khalid. As recorded by al-Tabari in his *History*, this passage does not state what happens if *jizya* is not paid, but rather what happens if the Muslims do not provide protection – in this circumstance the Muslims are not entitled to *jizya*. The actual text is:

> … you have a guarantee of security and protection, so that, if we protect you, we are entitled to the *jizyah*, but, if not, then not until we do protect you.[1]

To answer the rather different question of what happens if *jizya* is not paid, we can turn to the surrounding passages in al-Tabari. Earlier in the *History*, it had been reported of the same Saluba Ibn Nastuna that 'he had spared his blood by paying the *jizyah*.'[2] In another letter, also written by Khalid ibn al-Walid to Persian commoners at around the same time, it is made clear that the protection bought by the Persians with their *jizya* payments was from the 'people who love death', the Muslims themselves

> Embrace Islam so that you may be safe. If not, make a covenant of protection with me and pay the *jizyah*. Otherwise I have brought you a people who love death just as you love drinking wine.[3]

Yet another letter, sent this time to Persian rulers, was more intimidating, threatening conversion by force if it was not accepted willingly:

> … enter into our faith; we will leave you and your land alone and pass beyond you to others different from you. If not, that will happen [anyway],

---

1 al-Tabari, *The Challenge to the Empires. The History of al-Tabari*, vol. 11, p.40.
2 Ibid., p.3.
3 Ibid., pp.44-45.

even though you loathe [it], by force, at the hands of a people who love death just as you love life.[1]

The fact that the *jizya* purchased protection from Muslims is confirmed by a tradition from 'Ubaydallah, reported by al-Tabari:

> Khalid departed after the people of al-Hirah had written a document that he approved, stating 'We have paid the *jizyah* for which Khalid, the good servant [of God], and the Muslims, God's good servants, made a covenant with us, **on condition that they and their commander protect us from aggression from the Muslims** or others.'[2]

It is certainly true that an **additional** duty of protection against attack by third parties was assumed by Muslims, for the caliph 'Umar advised his successor to:

> ... take care of those non-Muslims who are under the protection of Allah and His Messenger in that he should observe the convention agreed upon with them, and fight on their behalf (to secure their safety) and he should not overtax them beyond their capacity.[3]

It was prudent for Muslims to protect *dhimmi* communities under their rule, because they were, like the land itself, a source of wealth for the *Umma*, and it would do no good to the *Umma* if their tribute went to another. However the first and foremost protection afforded by the *jizya* payments was the exemption from *jihad*, as we have already seen in considering the opinions of Quranic commentators.

Sources edited and translated by Muslims (and sometimes also non-Muslims) can selectively downplay the more confronting features of *dhimma* regulations. For example, Nuh Ha Mim Keller's edition of the *Reliance of the Traveller* sets side by side the original Arabic text with an English translation. In presenting the sections which deal with *dhimmis* (o11.1-5), he makes many cosmetic adjustments:

- Section o11.1, accurately translated, states: 'A dhimma may be made with Jews, Christians, Zoroastrians, those who entered the religion of Jews and Christians before it was corrupted, and Samaritans and Sabians ...' However Keller's translation reads 'A formal agreement of protection is made with citizens who are: Jews, Christians, Zoroastrians, Samarians and Sabians ...' There is nothing in the Arabic which refers to *dhimmis* as 'citizens', nor to a 'formal agreement of protection'.

---

1 Ibid., p.44. The interpolations in square brackets are from the translator.
2 Ibid., p.46. The interpolations in square brackets are from the translator.
3 *Sahih al-Bukhari*. The Book of *al-Jihad* (Fighting for Allah's Cause). 4:56:3052.

- Keller translates *jizya* as 'the non-Muslim poll tax'. This is misleading, as the *jizya* is not simply a tax upon non-Muslims.
- The Arabic states that punishment (*had*) is applied to *dhimmis* for adultery or theft (but not for drunkenness): this refers to the *hudud* punishments of stoning or amputation. Keller's translation softens this to 'they are penalized' (o11.5).
- Keller's translation correctly translates the stipulation that *dhimmis* are required to wear belts, but selectively omits to translate the requirement that they wear special bells in public baths, the prohibition on mounting horses, and the rule that asses or mules must be ridden side-saddle (o11.5). This selectivity is presumably to downplay the more humiliating *dhimma* regulations.
- Keller's translation states that Muslims should not say *al-salamu 'alaykum* (the standard Islamic greeting of peace) to 'non-Muslim subjects'. The Arabic simply states that Muslims are not to initiate a greeting to *dhimmis* (o11.5).
- Keller's translation states that *dhimmis* should keep to the side of the street. What the Arabic actually says is they should 'seek refuge in the narrow roads' (i.e. not travel at all on main roads). (o11.5).
- Keller's translation correctly states that *dhimmis* must not build their houses higher than those of Muslims, but incorrectly states that if they acquire a tall house it is not to be demolished. The Arabic refers to tall houses which they 'had acquired' (i.e. before conquest). (o11.5).
- Keller reports that a 'non-Muslim may not enter the ... Haram' (the sacred precinct in Mecca). What the Arabic actually says is 'idolater' (*mushrik*) (o11.7), which is a more offensive term.

The *dhimma* myths and spin, which have been concocted to conceal the reality of the *dhimmis'* condition, are a phenomenon of the modern era. The reality is that where there have been hard-won improvements to *dhimmis'* conditions in recent centuries, these were imposed upon Muslim societies under considerable external pressure, or as the result of European military occupation.

At the present time, the *dhimma* myths also serve to advance the missionary efforts of those who would propagate Islam (*da'wah*) in the West. They can also be used as propaganda for the jihadists, as, for example, the claim by Hamas and its supporters that for centuries Jews and Christians lived happily, 'coexisting' alongside Muslims under Islamic rule. Thus the Hamas Covenant states:

Article 6. ... under the wing of Islam followers of **all religions can coexist in security and safety** where their lives, possessions and rights are concerned. In the absence of Islam, strife will be rife, oppression spreads, evil prevails and schisms and wars will break out.

Article 31. Under the wing of Islam, it is possible for the followers of the three religions – Islam, Christianity and Judaism – to coexist in peace and quiet with each other. Peace and quiet would not be possible except under the wing of Islam. **Past and present history are the best witness to that.**

... Islam confers upon everyone his legitimate rights. Islam prevents the incursion on other people's rights.[1]

Bernard Lewis' comment on historical revisionism is entirely relevant and to the point:

It is only very recently that some defenders of Islam began to assert that their society in the past accorded equal status to non-Muslims. No such claim is made by spokesmen for resurgent Islam, and historically there is no doubt that they are right. Traditional Islamic societies neither accorded such equality nor pretended that they were so doing. Indeed, in the old order, this would have been regarded not as a merit but as a dereliction of duty. How could one accord the same treatment to those who follow the true faith and those who wilfully reject it? This would be a theological as well as a logical absurdity.[2]

Mawdudi's modern commentary on Q9:29 also makes some very pertinent criticisms of this kind of apologetic mythology, which commenced as early as the nineteenth century:

Some nineteenth-century Muslim writers and their followers in our own times never seem to tire of their apologies for jizyah. But God's religion does not require that apologetic explanations be made on its behalf. The simple fact is that according to Islam, non-Muslims have been granted the freedom to stay outside the Islamic fold and to cling to their false, man-made ways if they so wish. ...

One of the advantages of jizyah is that it reminds the Dhimmis every year that because they do not embrace Islam ... they have to pay a price – jizyah – for clinging to their errors.[3]

At the same time, one must acknowledge the existence of traditions which commend treating *dhimmis* reasonably, and not killing them,

---

1 Hamas Covenant 1988, viewed June 8 2009, <http://www.yale.edu/lawweb/avalon/mideast/hamas.htm>. Coauthored (dated 18 August 1988) by Sheikh Ahmad Yassin and Dr Abd al-Aziz al-Rantisi.

2 Bernard Lewis, *The Jews of Islam*, p.3.

3 Mawdudi, *Towards understanding the Qur'an*, vol.3: 201-2.

provided they have maintained the conditions of their *dhimma* pact. For example, on July 27, 2005, Sheikh al-Qaradawi issued a *fatwa* in the name of the International Association of Muslim Scholars which condemned attacks on certain kinds of non-Muslims, including tourists in Muslim countries:

> Islam considers killing others and taking their lives as one of the gravest of sins in the sight of Allah. ...
>
> The above ruling also applies to those who have a permanent pledge with Muslims. This category of people is named by Muslim jurists as Dhimmi or non-Muslims living under the protection of the Muslim state. This category is protected by the covenant of Allah, His Prophet, and the whole Muslim Ummah. They are known, according to all jurists, as ahl dar al-Islam or the people belonging to the abode of Islam; they are citizens who enjoy the same rights and bear the same responsibilities as Muslims.
>
> There is another category of people who have an interim pledge with Muslims, such as those who enter Islamic territories through the state authorities or any other recognized body such as travel agencies, etc. The individual pledge of security of a single person is as effective as the state pledge, and it prohibits any violation or cancellation of this individual pledge.
>
> With this in mind, Islam considers the act of issuing an entrance visa to a tourist to be a pledge of security given to this tourist, and hence it categorically prohibits transgressing the security given to tourists. The Prophet ... is reported to have said,[1] 'Anyone who kills a Dhimmi will not smell the fragrance of Paradise.'[2]

This *fatwa* contains some truth. It is indeed a crime, according to Islamic law, to kill a *dhimmi*, but not the capital offense that killing a Muslim would be. The *dhimma* pact does purchase the right to life of the non-Muslim who lives under Islamic conditions. At the same time, al-Qaradawi's statement perpetuates the untruth that *dhimmis* are 'citizens who enjoy the same rights and bear the same responsibilities as Muslims'. This statement is quite false. They were never 'citizens' in the sense modern political theory understands this term, and they did not have the same rights as Muslims. It also perpetuates the pernicious view that the right to life of non-Muslims is a concession granted by the Islamic state, in contrast to the inherent right to life which every individual Muslim enjoys.

---

1 *Sahih al-Bukhari.* The Book of *al-Jizya* and the Stoppage of War. 4:58:3166.
2 International Associate of Muslim Scholars, 'Bombing Innocents: IAMS's [sic] Statement.' 27 July 2005, viewed June 8 2009, <http://www.islamonline.net/English/In_Depth/ViolenceCausesAlternatives/Articles/topic08/2005/07/01.shtml>.

The impact

Demographic

The impact of the *dhimma* regulations was ultimately devastating for the conquered communities. Some communities, like the Christians of northwest Africa, southern Arabia and Afghanistan disappeared completely: the *dhimma* was not sufficient to protect them. In the 11th-12th centuries the Almohad persecutions eliminated Christianity in Muslim Spain by massacres, enslavement and enforced conversions.[1]

Other *dhimmi* communities steadily declined, gradually becoming assimilated into the Islamic community. Some changed their language and culture, like the Aramaic, Coptic and Greek-speaking peoples of Syria, Palestine and Egypt, who adopted Arabic, and ultimately embraced Arab identity in the twentieth century. Some communities kept their language, like the Armenians and Serbs, and retained their cultural identity more effectively.

Psychological

Like sexism and racism, dhimmitude is not only expressed in legal and social structures, but in a psychology of inferiority, and a will to serve, which the dominated community adopts in an attempt at self-preservation. As Maimonides put it, 'We have acquiesced, both old and young, to inure ourselves to humiliation ...'[2]

Bat Ye'or describes the condition of *dhimmis* as follows:

> The law required from *dhimmis* a humble demeanor, eyes lowered, a hurried pace. They had to give way to Muslims in the street, remain standing in their presence and keep silent, only speaking to them when given permission. They were forbidden to defend themselves if attacked, or to raise a hand against a Muslim on pain of having it amputated. Any criticism of the Koran or Islamic law annuled the protection pact. In addition the *dhimmi* was duty-bound to be grateful, since it was Islamic law that spared his life.
>
> The whole corpus of these practices ... formed an unchanging behavior pattern which was perpetuated from generation to generation for centuries. It was so deeply internalized that it escaped critical evaluation

---

1 The Jews, subject to the same repression, managed to hang on and were allowed to revert back to Judaism. Haim Z. Hirschberg, *A History of the Jews of North Africa*, vol. 1:114-39, 201-4. See also Bat Ye'or, *The Decline of Eastern Christianity under Islam*, p.89, citing Islamic historians al-Athir, Ibn Khaldun; and Hady Roger Idris, 'Les Tributaires'.

2 Andrew Bostom, 'Islamic antisemitism – Jew hatred in Islam.' In *The Legacy of Islamic Antisemitism*, p.22.

and invaded the realm of self-image, which was henceforth dominated by a conditioning in self-devaluation. ... This situation, determined by a corpus of precise legislation and social behavior patterns based on prejudice and religious traditions, induced the same type of mentality in all *dhimmi* groups. It has four major characteristics: vulnerability, humiliation, gratitude and alienation.

... The fundamental component of the *dhimmi* mentality is established from the moment he consents to submit to a system which removes his basic right to life.[1]

Early in the 20th century, Jovan Cvijic published *La Peninsule Balkanique*, which describes how the intergenerational fear of violence from the ruling Turks and Muslim Albanians produced typical adaptive psychological responses:

[they became] ... accustomed to belonging to an inferior, servile class, whose duty it is to make themselves acceptable to the master, to humble themselves before him and to please him. These people become close-mouthed, secretive, cunning; they lose all confidence in others; they grow used to hypocrisy and meanness because these are necessary in order for them to live and to avoid violent punishments.

The direct influence of oppression and violence is manifested in almost all the Christians as feelings of fear and apprehension. Whenever Moslem brigands or evil-doers made their appearance somewhere, entire districts used to live in terror, often for months on end. There are regions where the Christian population has lived under a reign of fear from birth until death. In certain parts of Macedonia, they don't tell you how they fought against the Turks or against the Albanians, but rather about the way that they managed to flee from them, or the ruse that they used to escape them. In Macedonia I heard people say: 'Even in our dreams we flee from the Turks and the Albanians.' It is true that for about twenty years a certain number of them have regained their composure, but the deep-seated feeling has not changed among the masses of people. Even after the liberation in 1912 one could tell that a large number of Christians had not yet become aware of their new status: fear could still be read on their faces.[2]

Matching the inferiority of the *dhimmi* is also the superiority of the Muslim, who is afforded a sense of being generous, having granted the *dhimmi* quarter, and refrained from taking his possessions. As one Iranian convert to Christianity put it 'Christianity is still viewed as the

---

1 Bat Ye'or, *Islam and Dhimmitude*, pp.103-4.

2 Jovan Cvijic, *La Péninsule Balkanique*, pp.487-88. Trans. by Michael J. Miller, in Andrew Bostom, 'Islamic antisemitism – Jew hatred in Islam.' In *The Legacy of Islamic Antisemitism*, p.144. This passage was first referenced in English by Bat Ye'or, *Islam and Dhimmitude*, p.108.

religion of an inferior class of people. Islam is the religion of masters and rulers, Christianity is the religion of slaves.'

This worldview is as pernicious for Muslims as it is humiliating for non-Muslims. Muslims injure themselves when they establish circumstances where they have no possibility of learning to compete on an even footing. Just as economic protectionism can cause the competitive ability of a whole nation to atrophy, so the 'religious protectionism' of the *dhimma* can mean that Muslims come to rely upon a false sense of superiority, which ultimately weakens them, and damages their ability to gain a true understanding of themselves and the world around them.

The system of dhimmitude engenders a set of deeply ingrained attitudes on both sides from generation to generation. Just as racism continues in America and other nations more than a century after race-based slavery was abolished, so the institution of dhimmitude continues to affect, indeed to dominate, relationships between Muslims and others, even when the *jizya* tax is but a distant memory. The dynamics can even extend to affect interfaith relations involving minority immigrant Muslim communities, in societies which have never been subject to the *Sharia*.

Collusion and the mimetic tendency

Dhimmis can appear to collude to conceal their own condition, finding themselves psychologically unable to critique or oppose it. The psychology of gratitude and inferiority can manifest in the *dhimmi* as denial or concealment of the condition. This can show itself in a mimetic tendency to imitate Muslims in every way, to attempt to disappear into the background, making oneself as inconspicuous as possible. This possibility was something which *Sharia* law had insisted was not to happen; for this reason specific regulations were developed to ensure that *dhimmis* would be instantly recognized as infidels.

The psychology of inferiority can mean that people from a *dhimmi* background are themselves the least able to analyze or expose their own condition. A powerful silence rests over the whole subject like a thick impenetrable blanket or a strong dose of anaesthetic.

A moving example of this is found in an interview between Nasser Khalili, Iranian-born Jew, and presenter of the Islamic Art exhibition referred to in the first chapter. When asked whether his work to present 'Islamic Art' might help Muslims understand that Jews are not inferior,

Khalili replied, 'I don't think there is a question of the Jews being inferior. I don't think that has ever crossed any Muslim's mind.'[1]

Nothing could be further from the truth. Throughout history Iranian Islam has produced some of the most aggressive anti-Jewish sentiments imaginable. Persian treatment of Jews before 1925 had been exceptionally harsh: the nineteenth century was littered with pogroms and forced conversions of Jews throughout the country.[2] In Shi'ite textbooks Jews are routinely named along with dogs, corpses and urine as one of the things whose contact makes a Muslim unclean (see Q9:28). It had only been the rise of Reza Pahlavi to power in 1925, and his modernizing influence, that had made conditions more bearable for Jews during the time of Khalili's childhood and youth. Even in 1977, anthropologist Loeb commented that 'Most Jews express the belief that it is only the personal strength and goodwill of the Shah that protects them: that plus God's intervention.'[3]

Stunningly, Khalili went on to state that:

> Virtually one third of the Qur'an, Surat al-Baqarah [Q2], is in the praise of the two other religions, Judaism and Christianity. I don't think that's a question at all. I think the problem is ignorance amongst people, and I can say, on your program, that I believe that the biggest and the real weapon of mass destruction is ignorance. If people try to understand their culture, their religion, their way of life, then they started to respect each other. I think that Maimonides' role was exactly that.[4]

The contributions of this statement to ignorance, Khalili's 'real weapon of mass destruction' include:

- Sura 2 (al-Baqarah) comprises 7% of the Quran, not a third.
- Far from being in praise of Christianity and Judaism, sura 2 largely comprises a long litany of retorts given to the Jews of Medina.[5]

---

1 Interview on *The Spirit of Things*: 'Arabesque, the Art of Islam.' Sunday July 1, 2007. ABC Radio, downloaded June 8 2009, <http://www.abc.net.au/rn/spiritofthings/stories/2007/1962358. htm>.

2 See the long section on Iranian Jewry under Shi'ite rule in Andrew Bostom, 'Islamic antisemitism – Jew hatred in Islam.' In *The Legacy of Islamic Antisemitism*, pp.130-51; and also David G. Littman, 'Jews under Muslim rule: the case of Persia', which provides 19th century documents from the archives of the Alliance Israélite Universelle, reproduced in Bostom, ibid., pp.131-32; 139-41.

3 Laurence Loeb, *Outcaste: Jewish Life in Southern Iran*, p.291.

4 Interview on *The Spirit of Things*: Arabesque, the Art of Islam. Sunday July 1, 2007. ABC Radio, downloaded June 8, 2009, <http://www.abc.net.au/rn/spiritofthings/stories/2007/1962358. htm>.

5 Ibn Ishaq gives the contexts for these interchanges, introducing them as follows: 'The first hundred verses of the *sura* of the Cow came down in reference to these Jewish rabbis and the

Included is a verse which says that Allah changed some Jews into apes (Q2:65), another which characterizes Islam as the 'religion of Abraham' in contrast to Judaism and Christianity (Q2:135), and another which alleges that the Jews forged their scriptures (Q2:79), to name but a few of the scores of anti-Jewish libels in this chapter. There is, it must be admitted, one verse which speaks positively of Jews: 'Surely they that believe, and those of Jewry … their wages await them with their Lord, and no fear shall be on them, neither shall they sorrow' (Q2:62).

- It is wrong to assert that dispelling ignorance necessarily leads to respect. Familiarity with Muhammad's polemics against Medinan Jews, which led to their destruction, need not improve one's respect for Muhammad. Ironically, Khalili's own expressions of respect for Islam appeal to ignorance.

- It is far from true that Maimonides, one of the great Jewish writers of the Middle Ages, had the role of promoting respect through understanding. After he was forced to flee persecution in Andalusia to Egypt, pretending to be a Muslim, he later had cause to write to the Jews of Yemen at a time when they were undergoing severe persecutions:

> … on account of our sins God has cast us into the midst of this people, the nation of Ishmael, who persecute us severely, and who devise ways to harm us and to debase us. No nation has ever done more harm to Israel. None has matched it in debasing and humiliating us. None has been able to reduce us as they have … the more we suffer and choose to conciliate them, the more they choose to act belligerently toward us.'[1]

Khalili's fantastic claims are in a sense predictable because the promotion of positive regard for Islam is required of *dhimmis*. Even highly cultured individuals can take this role upon themselves. It is expected of *dhimmis* that they should honor and praise Islam. This is also why religious liberty advocates, who call for the life and security of Christians in Muslim countries to be respected, can be attacked and contradicted by the Christians they are seeking to help, especially those who are leaders or members of the elites.

It is hardly surprising that *Sharia* conditions set different *dhimmi* communities against each other: Jews against Christians, Orthodox

---

hypocrites …' (Guillaume, *The Life of Muhammad*, pp.247-700).

1 Maimonides, *Epistle to the Jews of Yemen*, excerpted from Norman Stillman, *The Jews of Arab Lands*, pp.241-42.

Christians against Nestorian Christians, and so forth. Because each community was profoundly insecure, it can seem safer to undermine the other communities. The first Arabic translation of the notorious antisemitic fabrication, the *Protocols of the Elders of Zion*, was done by Christians in Jerusalem in 1926,[1] after a period of great insecurity for Christians in the Levant, who had witnessed genocidal massacres of Armenians and Assyrian Christians during the First World War. On the other hand, Turkish Jews worked during 2007 to oppose proposals for Washington to officially recognize the Armenian genocide, and they were successful in recruiting leading American Jewish organizations to their cause.[2]

Dhimmitude in retreat

The rise of the European powers and the decline of Islam was a long process, taking centuries. As European influence grew within Islamic regions, the situation of the *dhimmis* gradually got better. In 1788 a Muslim scholar, Hasan al-Kafrawi, regretted the improving conditions of the *dhimmis* of Cairo. His sense of offense related directly to their breach of *dhimma* regulations: Jews and Christians were dressing like Muslims and copying their accessories (e.g. riding ornamented saddles, holding batons, and the women were wearing veils); riding horses; building houses finer and taller than the houses of Muslims and churches more durable and taller than mosques; not getting out of the way for Muslims but instead pushing Muslims to one side; and openly buying and owning slaves (even Muslim ones):

> What do you say, O scholars of Islam, shining luminaries who dispel the darkness (may God lengthen your days!)? What do you say of the innovations introduced by the cursed unbelievers into Cairo, into the city of al-Muizz, which by its splendor in legal and philosophic studies sparkles in the first rank of Muslim cities?

> What is your opinion concerning these deplorable innovations which are, moreover, contrary to the Pact of Umar which prescribed the expulsion of the unbelievers from Muslim territory? ...

---

1 Bat Ye'or, *Islam and Dhimmitude*, p.169.
2 Ron Kampeas, 'Jews in the middle as Turks, Armenians fight over history.' *JTA*, 23 April, 2007, viewed 8 June 2009, <http://www.jta.org/cgi-bin/iowa/news/article/20070423turkscommission.html>.

Ought one to allow these things to the unbelievers, to the enemies of the faith? Ought one to allow them to dwell among believers under such conditions?[1]

The Baghdad Quranic commentator al-Alusi was commenting on the *jizya* payment ritual a few decades later in the first half of the 19th century, when he lamented the fact that *dhimmis* were being permitted to pay the *jizya* by means of an agent, thus escaping the degradation of having to pay it in person:

> Today none of these sayings [prescribing the *jizya* payment rituals] are in application. The people of *dhimma* have far more privileges over Muslims to the extent that it has become customary to receive *jizya* by the hand of an agent, although the most accurate of the sayings stipulated that we should not accept *jizya* this way ... They are to physically walk with it, walking not riding. All this is caused by the weakness of Islam.[2]

During the nineteenth and twentieth centuries, *dhimmi* laws were progressively set aside across most of the Islamic world under pressure from the Great Powers of Europe. During the nineteenth century the Turks pursued reforms (*Tanzimat*) to establish the equality of all their citizens under law. This was done under the influence and scrutiny of European governments, whose support Turkey needed against the Russians. The reforms helped to stave off interference from the Russians on behalf of Orthodox Christian *dhimmi* populations including the Greeks, Serbs and Armenians.

Such reforms were protested by local Muslim populations, many of whom were descendents of people who had escaped the *dhimma* through converting. Local Islamic populations resented and resisted the innovations, and change across the whole Ottoman world was slow in coming. For example, the Bosniak lords opposed the reforms. They deeply resented the new found freedoms of their Catholic and Orthodox neighbors, and the loss of privileges and financial advantages which their ancestors had converted to Islam to receive. Although Bosniak resistance was put down in 1850 by the Sultan's army, oppressive conditions continued for the Croats and Serbs, as the *dhimma* regulations were not only a matter of state legislation, but were an integral part of local political and economic conditions.[3]

---

1 Jewish History Sourcebook: 'Islam and the Jews: The Status of Jews and Christians in Muslim Lands, 1772 CE,' viewed 8 June 2009, <http://www.fordham.edu/halsall/jewish/1772-jewsinislam.html>.
2 *Ruh al-Ma'ani*. Commentary on Q9:29, viewed 21 February 2008, <http://altafsir.com>.
3 Bat Ye'or, 'The Tolerant Pluralistic Islamic Society'.

Despite much resistance, freedom did come to a considerable degree. Eventually, throughout the whole Islamic world most *dhimmi* populations experienced a degree of liberation through the intervention of European powers, in some cases completely throwing off the Muslim yoke. As early as the 1600's the Portuguese had assisted in the liberation of Abyssinia. The British ended Muslim Mughal rule and Hindu dhimmitude in India in 1857. The Greeks, Bulgarians, Romanians, Serbs, and Hungarians fought for their freedom with varying degrees of success. For some, like the Assyrians and the Maronites of Lebanon, the struggle ended in tragic failure, a failure which is still being worked out to its agonizing conclusion. The Armenians, with Russian assistance, did manage to establish freedom from the *dhimma* pact in present-day Armenia, although this represents but a small remnant of the ancient Armenian territories.

The founding of the state of Israel was another political manifestation of the period of liberation, providing sanctuary for hundreds of thousands of *dhimmi* Jews who left the house of Islam, abandoning the lands where they had lived for thousands of years, such as Egypt, Iran, Morocco, Turkey, Afghanistan and Yemen.

Today there is as yet no internationally recognized Islamic state which officially imposes a *jizya* taxation system on its non-Muslim citizens. However there are Muslim voices who argue that *jizya* should be reinstated, and there are contemporary examples of Muslims exacting the tax from their Christian neighbors. More than this, all throughout the Muslim world the institutions of dhimmitude are returning.

CHAPTER 8

The *Dhimma*'s Return

I'm becoming an alien in Malaysia, in my own country.
Dr Jacob George, President of the Consumers Associate of Sumban
and Shah Alam, Malaysia[1]

The persecuted church

Throughout the world today, Christians are victims of religious persecution. The British Secret Service reported in 2007 that around 200 million Christians are subject to persecution.[2] While it must be acknowledged that Christians have persecuted others on religious grounds throughout history, today the reverse is far more common.

Christians are persecuted in the name of diverse faiths and ideologies: by Buddhists in Laos, Sri Lanka and Bhutan, by Hindus in India, and by communists in Laos, Vietnam, China and North Korea. In some cases Christians also persecute other Christians, for example, in Ethiopia and Eritrea. However it is Islam which is the largest ideological contributor to anti-Christian persecution around the world today. In a May 2007 report, the Congressional US Commission on International Religious Freedom nominated six Muslim countries among its list of the worst 11 nations for religious persecution.[3] Open Doors, an organization which supports persecuted Christians, each year prepares a list of 50 nations (and some regions) where Christians are persecuted for their faith: in 2008 three quarters of these were majority Muslim areas.[4]

---

1 'Pressure on multi-faith Malaysia.' *BBC News*, 16 May 2006, viewed 8 June 2009, <http://news.bbc.co.uk/1/hi/world/asia-pacific/4965580.stm>.

2 'MI6 warns Pope: 200m Christians are in danger', *Sunday Express*, 17 June 2007; '200 million Christians in 60 countries subject to persecution', *Catholic News Agency*, viewed 27 September 2009, <http://www.catholicnewsagency.com/new.php?n=9669>.

3 These are the 'Countries of Particular Concern'. Annual Report, p.70. United States Commission on Religious Freedom. 2 May, 2007, downloaded 8 June 2009, <http://www.uscirf.gov/images/AR_2007/annualreport2007.pdf>.

4 Open Doors World Watch List 2008, viewed June 8 2009, <http://sb.od.org/index.php?supp_page=wwl_2008&supp_lang=en&PHPSESSID=cac24d4f0d6e24467c73821d7d03ccd9F:WWW>.

It is not that Christians are uniquely targeted by Muslims: people of all faiths can be persecuted in the name of Islam, for example, Sunnis and Shi'ites persecute each other in Iraq; Jews are persecuted in Iran; and Baha'is and Mandeans are cruelly treated in the several Middle Eastern nations.

Religious persecution happens for many reasons. Alongside ideological factors, base human motives such as greed can also play a role. The complicity of many ordinary Germans in the Holocaust was bought in kind through gifts of houses and land taken from the Jews. Islamic religious persecution can also have many contributing factors, including political conflicts, and local ethnic rivalries, but across the world it is the teachings of Islam which provide the most constant driver for religious persecution of others by Muslims. Islam itself – *the Quran*, the *Sunna* of Muhammad, and the laws of the *Sharia* – constitutes the 'compass of faith' which directs the character of religious persecution conducted by Muslims.

Dhimmitude and religious persecution

The human rights situation of Christians in many Muslim countries has been getting steadily worse over the past half-century. This deterioration has been directly linked to the world-wide Islamic revival and reinstatement of *Sharia* law. Most Muslim nations have taken steps, however small, towards re-implementing *Sharia*, and wherever this happens discrimination against non-Muslims increases. As Muslim women from Jakarta to Cape Town have been putting on the veil, so also Christians and other non-Muslims have been feeling the brunt of worsening human rights conditions.

Christians have been killed, subjected to forced conversions, enslaved, their churches destroyed, their property looted, the women raped and their fundamental human rights such as freedom of speech denied. In region after region the worldwide *Sharia* revival has been bad news for Christians. Battles are being fought over the return of dhimmitude. The Christians of Sudan have fought for more than 20 years at the cost of two million lives, because they refused to be made into *dhimmis* through the imposition of *Sharia* law by the north.

A report from the Lausanne Forum on World Evangelization highlighted this trend, and identified several theological motivations which underpin it, such as the beliefs that Allah has determined that Islam and Muslims should be dominant; non-Muslims must not exercise authority over Muslims; and Christians are pact-breakers, betrayers, infidels and rejecters (and thus unworthy of protection).[1]

The dhimma as the model for persecution

The key to understanding increasing Islamic persecution of Christians and other non-Muslims throughout the world today is that persecuting behaviors closely track ancient *dhimma* regulations. The principles of discrimination described in chapters 6 and 7, to which *dhimmi* Christians were subjected in pre-modern times under the *dhimma*, also account for most discrimination against Christians in Muslim contexts today. In Indonesia, Egypt or Turkey – to name but a few examples – it is very difficult for Christians to gain a permit to build a church. Why? The ultimate cause is that the *dhimma* stipulates that there will be no new churches after Islamic conquest. Such restrictions apply even in a state which is not officially Islamic, such as Indonesia, or is officially secular, such as Turkey. A state need not have formally embraced the *Sharia* for laws to be shaped by its principles, which include the *dhimma* regulations.

The influence of the *dhimma* extends well beyond official legislation. In Pakistan or Denmark, non-Muslim girls are at risk of being kidnapped and raped by Muslim men. Pipes and Hedegaard report that while Muslims make up around one in twenty of the population of Denmark, they make up the majority of the country's convicted rapists, and 'practically all the female victims are non-Muslim'.[2] On the other side of the globe, in Islamic Pakistan, the kidnapping and rape of Christian women by Muslim men is a serious problem for the minority Christian community.[3] These manifestations are produced by the dynamics of dhimmitude, whether home-grown or imported through immigration.

Retheologizing the dhimma as 'freedom of choice'

In recent years a good deal of theological groundwork has gone into preparing the way for bringing back the *dhimma*, together with the *jizya*. A modern discussion of this subject by Sayyid Qutb (d. 1966) is found in his widely used and influential commentary *In the Shade of the Quran*.

---

1 'The Persecuted Church.' Lausanne Occasional Paper No. 32, produced by the Issue Group on the Persecuted Church at the 2004 Forum for World Evangelization in Pattaya, Thailand. The principal writer was Patrick Sookhdeo. Published 2005.
2 Daniel Pipes and Lars Hedegaard, 'Something rotten in Denmark?'
3 *Human Rights Monitor – 2001* and *Human Rights Monitor – 2002*.

In his explanation of Q9:29 Qutb acknowledges the contrast between the Meccan and Medinan *suras* in their rulings concerning Jews and Christians, and argues that the correct application of these verses depended upon the attitudes of Jews and Christians towards Islam: the hostility of Jews and Christians was the reason for the final command of Q9:29 to fight and subjugate them. Today, because Jews and Christians show the same characteristics as they did during the Medinan period – Qutb calls them polytheists and disbelievers – the command to fight these groups is still valid, and cannot be denied.

The reason Qutb gives for applying *jizya* and the *dhimma* is to ensure that, by 'smashing the power' of false religions, there will be no obstacles to propagating Islam. According to Qutb, only under the conditions of the *dhimma* will non-Muslims agree to provide no obstacles to Islam's spread, and only when this happens can every individual be provided with true freedom of choice to accept Islam:

> When this happens [i.e. *jizya* is paid] the process of liberating mankind is completed by giving every individual the freedom of choice based on conviction. Anyone who is not convinced may continue to follow his faith. However he has to pay the submission tax to fulfill a number of objectives … by paying this tax, known as *jizyah*, he declares that he will not stand in physical opposition to the efforts advocating the true Divine faith.[1]

Many would consider Qutb's argument, that the *jizya* ensures complete 'freedom of choice based on conviction', to be absurd. However it must be understood that Qutb is using the expression 'freedom of choice' in a way which is shaped by his theological assumptions. In his view, it is only the freedom to choose Islam that mankind has any duty to promote, and non-Muslims will only enjoy **this** 'freedom' when non-Muslim faith communities are completely subjugated under the *dhimma*. If non-Muslims' status was superior or even equal to that of Muslims, this could be an 'obstacle' to people entering Islam. In Qutb's view, it is all such 'power' which Islam must 'smash' to ensure that people experience no obstacles to entering Islam. This is why the *dhimma* must be imposed upon them.

What is deceptive about Qutb's rhetoric is that it utilizes words such as *freedom* and *choice*, but utterly rejects Western concepts of equality and reciprocity which give these words meaning.

---

1 Sayyid Qutb, *In the Shade of the Qur'an*. Commentary on Q9:29. Excerpted in Bostom, *The Legacy of Jihad*, p.134.

Islamic revolutions

There is a direct link between the state of the Islamic community and the re-implementation of *dhimma* conditions. For the best part of a century, the world wide Islamic movement has been progressively transforming Muslim societies, and this has gone hand-in-hand with the return of the conditions of the *dhimma*. It was a measure of the confidence of the Taliban in the success of their Islamic revolution that they reintroduced *dhimmi* laws against non-Muslim Hindus in Afghanistan, such as colored clothing patches.

When the Ayatollah Khomeini ushered in the Iranian Islamic revolution in 1979, Muslims greeted this event with enthusiasm all over the world. At last, or so it was thought, Islam would be implemented rigorously to reinstitute an Islamic utopia on earth. Yet along with the Islamization of Iran came the return of the laws of the *dhimma*. The Iranian democracy activist Frank Nikbakht describes the changes after 1979:

> Non-Muslims had become "Dhimmis", second class citizens with limited rights, or non-citizens with absolutely no rights, just based on their beliefs. The Jews, Christians and Zoroastrians were given certain rights but their lives were legally valued as less than ½ or ⅛th of a Muslim's life (depending on which source of Shari'a a judge decided to use in cases of compensations for loss of life or limb). They lost their right to testify in court against Muslims and they lost all sorts of imaginable rights to material and social status which might demonstrate any semblance of superiority or power over Muslims.[1]

It has also been reported that the Iranian government has considered reintroducing discriminatory clothing for *dhimmis*.[2]

Reviving the jizya

There are many other signs that the *dhimma* and the *jizya* have once again come knocking at the door of the world:

- In recent decades Islamists have been reported to have extorted *jizya* from Copts in Egypt.[3]
- Dr. Amani Tawfiq, Professor at Mansoura (Egypt) University, proposed that Egypt solve its economic problems by reintroducing *jizya*: 'If Egypt wants to slowly but surely get out of its economic

---

1 Jamie, Glazov. 2008 (March 5). 'Iran's killing fields.' *Fontpagemag.com*, viewed June 8 2009, <http://www.frontpagemag.com/readArticle.aspx?ARTID=30138>.

2 Andrew Bostom, 'Islamic antisemitism – Jew hatred in Islam.' In *The Legacy of Islamic Antisemitism*, p.148.

3 Ana Belén Soage, 'Faraj Fawda, or the cost of freedom of expression.'

situation and address poverty in the country, the Jizya has to be imposed on the Copts.'[1]

- Palestinian Sheikh Muhammad Ibrahim al-Madhi stated in a sermon broadcast on Palestinian Authority Television from Gaza that Jews are welcome in Palestine as long as they accept *dhimmi* status:

> We welcome the Jews to live as Dhimmis, but the rule in this land and in all the Muslim countries must be the rule of Allah.[2]

- Saudi Sheikh Muhammad bin 'Abd al-Rahman al-'Arifi, Imam of the King Fahd Defence Academy declared in 2002:

> We will control the land of the Vatican; we will control Rome and introduce Islam in it. Yes, the Christians … will yet pay us the jizya in humiliation, or they will convert to Islam.[3]

- Palestinian Authority Undersecretary for Awqaf [Religious Endowment], Sheikh Yussef Salamah, represented the PA at a May 1999 'Inter-Cultural Conference', held in Tehran, where he held up the *dhimma* as the proper paradigm for relations between Muslims and Christians today. 'Islam', he argued, 'respected people of [other] religions and did not hurt them.'[4]

- Hassam El-Masalmeh, leader of the Hamas representatives on the municipal council of Bethlehem, in 2005 announced Hamas' intention to reinstate *jizya* in a Palestinian state, in which all non-Muslims would be 'welcome' to live as *dhimmis*, if they submit to *Sharia* norms:

> We in Hamas intend to implement this tax (i.e., the jizya) someday. We say it openly – we welcome everyone to Palestine but only if they agree to live under our rules.[5]

---

1 Emmi El Masry, 'Imposing JIZYA on Christians to address poverty!!!' January 7, 2009, viewed 8 June 2009, <http://voiceofthecopts.org/en/articles/imposing_jizya_on_christians_to_address_poverty.html>.

2 'A Friday sermon on PA TV …' June 6, 2001. Middle East Media Research Unit, Special Dispatch No. 240, viewed 8 June 2009, <http://memri.org/bin/articles.cgi?Page=archives&Area=sd&ID=SP24001>.

3 Steven Stalinsky, 'The next Pope and Islamic Prophecy.' *FrontPageMagazine.com.* April 14, 2005, viewed 8 June 2009, <http://www.frontpagemag.com/readArticle.aspx?ARTID=8931>.

4 *Al-Hayat Al-Jadida*, May 12, 1999. Translated in MEMRI Special Dispatch No. 41, August 2, 1999: 'Muslim-Christian Tensions in the Israeli-Arab Community,' viewed August 21, 2009, <http://memri.org/bin/articles.cgi?Page=archives&Area=sd&ID=SP4199#_edn1>.

5 Interview by reporter Karby Legget, published in the December 23-26, 2005 edition of *The Wall Street Journal*.

- Human rights reports from Yemen indicate that in January 2007, the tiny remnant community of Jews in Sa'ada was being forced to make *jizya* payments.[1]

- Christians were compelled in 2007 to pay *jizya* in Durah, the Christian district of Baghdad. Otherwise, they had to convert to Islam and give their daughters to the jihadists. Moreover, if they fled, they were required to leave their possessions behind for the Muslims.[2]

- A Pakistani lawyer has argued that reinstating the *jizya* would improve harmony between Christians and Muslims, and that leaders had done away with the *jizya* 'to selectively victimize the Christian minority of Pakistan'[3] (i.e. Christians will not be safe unless and until they pay *jizya*).

- Some time before March 2008, a *fatwa* was issued to al-Qaida jihadists in Algeria, with instructions demanding the imposition of *jizya* on Christians there, and forbidding them from manifesting their religion. The letter is entitled: 'The severe cutting sword upon the necks of Algerian Christians'. It has been attributed to Abu Turab al-Jaza'iri, an al-Qaida leader in Iraq.[4] The letter states that 'Allah commands us not to remove the sword from them' until they pay *jizya*, which must be taken by force because 'while we take it from them we have the power and the upper hand over them', and 'Allah commands us to humiliate them at the time we extract it from them.' The al-Qaida operatives should 'Smite, and do not remove the sword until they pay *jizya* out of hand and are belittled as we were commanded.'[5]

- In July 2008, Catholics on Basilan in the Philippines received letters from Islamic militants with an ultimatum giving them three choices: convert, pay *jizya* or face the sword:

---

1 Andrew Bostom, 'Islamic antisemitism – Jew hatred in Islam.' In *The Legacy of Islamic Antisemitism*, p.164.

2 'Muslims forcing Christian Assyrians in Baghdad Neighborhoods to pay 'protection tax,' a news release dated 18 March 2007, the Assyrian International News Agency; a report in *al-Bayyinah*, the Iraqi daily on 10 May 2007; 'Islamic groups impose tax on Christian "subjects"', March 19 2007 in *Asia News*, viewed 8 June 2009, <http://www.asianews.it/index.php?1=en&art=8773$size=A#>; and a report from *Al-Sharq Al-Awsat*, May 1 2007 (see Memri Blog report, 1 May 2007, viewed April 27 2009, <http://www.thememriblog.org/blog_personal/en/1426.htm>).

3 Patrick Sookhdeo, *A People Betrayed*, p.249.

4 The Arabic text was posted on March 5, 2008 on Aljazeera Talk, viewed April 23 2009, <http://www.aljazeeratalk.net/forum/showthread.php?t=124389>. See also <http://www.thememriblog.org/blog_personal/en/11784.htm>, viewed April 27 2009.

5 Ibid.

The Qur'an's instruction is that if there are Christians living in a place for Muslims, they have to be converted to Islam. If they don't want to convert to Islam, they have to pay the jizya. If they refuse to pay, they can be subjected to violence! We are giving you 15 days to respond. If we don't get an answer from you, we will consider you our enemies.[1]

- In April 2009, a group of Sikhs in Pakistan's Orakzai Agency abandoned their homes and moved elsewhere because local Taliban authorities had demanded they pay the *jizya*.[2] Others stayed and paid up.[3] In June 2009, Catholic authorities protested the imposition of *jizya* in Orakzai and Khyber Agencies on more than 700 non-Muslim families, stating that 'Pakistan is a democratic country that cannot allow religious minorities to be subjected to such discrimination and economic injustice because they are equal citizens and not a conquered people.'[4]
- In August 2009, Younus Abdullah Muhammad was street preaching in New York when he cried out 'We ask that Allah give victory and collect the *jizya* from the Jews and the Christians and establish Islam all over the *dunya* ['world'] during our lifetime.'[5]

The trend of *Sharia* reimplementation and persecution

During the past half century, most Muslim nations have taken steps, however small, towards reimplementing *Sharia*, and wherever this happens discrimination against non-Muslims increases. The story of Islamic persecution of non-Muslims around the world is simply that dhimmitude is returning as part and parcel of the *Sharia* revival.

---

1 Elizabeth Kendal, 'Southern Philippines: Terror on Basilan Island'. *Religious Liberty Prayer Bulletin*, No. 488, Wed 23 July, 2008, viewed 8 June 2009, <http://www.ea.org.au/default.aspx?id=68bee070-0953-40ca-afe3-7790ed22b673>.

2 Abdul Saboor Khan, 'Sikh families leave Orakzai after Taliban demand jizia'. *Daily Times*, Wednesday 15 April 2009, viewed 8 June 2009, <http://www.dailytimes.com.pk/default.asp?page=2009\04\15\story_15-4-2009_pg7_5>.

3 'Sikhs in Pakistan pay jizia (tax) of Rs.20 mn to Taliban.' Thursday 16 April 2009, viewed 8 June 2009, <http://islamicterrorism.wordpress.com/2009/04/16/sikhs-in-pakistan-pay-jizia-tax-of-rs20-mn-to-taliban/#respond>.

4 'Pakistani Catholic leaders come out against the Taliban and the imposition of the jizya.' *Asia News*, June 5, 2009, viewed June 8 2009, <http://new.asianews.it/index.php?l=en&art=15435>.

5 'Street Dawa 8 14 09 Part 2', YouTube. Viewed August 29, 2009, <http://www.youtube.com/watch?v=KCooZBxBn-k>.

An extreme expression of this trend was the reintroduction of identifying clothing patches for Hindus in Afghanistan under the Taliban.[1] More typical are less visible discriminations which limit and restrict the freedom of non-Muslims in society, for example the sequence of legal and constitutional changes in Pakistan over 60 years has followed a steady trend towards Islamization, accompanied by worsening human rights conditions for non-Muslim minorities.

Case Study: Pakistan

The case of Pakistan is illustrative of the steady character of *Sharia* reimplementation, and the growing discriminations which have accompanied it:

- In 1947 Pakistan was established as a secular state, its founding father Muhammad Ali Jinnah declaring in a speech three days before partition 'You may belong to any religion or caste or creed – that has nothing to do with the business of the State.'[2]
- In 1956 Pakistan was proclaimed an 'Islamic Republic'.[3]
- During 1979-80 a *Sharia* court was established, and laws introduced to enforce penalties for alcohol, theft and adultery.
- In 1984 a new Law of Evidence was promulgated, which downgraded non-Muslims' testimony in court cases.
- In 1985 the national constitution was radically Islamized.
- In 1986 blasphemy against Islam was declared a capital offense. This is a key aspect of the classical anti-*dhimmi* legal structures, being designed to prevent criticism of Islam by non-Muslims.
- In 1991 the *Sharia* was declared to be 'the supreme law in Pakistan'.[4]
- In 1993 the Supreme Court ruled that fundamental constitutional rights are subject to 'the injunctions of Islam as contained in the Quran and *Sunna*'.[5]
- In 1998 John Joseph, Catholic bishop of Faisalabad, committed suicide in protest against the worsening plight of Christians in his nation.

The steadily worsening human rights situation for minorities in Pakistan, accompanying these political developments, have been noted

---

1 'Taliban Order Will Require Hindu Identity Tags.' *U.N. Wire.* 23 May, 2001, viewed 8 June 2009, <http://www.unwire.org/unwire/20010523/14906_story.asp>.
2 Patrick Sookhdeo, *A People Betrayed*, p.77.
3 Ibid., p.82.
4 Ibid., p.145.
5 Ibid., p.102.

by international agencies for many years. Two independent reports of religious discrimination in Pakistan point to a foundation in the *Sharia*. These are *A People Betrayed* by Patrick Sookhdeo, and US Department of State's *International Religious Freedom Report 2006*. Here is a summary of reports of *dhimma*-tracking human rights violations from Pakistan:

- **Conversions.** Although there is no law on the statute books against apostasy, converts out of Islam must be secret and forced conversions are regularly reported.
- **Marriage.** Marriages between Muslim women and non-Muslim men are not recognized. Children born to such women are considered illegitimate. If a woman converts to Islam, her marriage to a non-Muslim is considered dissolved.
- **Abduction of women.** There have been increasing reports of abductions of non-Muslim women. Muslim men who abduct, rape or forcibly convert Christian women (thereby annulling the women's marriages) are rarely brought to justice, the evidence of a Christian women carrying only a quarter of the weight of Muslim man.
- **Worship restrictions.** Although in principle religious minorities may establish places of worship, in practice this right is restricted. A Pastor, the Revd Noor Alam, was killed, apparently because it was thought he had plans to build a church building.[1] There are also restrictions on publicly displaying non-Muslim religious images. State funding supports mosques and Muslim clergy, but not non-Muslim religions.
- **Restrictions on criticizing Islam.** Christians have been falsely charged under blasphemy laws. Extra-judicial killings of Christians accused of blasphemy are rarely prosecuted. Laws which prohibit injuring others' religious sentiments are rarely used to protect the sentiments of non-Muslims.
- **Legal vulnerability.** Courts can decide to reject a Christian's evidence, in accordance with Islamic law. They are unlikely to act objectively in cases of discrimination against religious minorities. In compensating victims of crime, courts award far lower restitution to non-Muslims. Forced evictions of Christians are common, rarely with legal restitution. Confiscations of church property, without legal redress, have been reported.
- **Loyalty to Islam.** All government officials, irrespective of their faith, must swear on oath to protect the country's Islamic identity.

---

1 Ibid., p.180.

- Social status and public office. Religious minorities are discriminated against in government hiring and promotions. Non-Muslims rarely rise to high rank in the armed forces. The majority of bonded laborers (a form of slavery) are Christians. Most 'sweepers' are Hindus or Christians.
- Appearance, and status. Passports display the holder's religion. Students must declare their religion on entrance applications to state institutions, and are discriminated against. Non-Muslim prisoners received poorer facilities in state prisons. Christian villages received poorer essential services.
- Violence. Violent attacks on Christians have been increasing, including by police. These are rarely prosecuted.

Other nations: Egypt, Malaysia, Nigeria, Iran

Here a group of five states are considered together. This summary is mainly based upon US Department of State's *International Religious Freedom Report* for 2006.

Restrictions relating to conversion

Malaysia: Muslims are not legally permitted to convert to other religions, unless a *Sharia* court approves their apostasy. In practice such approvals are routinely denied. Proselytizing of Muslims is strictly prohibited: proselytizing of non-Muslims is not restricted but is facilitated by government policy and structures.

Egypt: converts out of Islam are unable to change their religion legally without a state court verdict. They are at risk of violent retribution, arbitrary detention and harassment by security forces. In contrast, converts to Islam receive state support.

Iran: apostasy from Islam can attract the death penalty.

Restrictions on marriage

Malaysia: women considered by the state to be Muslims may not marry non-Muslims, so female converts to Christianity are unable to marry fellow Christians.

Egypt: Muslim men can marry Christian women but Muslim women are prohibited from marrying Christian men. If a Muslim man marries a Christian woman, any marital disputes must be settled according to *Sharia* law. Christian widows of Muslims have no automatic inheritance rights. If a Muslim woman marries a Christian man, she could be arrested for apostasy, and any children can be taken and placed into the custody of a male Muslim guardian according to the principle of 'no jurisdiction of a non-Muslim over a Muslim'.[1] If a Christian woman married to a Christian converts to Islam, she is automatically divorced after the husband has been given an opportunity to follow her into Islam. If either parent converts to Islam, the minor children – and in some cases the adult children – are automatically classified as Muslims and placed in the Muslim parent's sole custody.

Restrictions on worship and practice of faith

Malaysia: restrictions on distribution of Christian publications apply in some states. The film *The Passion of the Christ* was forbidden to be viewed by Muslims in 2004. Approvals for non-Muslim places of worship are subject to long delays. Unregistered places of worship may be demolished by the state.

Egypt: Christians face great difficulties in obtaining permits to repair and build churches, which until 1999 required presidential approval. Permission for repairs has now been devolved to local government, while the president still has power to decide on the building of new churches. Applying for either kind of permission is a long, slow process with no guarantee of success. A rumor of plans to extend a church in Bimha south of Cairo was the pretext for a pre-mediated and violent mob attack by 2000 people against the Christian community on May 11, 2007.[2]

Nigeria: Christians in predominately Muslim areas report that local Muslim government officials block church building projects.

Prohibition on critiquing Islam

Malaysia: Several Muslim organizations rejected formation of an interfaith council in 2005, condemning it on the grounds that 'matters concerning Islam could only be discussed by Muslims'.[3]

Nigeria: In Bauchi State in February 2006 a Christian teacher confiscated a Quran from a student. The teacher was threatened by students for handling the book, and in a subsequent demonstration two churches were burned and approximately 20 Christians were killed. A Christian

---

1 US Department of State. Egypt. Religious Freedom Report 2006.
2 Elizabeth Kendal, 'Egypt: Keeping the Copts subjugated'. 29 May, 2007. World Evangelical Alliance Religious Liberty News and Analysis, viewed 8 June 2009, <http://wwwworld evangelicalalliance.com/news/view.htm?id=1148>.
3 US Department of State. Malaysia. *Religious Freedom Report* 2006.

nursing student in Sokoto was accused of having made critical remarks about Islam. The school was closed for weeks, and the student had to be relocated under police protection to another state. In December 2004 the head of a campus Christian group was killed for insulting Islam.[1]

Legal vulnerability

Egypt: In an infamous case, the Muslim killers of 21 Christians in Al-Kosheh in 1999-2000 were never brought to justice. A court acquitted 94 of 96 suspects held in connection with the killings, and no one was sentenced for the killings.[2]

Nigeria: the abduction and murder of a Christian student leader in Bauchi State in 2005 resulted in no arrests or prosecutions.

Rendering assistance and loyalty to Muslims

Egypt: After the large mob attack of May 2007, the Christians of Bimha agreed through reconciliation to forfeit their complaints, and surrender all rights to request compensation. All criminal charges were dropped against offenders.[3]

Restrictions on holding public office

Egypt: Christians are rarely found in higher-level civil or military positions. Christians constitute between 10% and 20% of the population, but are under-represented in parliament. Since the Nasser coup of 1952, no Christian has been prime minister, speaker in the Legislative Assembly, or Minister for the Interior, Foreign Affairs or Defence.[4] There are no known Christian university presidents or deans, and very few judges.[5]

Iran: Non-Muslims may not occupy political elected offices, and are excluded from senior government positions. No non-Muslim can hold a military position over a Muslim.

---

1 US Department of State. Nigeria. Religious Freedom Report 2006.
2 Nina Shea, Briefing on 'Religious Freedom in Egypt: Recent Developments.' Before the Task Force on Religious Freedom of the United States House of Representatives. May 23, 2007.
3 Elizabeth Kendal, 'Egypt: Keeping the Copts subjugated'. 29 May, 2007. World Evangelical Alliance Religious Liberty News and Analysis, viewed 8 June 2009, <http://www.world evangelicalalliance.com/news/view.htm?id=1148>.
4 Khair Abaza and Mark Nakhla. 'The Copts and their political implications in Egypt.' October 25, 2005. PolicyWatch #1039. The Washington Institute, viewed 8 June 2009, <http://www. washingtoninstitute.org/templateC05.php?CID=2386>.
5 US Department of State. Egypt. Religious Freedom Report 2006.

Restrictions on housing, public appearance, status and behavior

Egypt: Religion is recorded on identity cards. In general, public university training for Arabic language teachers bars non-Muslims because the curriculum involves the study of the Quran. There has reportedly been only one Christian appointed to a university teaching position in Arabic language in several decades.[1]

Violent attacks

Egypt: The Ibn Khaldoun Research Center has documented over 120 major attacks on Copts during the past 40 years.[2] In February 2007 several Christian-owned shops were arsoned due to rumors of a relationship between a Muslim woman and a Christian man.[3]

Abduction of women

Egypt: There have been many reports of rapes, abductions, forced conversion and marriages of Christian girls.

ooooo

There is no state in the world today that applies the *dhimma* in its classical form. Nevertheless state after state throughout the world imposes conditions of non-reciprocity and inferiority upon non-Muslims, which can only be accounted for in terms of influence of the *dhimma*. This is true of the most extreme Islamic regimes like Iran, as well as the more tolerant ones like Turkey or Indonesia.

Mutilated speech and the *dhimmi* syndrome

The situation for Christians living under Islam has been made worse by certain political and intellectual developments in which *dhimmis* themselves have often taken the lead. These not only impact negatively upon Christians living under Islam: they are also shaping attitudes of the West to Islam and its treatment of non-Muslims, as well as to the Israeli-Palestinian conflict.

---

1 Nina Shea, Briefing on 'Religious Freedom in Egypt: Recent Developments.' Before the Task Force on Religious Freedom of the United States House of Representatives. May 23, 2007.

2 Elizabeth Kendal, 'Egypt: Keeping the Copts subjugated'. 29 May, 2007. World Evangelical Alliance Religious Liberty News and Analysis, viewed 8 June 2009, <http://www.world evangelicalalliance.com/news/view.htm?id=1148>.

3 Nina Shea, Briefing on 'Religious Freedom in Egypt: Recent Developments.' Before the Task Force on Religious Freedom of the United States House of Representatives. May 23, 2007.

Arab nationalism

The Arab nationalist or Pan-Arabist movement, which first arose in Christian circles in the nineteenth century, can be understood as a product of the *dhimmis'* mimetic tendency. This movement hoped to establish a multicultural secular Arab identity, expressed in a territorially expanded Syria, and incorporating Lebanon and Palestine, in which Christian and Muslims would be forged together into one nation. Bat Ye'or describes how Syrian Christians, as part of this project, committed themselves, not only to be Arabs together with Muslims, but to identify with the ideological cause of the *Umma*:

> Traumatized by [the Armenian and Assyrian massacres], the Syrian Christians committed themselves totally to the doctrine of Arab nationalism. The most intransigent exponents of a Muslim-Christian brotherhood, they dedicated themselves to extolling at both a political and a literary level the greatness and tolerance of Islamic civilization.[1]

One danger of giving in to the mimetic tendency is that it can undermine a *dhimmi* community's identity and ultimately threaten its very existence. Arab nationalism has, by the end of the twentieth century, become an instrument of Islamization. Walid Phares has identified what he calls the 'Arabist strategy', which 'since the forties' has been to:

- claim that the Middle East is an Arab and Muslim region – this is directed not only against Israel, but all non-Arab, non-Muslim populations in the region;
- isolate non-Arab, non-Muslim groups one from another; and
- eliminate minorities within their borders, by one means or another.[2]

This policy is now leading to the destruction of Christian minorities, as Christians flee the Middle East in a massive demographic collapse.[3]

Edward Said's Orientalism

Another leading instance of the pathological influence of the mimetic principle is found in the writings of Professor Edward Said (d. 2003),

---

1 Bat Ye'or, *Islam and Dhimmitude*, p.159.
2 Walid Phares, 'The oppression of Middle East Christians: a forgotten tragedy.' In Robert Spencer, *The Myth of Islamic Tolerance*, p.230.
3 'Abd al-Nasser al-Najjar, 'Palestinian Columnist: Muslims are harming Christian culture.' MEMRI Special Dispatch No. 2112, November 12, 2008. Excerpted from *Al-Ayyam* (Palestinian Authority) October 25, 2008, viewed 8 June 2009, <http://www.memri.org/bin/latestnews.cgi?ID=SD211208>. See also Amira El Ahl, Daniel Steinvorth, Volkhard Windfuhr and Berhard Zand, 'A Christian Exodus from the Arab World.' Spiegel Online. 10 January, 2007, viewed 8 June 2009, <http://www.spiegel.de/international/spiegel/0,1518,457002,00.html>.

formerly of Columbia University. A Middle Eastern Christian by birth, Said's enormously influential *Orientalism*, has, according to Ibn Warraq, had a 'totally pernicious' influence on the ability of the West to criticise Islam.[1] By leveling the label of 'racism' against generations of Western scholars of Islam, Said has intimidated many researchers into silence. By blaming the problems of the Arab world on 'orientalism' – the wicked West's allegedly racist perspective on the East – he made it very difficult for non-Muslims to critique Islamic ideology. By demonizing the West, and silencing a whole generation of Western critics of Islam, Said has 'encouraged Islamic fundamentalists'.[2]

The silence of the dhimmis

For those living under Islamic law, to criticise the *dhimma* is forbidden. *Dhimmi* testimony against Muslims was prohibited. It was never permitted for the *dhimmis* themselves to expose or analyze their own plight: it sufficed rather that they be grateful for it. Asking challenging questions was not permitted. Criticism of Islam was prohibited to non-Muslims under *Sharia* conditions: this was one of the crimes which cancelled the *dhimmis*' protection. The whole institution of the *dhimma*, including the history of Islamic conquest, became a taboo subject for the *dhimmis* themselves. Bat Ye'or writes:

> The concealment of the *dhimmis*' history arises from the silence imposed on them and the ban on any criticism. ... In the dominating group, this refusal of testimony by the suppression of speech – the distinctive sign of humanity – reflects a denial of rights. This mutilated speech, this rejected testimony, is transposed from the individual to the group and is perpetuated in time. History being also the testimony of a people and the foundation of its rights, the effacement of the past abolishes its rights.[3]

The Muslim Palestinian writer 'Abd al-Nasser al-Najjar, lamenting confiscations of Christian lands by Muslims in Bethlehem and elsewhere, reported that Christians are silent 'so as not to attract attention', and when they do attempt to take steps to retrieve their property, they can be subjected to death threats.[4]

---

1 Ibn Warraq, 'Edward Said and the Saidists.' In Robert Spencer, *The Myth of Islamic Tolerance*, p.474.
2 Ibid., p.512.
3 Bat Ye'or, *The Decline of Eastern Christianity under Islam*, p.240.
4 'Abd al-Nasser al-Najjar, 'Palestinian Columnist: Muslims are harming Christian culture.' MEMRI Special Dispatch No. 2112, November 12, 2008. Excerpted from *Al-Ayyam* (Palestinian Authority) October 25, 2008, viewed 8 June 2009, <http://www.memri.org/bin/latestnews.cgi?ID=SD211208>.

The extent to which *dhimmis* will go to maintain their silence can be astounding. In 2000 Abe Ata, a Palestinian Christian, published a study of patterns of interfaith marriage among Palestinians entitled *Intermarriage between Christians and Muslims.* The overwhelming pattern, in 96% of cases, is that Christian women are marrying Muslim men. Usually the children are raised as Muslims, and more often than not the wives convert to Islam. All this is in conformity with the *Sharia.*

What is remarkable is that although this fundamental asymmetry is foundational for understanding Palestinian mixed marriages, it is rendered almost invisible in Ata's book. Not until the final few pages is the religious gender imbalance acknowledged clearly.[1] In its suppression of the contribution of the *Sharia* to Palestinian mixed marriages, Ata's work is a breathtakingly consistent exercise in denial.

Dhimmi clergy

While Abe Ata's silence is maintained faithfully through scholarship, published far away in Australia, in the Palestinian territories the devastating impact of such silence threatens the continued viability of the Christian Arab community.

Justus Reid Weiner, in his investigation of the deteriorating human rights situation of Christians living under the Palestinian Authority, pointed out that there is a widespread distrust of religious leaders among Palestinian Christians, who 'obfuscate the situation as it affects their constituents'.[2] One Christian man said, 'Our leaders are liars: They tell the newspapers that everything is OK. But when Christians go to the market, they're afraid to wear crosses.'[3]

Weiner identifies the two main reasons for the denial:

- Fear and intimidation – one Palestinian woman said 'We are afraid. They have knives [and] guns and can do whatever they want. They can kill you simply … [for] speaking bad about them.'[4]
- Identification with the abuser – one Christian cleric 'compared the behavior of Christian *dhimmis* to that of battered wives and

---

1 The acknowledgement is on p.96. The book could have revealed the religious non-reciprocity at Table 4.2, on p.50. However the table reverses the statistics, reporting, falsely (!) that it is overwhelmingly Christian men who are marrying Muslim women. This 'Freudian typo' serves only to deepen the impact of Ata's silence.

2 Justus Reid Weiner, *Human Rights of Christians in Palestinian Society*, p.22.

3 Ibid., p.23.

4 Ibid., p.23.

children, who continue to defend and even identify with their tormentor even as the abuse persists.'[1]

What Weiner describes is a vicious cycle, where *dhimmis*, eager to placate the Muslims and afraid if they do not, identify strongly with Palestinian nationalist aspirations (including anti-Israeli rhetoric). This 'leads them to deny the persecution of their community'. As an example, Father Labib Kobtl, from the Latin Patriarch in Jerusalem, urged others to:

> ... refuse ... the propaganda that wants to prove that there were any studied or willed persecution from our Muslim brothers and sisters of the Christians. We consider it as a mere propaganda against Islam, a cold war against our Muslim brothers that only benefits the Zionists of Israel.[2]

Displays of devotion to the *Umma* such as this may appear to purchase some degree of temporary immunity from Muslim extremists, but they reinforce the cloak of silence over the sufferings of the Christian community, and contribute to the worsening human rights situation.

In 2008 the Egyptian Muslim writer Ahmad al-Aswani lamented the escalating attacks on Copts in his nation, which have been egged on by Islamic leaders. Al-Aswani held Christian clergy partly responsible for denying that Islamic sentiment was behind the abuse. He writes that after attacks:

> Of course, the usual Coptic notables deny any suspicion of sectarianism, and affirm national unity, and the sheikh and the priest embrace.
>
> ... one saddening thing is that some prominent Copts voluntarily deny any suspicion that sectarianism is fueling recent events [even] before the truth becomes known. I do not know whether they are aware that their words both increase the suffering and will fail to end this series [of incidents]. [Instead,] why don't they use their media presence to defend their people, the Copts, and to urge the enactment of laws to prohibit what is happening, and to purge the educational system and media of the explosive mines of sedition, discrimination, and incitement? ...
>
> What is happening is an attempt to terrorize Egypt's Copts, and to force them either to emigrate from the homeland once and for all, or to convert to Islam to protect themselves and their families [from harm] and to protect their property from the confiscation mentioned by many Islamic publications.
>
> It causes me regret, and as an Egyptian it makes my heart bleed, to see this farce endlessly repeated ... lives and property are taken with impunity, and

---

1 Ibid., p.23, citing David Raab, 'The beleaguered Christians of the Palestinian-Controlled Areas.'
2 Ibid., p.24.

clearly with the authorities' collusion – with no fear of effective response, and with the confidence of all that, as always, the matter will end with beard-kissing and forgetting.[1]

The Iraqi scholar Kanan Makiya has made the point that 'The ironical fact is that [Edward Said's *Orientalism*] was given the attention it received in the "almost totally ethnocentric" West largely because its author was a Palestinian.'[2] It is a difficult and painful reality that Middle Eastern '*dhimmi* clergy' play a key strategic role in preventing the international community from understanding the suffering of Christians living under Islam, and its foundations in the *dhimma*. By embracing a culture of denial, *dhimmi* Christian leaders use their positions of leadership to promote the cause of the Islamists to the West. In the case of the Palestinian church:

> ... although certain Christian religious leaders such as Bishop El-Assal [former Anglican Bishop of Jerusalem, responsible for Palestine, Israel, Jordan, Lebanon and Syria] enjoyed close connections with Arafat over the years, these mutually supportive relationships bear no resemblance to the difficult, often dangerous, circumstances in which common Palestinian Christians live. These leaders are given special access to the media and used this opportunity to gain sympathy and political support from Christian countries for Arafat and his policies.[3]

The silence of the *dhimmis* continues to have a profound impact upon the attitude of the rest of the world to Islam and its history. When spokespeople of a *dhimmi* background – like Edward Said or Bishop El-Assal – take up Islam's causes as their own, they are heeded in the West. The West assumes that local sources, from 'on-the-ground' Christians, will have better insight and be more credible than any objective analysis from outside.

This is debilitating to the West, because for a Western Christian to take up the cause of the persecuted church they must expose the denial and deception which is at the heart of dhimmitude, and this includes challenging the account being given by '*dhimmi*' Christian spokespeople. Many do not like to do this, not only because it seems

---

1 Ahmad al-Aswani 'It's "Open Season" on Egypt's Copts'. June 7, 2008, viewed 8 June 2009, <http://www.aafaq.org/masahas.aspx?id_mas=1905>. MEMRI Special Dispatch No. 1955, June 11, 2008. Egypt/Reform Project, viewed 8 June 2009, <http://www.memri.org/bin/articles.cgi?P age=subjects&Area=reform&ID=SP195508>.

2 Ibn Warraq, 'Edward Said and the Saidists.' In Robert Spencer, *The Myth of Islamic Tolerance*, p.510.

3 Justus Reid Weiner, *Human Rights of Christians in Palestinian Society*, p.23.

rude and confrontational, but also because the West has taught itself to feel guilty. So Western Christians remain silent too.

But as Weiner grimly observes, the *dhimmi* leaders' strategy of buying immunity through service to the *Umma* 'may prove self-destructive in the long run'.[1]

The great Maimonides came to the same conclusion in the Middle Ages: '... the more we suffer and choose to conciliate them, the more they choose to act belligerently toward us'.[2] In practice what this has meant for the Palestinians is an inexorable move towards reinstatement of that very condition which the *dhimmi* leaders deny so vehemently: the *dhimma* itself.

The silence of the historians

Dating back at least to the Enlightenment, there has been a trend in western historical writings to conceal the historical condition of *dhimmis*. The reasons for this are complex, and its manifestations diverse. Ibn Warraq has identified a trend among Western intellectuals, including Voltaire and Montesquieu, to use the 'putative tolerance' of Islam 'to belabor Christianity and her relative intolerance'.[3] Building on this tradition, 19th century Jewish historians promoted the myth of an Islamic golden age to garner support against the rise of racism across Europe. Gerber has observed that 'The cult of a powerful, dazzling and brilliant Andalusia in the midst of an ignorant and intolerant Europe formed an important component in these contemporary intellectual currents.'[4]

Another political factor during the 19th century was the alliance of western Europeans with the Ottomans against Russian and Austrian designs, and the resulting polemical propaganda that the Christian provinces of the Ottoman Empire were thriving under Islamic 'tolerance'.[5] A military manifestation of this alliance was the Western nations' participation in the Ottoman *jihad* known as the Crimean War.

---

1 Ibid., p.24.

2 Maimonides, *Epistle to the Jews of Yemen*, excerpts from Norman Stilman, *The Jews of Arab Lands*, pp.241-42.

3 Ibn Warraq, 'Foreword' to Andrew Bostom, *The Legacy of Islamic Antisemitism*, p.24.

4 Jane Gerber, 'Towards an understanding of the term "The Golden Age" as an historical reality.' In Aviva Doron, ed. *The heritage of the Jews in Spain*, p.16. See also Marc Cohen, *Under Crescent and Cross*, p.3ff. Cohen's thesis of 'myth and countermyth' had already been presented in the *Jerusalem Quarterly* in 1986, and was rebutted by Bat Ye'or the following year in the same journal ('Islam and the *Dhimmis*').

5 See Bat Ye'or, *The Decline of Eastern Christianity under Islam*, pp.248-50.

At the time it was politically expedient for Europeans to whitewash the conditions of Christians and Jews who were living under the rule of their Ottoman ally.

The historian Bernard Lewis, writing in the second half of the 20th century, continued this theme:

> The dhimma on the whole worked quite well. The non-Muslims managed to thrive under Muslim rule, and even to make a significant contribution to Islamic civilization. The restrictions were not onerous and were usually less severe in practice than in theory ...[1]

Lewis compared the example of medieval Islam favorably to that of Christian Europe:

> If we compare the Muslim attitude to Jews and treatment of Jews in medieval times with the position of Jews among their Christian neighbors in medieval Europe, we see some striking contrasts. Even the hostilities of the two majority communities differ considerably. **In Islamic society hostility to the Jew is non-theological. It is not related to any specific Islamic doctrine, nor to any specific circumstance in Islamic sacred history. For Muslims, it is not part of the birth pangs of their religion,** as it is for Christians. It is rather the usual attitude of the dominant to the subordinate, of the majority to the minority, without that additional theological and therefore psychological dimension that gives Christian anti-Semitism its unique and special character.[2]

Lewis' statements in bold (my emphasis) are baseless. Islamic hostility to the Jews is theological to its bootstraps. It is founded upon very many verses from the Quran and the traditions of Muhammad. As we have already seen, there are many dogmas of Islamic theology which underpin Islam's treatment of Jews. One can point, for example, to the seventeen daily recitations of *al-Fatihah* by every observant Muslim, which characterize Jews – according to a *hadith* of Muhammad – as those 'who have incurred Allah's wrath', as well as the repeated denunciations of the Jews throughout the second *sura* of the Quran.

Not only this, but Muhammad's hostility to the Jews is a key part of his personal life-story, which is the bedrock of Islam's genesis. (This is elaborated in chapter 5). Virtually **all** of Muhammad's life is of

---

1 Bernard Lewis, *Islam from the Prophet Muhammad to the Capture of Constantinople*, vol. 2, p.217.
2 Bernard Lewis, *The Jews of Islam*, p.85. See also Bat Ye'or, *The Decline of Eastern Christianity under Islam*, pp.255ff on the 'Method of Comparative History,' which discusses the problems involved with comparing Christians' treatment of the Jews with the *dhimma*. On Lewis, see Hugh Fitzgerald, 'Reflections on Bernard Lewis', 17 June, 2004, viewed 8 June 2009, <http://www.jihadwatch.org/dhimmiwatch/archives/002247.php>.

theological significance in Islam, and his theological debates with the Jews and ensuing military hostilities against them contributed essential building blocks of Islamic sacred history and law. Indeed, the conquest of the Jews of Khaybar is cited by Islamic authorities as the theological precedent in Muhammad's life for the whole *dhimma* system.

Lewis' astounding claim that Islamic antisemitism has no theological basis in Islam has been relied upon by many Western intellectuals, corrupting their understanding of Islamic history. As the error is so blatant, and so easily refuted, one must be astonished at the degree to which a capable scholar could be so blinkered.[1] Lewis' denial is testimony to the hypnotic power of the *dhimma* to shape the worldview even of those who study it.

The bloody cost of repressed history

A group's historical worldview determines its own self-understanding, including its claim to political rights. When national worldviews are distorted by the concealment of *jihad* and dhimmitude, it can make it virtually impossible for different groups to live together peaceably in the same space. The conflicting historical claims of the Orthodox Christian Serbs and Muslim Bosnians offer a classic example.[2]

On the one hand the Bosnians claim the precedent of five centuries of 'harmonious and peaceful coexistence' under Islamic rule. When the Canadian UN commander, Major-General Lewis W. MacKenzie spoke of 'both sides' in the war being filled with hatred, he was vilified as an 'ignorant man' by Bosnian President Alija Izetbegovic for knowing nothing of Sarajevo's Muslims and their '500-year tradition of tolerance'.

Yet this was the same Izetbegovic who had published an 'Islamic Declaration' in 1970 stating:

> There can be neither peace nor coexistence between the Islamic faith and non-Islamic social and political institutions ...

> The Islamic movement must, and can, take over power as soon as it is morally and numerically so strong that it can not only destroy the existing non-Islamic power, but also build up a new Islamic one.[3]

---

1 For a more comprehensive rebuttal of Lewis' claim that Islamic antisemitism is not theological, see Andrew Bostom, 'Islamic antisemitism – Jew hatred in Islam,' in *The Legacy of Islamic Antisemitism*, pp.164-69.

2 This section is based upon Bat Ye'or's analysis in *Islam and Dhimmitude*, p.202.

3 John Zametica. *The Yugoslav Conflict*, pp.38-39.

On the other hand, as Bat Ye'or has pointed out, the previous five hundred years is remembered by the Serbs as a period of 'massacre, pillage, slavery, deportation, and the exile of Christian populations'.[1] As recently as the period of Nazi occupation, Muslim Slavs had collaborated in the 'genocide of hundreds of thousands of Orthodox Serbs, Jews and gypsies'.[2]

The result of these conflicting historical worldviews, including barbaric war crimes committed against Bosnians by Serbian forces in the mid-1990's, was not unpredictable:

> Bosnian Serbs recognized the *shari'a* system which had decimated them. Hence, the cruelty of the fighting in Bosnia reflected the historical confrontation which, instead of being settled by dialogue, erupted in hatred. Its barbarity expresses the revenge of repressed history, a parody of the distorted myth of idyllic coexistence.[3]

Silent bells

When Hamas took control of Gaza in 2007 they lost no time in announcing to the tiny Christian community that they were now in a full Islamic system and had to accept Islamic law. Sheikh Abu Saqer declared that Christians 'must be ready to accept Islamic rule if they want to live in peace'.[4] In the light of this statement, it is hardly surprising that the Gazan Christians' church bells have fallen silent, in submission to one of the age-old requirements of the *dhimma*. Katya Adler, BBC News reporter from Gaza city describes a moving scene during a Christmas service at which the Latin Patriarch was presiding:

> As the crowded church was belting out hallelujahs, I stepped into the church courtyard for some fresh air. The Muslim call to prayer was beginning to echo from the myriad of mosques all around.
>
> I thought how this reflected the situation in Gaza in Christmas 2007 – that while the muezzin were on loudspeaker, the church bells here are played from a cassette tape. A nervous young nun adjusted the volume – loud enough to peel through the church but not to penetrate its walls – it might risk offending Muslim Gazans passing by.[5]

---

1 Bat Ye'or, *Islam and Dhimmitude*, p.201.
2 Ibid., p.201.
3 Ibid., p.202.
4 Aaron Klein, 'Christians warned: accept Islamic law.' World Net Daily, 19 June, 2007, viewed 8 June 2009, <http://www.worldnetdaily.com/news/article.asp?ARTICLE_ID=56241>.
5 Katya Adler, 'Christmas under Hamas rule.' BBC News, December 22, 2007, viewed 8 June 2009, <http://news.bbc.co.uk/2/low/programmes/from_our_own_correspondent/7154134.stm>.

Ironically, Adler sugar-coats her report: 'There is no evidence to suggest the Hamas government here officially discriminates against Christians ...' She crucially misinterprets the silence of the bells as a Christian gesture to avoid offending Muslims – a sign of interfaith tolerance – instead of correctly identifying it as evidence that the Christians of Gaza are, quite simply, living under the *dhimma*.

A regime of silence has descended over the subject of the history of *dhimmi* peoples. Today many who write and speak about Islam, if they refer to the *dhimma*, will describe it in as glowing terms which are nothing but misleading, and which do not accurately reflect fourteen hundred years of Islamic thought and practice on this subject, let alone the sufferings of millions of non-Muslims.

Dhimmitude is concealed. Yet it is of great importance as a whole tendency of thought influencing our world today. It is as important for understanding Christian-Muslim relations as racism is for understanding slavery, or sexism for understanding gender relations. In our era this taboo of silence needs to be deliberately and comprehensively broken. There is a lot of ground to be made up.

The dhimmitude of the West

Today Islam is exerting an increasingly important influence in the destiny of Western cultures.[1] Through mass immigration, oil economics, cultural exchange and even terrorism, the remnants of what was once Christendom now find themselves having to respond to Islam and its distinctive 'take' on the world. One of the great challenges is that the West, in seeking to find a response, is already coming under the influence of the worldview of dhimmitude.

Within the Islamic worldview, there are limited options for the roles that non-Muslims communities can play. In classic Islamic theology, the dogma of the 'three choices' meant that the only real alternative to 'enmity to Allah', apart from conversion, was dhimmitude.

The requirement that non-Muslims – at least those who are not enemies – embrace dhimmitude, and affirm, appease and serve Islam, greatly limits the repertoire of responses that Christians can have towards it.

---

1 The expression 'Dhimmitude of the West?' – with a question mark – was introduced into English in 1996 by Bat Ye'or in *The Decline of Eastern Christianity under Islam*, p.217. This section draws in part on an article also entitled 'Dhimmitude of the West' which I published in 2002 in the *Newsletter for the Centre for Islamic Studies*.

Where there are grounds for confrontation, the only way of struggling permitted to the *dhimmi* is by saying soft things. Direct confrontation is discouraged, penalized, made illegal, and ostracized.

This is a key reason for the weak international response today to the persecution of Christians under Islam. The media provides many reports of the Israeli-Palestinian conflict, but over two million African Sudanese have perished in the Sudanese *jihad*. Such asymmetries, which are hidden from many Westerners, are only too obvious to African Christians.

Such political correctness is itself an injustice that needs to be exposed and challenged. Yet at the same time, *jihad* is claimed as a divine right of Islam without apology of any kind. Even in non-Muslim societies, some Muslims can be extremely aggressive and confrontational in pressing for their rights, and yet take offense when non-Muslims insist on theirs.

This, combined with the pressure to act like *dhimmis*, can intimidate and weaken Christians and others who are free and do not live under Islam. The cumulative effect can be that the gross injustices come to seem as somehow excusable or unexceptional to Western non-Muslims.

Dhimmi politicians

There is a good deal of evidence that senior Western political leaders are submitting to the worldview of dhimmitude. In the wake of the post-9/11 declaration by George Bush that 'Islam is a religion of peace', European leaders have been lining up to praise Islam.

On a visit of Saudi Arabia in January 2008, President Sarkozy of France gave a speech declaring that Islam is 'one of the greatest and most beautiful civilizations the world has known'.[1]

Mary Robinson, former president of the nation of Ireland, one of the most Christian societies in Europe, was the UN High Commissioner for Human Rights in 2002 when she read a statement to an *Organization of Islamic Conference Symposium on Human Rights in Islam* held at the Palais des Nations in Geneva in 2002. After offering praise, Robinson adopted the strategy of affirming the inherent righteousness of Islam:

> It is important to recognize the greatness of Islam, its civilizations and its immense contribution to the richness of the human experience, not

---

1 FaithWorld: Religion, Faith and Ethics. Reuters Blogs, 15 January 2008, viewed 8 June 2009, <http://blogs.reuters.com/faithworld/2008/01/15/in-riyadh-sarkozy-praises-god-islam-and-saudi-arabia/>.

only through profound belief and theology but also through the sciences, literature and art.

No one can deny that at its core Islam is entirely consonant with the principle of fundamental human rights, including human dignity, tolerance, solidarity and equality. Numerous passages from the Quran and sayings of the Prophet Muhammad will testify to this. No one can deny, from a historical perspective, the revolutionary force that is Islam, which bestowed rights upon women and children long before similar recognition was afforded in other civilizations.

... And no one can deny the acceptance of the universality of human rights by Islamic States.[1]

Observe here the dhimmitude themes of gratitude (for bestowing rights upon women), affirmation of the moral superiority of Islam (with the implication of inferiority of the infidel), and silencing any possible voice of protest by the repeated phrase 'no one can deny ...'

The same censorious tone prohibiting criticism of Islam came out loud and clear in the comments of British Home Secretary Jacqui Smith, when she commented immediately after the Glasgow attempted bombing: 'Any attempt to identify a murderous ideology with a great faith such as Islam is wrong, and needs to be denied.'[2]

It is an age-old *dhimmi* strategy to avoid confrontation by affirming what is best in Islam. Change for the better is only allowed to arise from values which Muslims will admit as springing from their faith itself. Under the *dhimma*, Christians are not supposed to confront Islam, but they are permitted to look for the best in Islam and affirm it. They may challenge it only by praising it. This strategy conceals and disempowers the moral worth of non-Muslim value systems. It is the strategy of those whose existence is marginal and threatened. If you adopt the posture of praising Islam, you are already acting like a defeated or a threatened person.

Tony Blair manifested *dhimmi*-like self-rejection and denial when he made the following public statement at the 'Islam and Muslims in the World Today' conference in June 2007, announcing a grant of one million pounds to support the study of Islam in British universities:

---

1 Mary Robinson, Speech given to the UNHRC March 15, 2002. 'UN's top human rights official urges action to combat "Islamaphobia"'. UN News Service, viewed 8 June 2009, <http://www.un.org/apps/news/story.asp?NewsID=3128&Cr=Robinson&Cr1=>. See critique by David G. Littman, 'Human rights and human wrongs', *National Review Online*, 19 January, 2003, viewed 8 June 2009, <http://www.nationalreview.com/comment/comment-littman011903.asp>.
2 Mark Steyn, 'Denial is a river in Washington'. SteynOnline. July 31, 2007.

The voices of extremism are no more representative of Islam than the use in times gone by of torture to force conversion to Christianity represented the teachings of Christ.[1]

In putting Christian transgressions forward as part of his strategy of evaluating the moral worth of Islam, Blair engages in a display of self-rejection, but without truth: he is denying the reality that Islam has genuinely violent strands in its canon (Quran and *Sunna*). In reality the precedents for violence in Muhammad's life have absolutely no parallels in the life of Christ, and the comparison Blair makes is baseless.

Finally, while addressing the Turkish parliament on April 6, 2009, Barack Obama added his own expression of gratitude to Islam for what it has done to 'shape' the United States of America:

> We will convey our deep appreciation for the Islamic faith, which has done so much over the centuries to shape the world – including in my own country.[2]

Aid or Jizya?

One can also ask some troubling questions about the flow of funds from Western governments to organizations and nations which are committed to Islamization. This includes what is known as 'international aid', but might just as easily be called tribute. Some of largest aid grants from the USA and the European Union have been going to Islamic communities which are producing large numbers of radicals, such as Egypt and Pakistan. Professor Moshe Sharon, emeritus Professor of Islam at the Hebrew University in Jerusalem has written:

> ... the billions of dollars which stream from the EU to Muslim terror groups under various disguises **are nothing less than Jizyah money paid by the dhimmis of Europe to the Muslim rulers**. ... European money is the collective Jizyah paid by the Europeans in the (false) hope that it will secure for them the protected status of the dhimmi.[3]

It is an irony that clerics funded by the Palestinian Authority, who live off European and US aid, have denounced Western governments on Palestinian Television, declaring the inevitable victory of Islam over the whole world. For example, Sheikh Muhammad Ibrahim al-Madhi, a

---

1 Full text: Blair speech on Islam, *BBC News,* June 4, 2007, viewed 8 June 2009, <http://news.bbc.co.uk/2/hi/uk_news/politics/6719153.stm>.

2 'Remarks by President Obama to the Turkish Parliament,' April 6, 2009, viewed 8 June, 2009, <http://www.whitehouse.gov/the_press_office/Remarks-By-President-Obama-To-The-Turkish-Parliament/>.

3 Moshe Sharon, 'Reviving the Caliphate,' *Daily News,* January 1, 2008, viewed 8 June 2009, <http://www.israelunitycoalition.org/news/article.php?id=2264>.

Palestinian authority employee, preached a sermon broadcast on PA Television on April 12, 2002, in which he prophesied the defeat of every nation on the earth:

> Oh beloved, look to the East of the earth, find Japan and the ocean; look to the West of the earth, find [some] country and the ocean. Be assured that these will be owned by the Muslim nation, as the Hadith says … from the ocean to the ocean'…[1]

Loving your abuser

Immediately after September 11, Muslims reported a rash of conversions to Islam across the West. A Muslim friend shared with me the testimony of a man who recited the *shahada* a few days after the September 2004 Beslan massacre. Why? One possible explanation is fear. The Stockholm Syndrome is that some decide to love their captors. It is easier to embrace Islam, and deny the problem of potential violence, than to face the alternative of fear. It is safer to feel good thoughts about Islam, than to have to deal with hard truths.

It was a Palestinian Christian who quite appropriately invoked the battered-wife syndrome to account for his community's complicity in their persecution.[2] The battered woman is conditioned to believe that her punishment is her fault, and she should feel grateful to her abusive partner for sparing her. The only strategy she is allowed to use to protect herself is to appeal to his good side through soft talk and grateful praise, all the time acknowledging her own guilt. She can never confront and challenge his bad side with direct truth.

Dhimmitude at the United Nations

Not only are significant western Christian leaders embracing the *dhimmi* syndrome, but the United Nations, in which Muslim nations form a powerful voting block, has been a scene of much dhimmification.[3]

A 'Universal Islamic Declaration of Human Rights', was proclaimed at UNESCO in 1981 and followed by the 'Cairo Declaration on Human Rights in Islam', adopted in August 1990 by the Nineteenth Conference

---

1 Sheikh Ibrahim Madhi, 'Friday Sermon on Palestinian Authority TV', MEMRI Special Dispatch Series No. 370. April 17, 2002, viewed 8 June 2009, <http://memri.org/bin/articles.cgi ?Page=archives&Area=sd&ID=SP37002>

2 Justus Reid Weiner, *Human Rights of Christians in Palestinian Society*, p.23, citing David Raab, 'The beleaguered Christians of the Palestinian-Controlled Areas.'

3 David Littman has published an overview of this issue with his chapter 'Human Rights and Human Wrongs at the United Nations' in Robert Spencer, ed. *The Myth of Islamic Tolerance*, pp.305-472.

of Foreign Ministers of the then 45 Organization of the Islamic Conference (OIC) countries. The Cairo Declaration was subsequently published by the Office of the UN High Commissioner for Human Rights in 1997.[1] At the 1993 World Conference on Human Rights, held in Vienna, Iran proposed, with the support of several other states, that the Cairo Declaration be adopted as an alternative to the Universal Declaration of Human Rights.[2]

Article 24 of the Cairo Declaration states that its provisions are 'subject to the Islamic *Sharia*', and article 25 confirms that *Sharia* 'is the only source of reference for the explanation or clarification of this Declaration.' The essence of these statements is that the example of Muhammad (the *Sunna*), which is the root of *Sharia*, has supremacy in the domain of human rights. This includes the principles of the *Sharia*'s *dhimma* legislation. Moreover, article 25 makes clear that the *Sharia* has primacy over all universal human rights declarations, including the Universal Declaration of Human Rights, and all other UN covenants.

Mary Robinson's 2002 statement, referred to above, must be read against the background of the Islamic challenge to the Universal Declaration in the form of the Cairo Declaration. Instead of standing up for the UN's own human rights framework, Mary Robinson adopted an attitude of humble gratitude to the *Sharia*.

In 2005 the Organization of the Islamic Conference adopted a 'Ten Year Action Plan' to address challenges facing Muslims in the world today. Item 6 on their plan was to combat Islamophobia, and one of their strategies was to get the United Nations to 'adopt an international resolution on Islamophobia, and call on all States to enact laws to counter it, including deterrent punishments'.[3]

At the December 2006 meeting of the OIC a decision was taken to create an 'Observatory' to monitor all reports of 'Islamophobia'. This strategy proved effective. In August 2007, Mr Doudou Diene, the UN Special Rapporteur on Contemporary Forms of Racism, Racial Discrimination, Xenophobia and Related Intolerance, presented a

---

1 The Cairo Declaration is the last document included in: *Human Rights: a Compilation of International Instruments: Volume II: Regional Instruments* (OHCHR, Geneva: New York and Geneva).

2 'The Cairo Declaration and the Universality of Human Rights'. A joint written statement by the International Humanist and Ethical Union (IHEU), the Association of World Education and the Association of World Citizens to the Human Rights Council, 7th session, 2008. (A/HRC/7/NGO/96).

3 Organization of the Islamic Conference. 'Ten Year Program of Action', viewed 8 June 2009, <http://www.sciencedev.net/Docs/OIC%2010%20year%20plan.htm>.

report to the UN Human Rights Council on 'the manifestations of defamation of religions and in particular on the serious implications of Islamophobia on the enjoyment of all rights'.[1] After this, the OIC's 'anti-defamation of religion' resolutions were passed, first by the UN Human Rights Council, and then at the General Assembly in December 2007.[2]

An ensuing 'Observatory Report' was presented to the 11th session of the OIC, meeting in Senegal in March 2008. Elizabeth Kendal, human rights activist, commented that the Report asserts:

> ... that in order to have peace, the correct (OIC-approved) version of history and of Islam must be understood, accepted and promoted (anything else is 'baseless' Islamophobia or inciteful 'defamation' of Islam)[3]

At the June 16, 2008 session of the UNHRC, Muslim delegates repeatedly interrupted a NGO presentation by David Littman addressing the human rights of women under Islamic law. As a result, the President ruled that no speakers were to make 'judgments or evaluations' about religions.[4] By this ruling the *Sharia* became in effect above criticism at the Council.

In such ways, Muslim nations are seeking to impose a *dhimma* regulation **upon the whole world**, namely that non-Muslims must not criticize Islam.

Islamizing history

A similar response can be seen in history text books, increasingly appearing in the school systems of Western nations, which downplay all talk of *jihad*, battle or conquest in accounts of the advance of Islam, and blame terrorism on 'colonial domination'.[5]

1 Elizabeth Kendal, 'OIC: Eliminating "defamation" of Islam'. (World Evangelical Alliance Religious Liberty News & Analysis), viewed 8 June 2009, <http://www.worldevangelicals.org/news/article.htm?id=1725>.

2 UN General Assembly Resolution 62.154 'Combating defamation of religions' of which a summary was reproduced as a General Assembly document A/HRC/9/G/2.

3 Elizabeth Kendal, 'OIC: Eliminating "defamation" of Islam'. (World Evangelical Alliance Religious Liberty News & Analysis), viewed 8 June 2009, <http://www.worldevangelicals.org/news/article.htm?id=1725>. See also Elizabeth Kendal, 'Apostasy, Apostaphobia and postmodernism'. (Religious Liberty Trends, World Evangelical Alliance Religious Liberty News & Analysis), viewed 8 June 2009, <http://www.worldevangelicals.org/news/article.htm?id=1666>.

4 David G. Littman, UN Human Rights Council: Any mention of the word "sharia" is now taboo, Jihad Watch, 21 June, 2008, viewed 8 June 2009, <http://jihadwatch.org/archives/021461.php>. The video of the session is available at <http://www.youtube.com/watch?v-03dOu-DNLec> (viewed 8 June 2009).

5 Gilbert T. Sewall, 'Textbook lies about Islam.' *New York Post*. August 17, 2008, viewed 8 June 2009, <http://www.nypost.com/seven/08172008/postopinion/opedcolumnists/textbook_lies_

A repeated theme in these school texts is that the West should be grateful to Islamic civilization for preserving Greek philosophy.[1] The narrative offered to justify this gratitude is that during the Dark Ages the Islamic world underwent a golden age of cultural and scientific development, preserving Greek learning, which then kick-started the Western Renaissance.

Of course Greek civilization did not need 'rescue-by-conquest': indeed it continued in Constantinople all through the European dark ages. It is true that when the Europeans translated Arabic texts into Latin, this did stimulate the development of Western philosophy and science. Many terms passed over into Arabic into European languages as a result, including *sherbet*, *zero* and *zenith*.[2] However the fact that elements of Greek philosophy and science were transmitted to Europe via Arabic was not something for which Western children should be schooled to feel grateful. If Arab conquest had never happened, we can assume that Greek culture and philosophy would have continued to develop in Alexandria, Damascus and Constantinople to the present day.

In reality, as Crombie pointed out in *Augustine to Galileo*, the conquest of the heart of the Greek-speaking world by Islam, and resulting Arab control of the Mediterranean, stunted scientific progress in Europe:

> ... it was the eruption of the Mohammedan invaders into the Eastern Empire in the 7th century that gave the most serious blow to learning in Western Christendom. The conquest of much of the Eastern Empire by the Arabs meant that the main reservoir of Greek learning was cut off from Western scholars for centuries ...[3]

Islam's disruption of Mediterranean civilization ushered in the so-called European 'Dark Ages', as historian Henri Pirenne concluded in his classic study, *Mohammed and Charlemagne*:

> The cause of the break with the tradition of antiquity was the rapid and unexpected advance of Islam. The result of this advance was the final separation of East from West, and the end of the Mediterranean unity. ... The Western Mediterranean, having become a Musulman lake, was no longer the thoroughfare of commerce and of thought which it had always been. The West was blockaded and forced to live upon its own resources.[4]

---

about_islam_124840.htm>.

1 See Gilbert T. Sewall, *Islam and the Textbooks*.
2 A.C. Crombie, *Augustine to Galileo: the History of Science AD 400-1650*, p.32, 35.
3 Ibid., p.4.
4 Henri Pirenne, *Mohammed and Charlemagne*, p.284. See also John J. O'Neill, *Holy Warriors: Islam and the Demise of Classical Civilization*.

It is disappointing that today history books are teaching a dhimmified version of history, according to which children are schooled in feeling grateful to Islam for rescuing Western and Christian culture from Islam itself. This is exactly the *dhimmi* condition, and the essential meaning of the *jizya* payment ritual: to render gratitude to Islam for being rescued by conquest.

For more than a century, Christians have been re-examining their history, and apologizing for their errors. Reconciliation with Jews and with indigenous victims of colonization is well advanced. Popes too have uttered their apologies. But the Muslim world has not to this day apologized to non-Muslims for *jihad* and dhimmitude. Muslims have not allowed themselves to confront their bitter past. For example, secular Turks, having a historical consciousness shaped by Islam, still deny the genocide of the Armenians, and bitterly oppose commemorations of this event by its survivors.

Law and disorder

Distortions are also creeping into the fabric of Western societies. One common pattern is the privileging of Islam by community leaders and institutions.

In the New York Public school system, Muslims asked for prayer rooms to be set apart for Ramadan during 2001. Harold Levy, the Governor of the New York City schools system agreed. Then the Christians and Jews asked for the same privilege – a dedicated prayer room. Annoyed, Levy withdrew his permission.[1]

Many cases have been reported in Western nations where violent attacks by Muslims against non-Muslims have been mishandled by the police, in ways which are reminiscent of the difficulty which *dhimmis* have in securing justice under Islamic rule.[2] An example of such mishandling was the statement by Elly Florax, spokeswoman for the Amsterdam police force, just hours after the killing of Theo Van Gogh, that the killer had possibly been disguised as a Muslim.[3]

---

1   Joseph D'Agostino, 'New York Schools Flip-Flop on Ramadan,' Human Events, 26 November 2001, viewed 8 June 2009, <http://findarticles.com/p/articles/mi_qa3827/is_200111/ai_n9004766>.

2   Daniel Pipes, 'Denying [Islamist] terrorism,' viewed 8 June 2009, <http://www.danielpipes.org/blog/403>; Daniel Pipes, 'More incidents of denying Islamist terrorism,' viewed 8 June 2009, <http://www.danielpipes.org/blog/2005/02/more-incidents-of-denying-islamist-terrorism.html>.

3   Johannes J.G. Jansen, 'Dhimmitude'.

Some western governments have been funding information campaigns about Islam which cross a line in embracing denial. In Australia, Victoria's Equal Opportunity Commission put out 'fact sheets' on Islam in 2002 which stated that 'Islam gives its followers the right to absolute and complete equality before the law.' This statement conceals the truth that Islam discriminates against female Muslims and slaves, and it is misleading because it glosses over the fact that the *Sharia* does **not** grant equality to non-Muslims.

At the start of 2007, Channel 4 in the UK screened a program titled 'Undercover Mosque' which presented video clips of Muslim preachers in Britain.[1] The preachers' remarks incited hatred and violence against women, Jews, homosexuals and non-Muslims. However, the *Telegraph* reported that the police and crown prosecutor, instead of investigating the Muslim preachers, investigated the television station.[2]

In May 2008 two Christians reported being threatened with arrest if they continued to hand out leaflets promoting Christian beliefs in Birmingham. Arthur Cunningham and Joseph Abraham reported that the policeman told them that they were in a Muslim area, and were committing a hate crime by telling Muslims to leave Islam.[3]

On July 14, 2008, two English schoolboys were given class detentions for refusing to bow and pray to Allah in a religious studies class. One of the parents, Sharon Luinen complained to the *Daily Mail*: 'what got me is that they were told they were being disrespectful'.[4]

In 2008 both the Archbishop of Canterbury, Rowan Williams and Nicholas Phillips, Lord Chief Justice of England and Wales suggested that the United Kingdom could consider, in the words of Phillips, 'embracing *Sharia* Law'. Phillips argued that 'There is no reason why principles of *Sharia* Law, or any other religious code should not be the basis for mediation or other forms of alternative dispute resolution.'[5]

---

1 *Undercover Mosque* (Video), viewed 8 June 2009, <http://video.google.com.au/videosearch?q=un dercover+mosque&hl=en&emb=0&aq=f#>.

2 'Channel 4 wins Muslim "preachers of hate" case', *The Telegraph*, May 15, 2008, viewed 8 June 2009, <http://www.telegraph.co.uk/news/uknews/1955818/Channel-4-wins-Muslim%27 preachers-of-hate%27-case.html>. Channel 4 later ran a successful libel suit against the Police.

3 David Harrison, 'Christian preachers face arrest in Birmingham.' *The Telegraph*, 6 February, 2008, viewed 8 June 2009, <http://www.telegraph.co.uk/news/uknews/2058935/Police-advise-Christian-preachers-to-leave-Muslin-area-of-Birmingham.html>.

4 'Boys punished with detention for refusing to pray to Allah.' July 4, 2008. WorldNet Daily, viewed 8 June 2009, <http://wnd.com/index.php?fa=PAGE.view&pageId=68785>.

5 Lord Chief Justice Phillips, 'Equality before the law.' Speech presented at the East London Muslim Centre, 3 July, 2008.

Williams commented 'it's not as if we're bringing in an alien and rival system.'[1]

The long litany of such incidents points to a drift in Western nations to adopt the stance of the *dhimmi* in relating to Islam and Muslims. We are seeing the privileging of Islam in the public square, mandating of compulsory respect for Islam, erosion of the principle of reciprocity and equality, implementation of *Sharia* restrictions on freedom of speech and religious practice, denial and deception about the teachings of Islam including *jihad* and the *Sharia*, and denial about the religious motivations of some Muslims who engage in intimidation and criminal acts.

Dhimmi church leaders

The problem which non-Muslims living under Islam have with *dhimmi* clerics has also been exported to the West. Patrick Sookhdeo has reported:

> In south London Muslim gangs armed with guns have targeted Christians saying if they do not convert they will be killed. In Bradford, a Christian family converted from Islam have had their lives threatened. ... Their car has been arsoned and they have been threatened with violence. The Bishop of Bradford met this family with his interfaith advisor. At this meeting he stated that the Diocese of the Anglican Church would not welcome such converts into it. ... He did not want Muslim converts into the Anglican Church. The convert was extremely disappointed and deeply saddened by the stance of the bishop. He felt that the bishop was more concerned with his relationship with the Muslim leaders in Bradford than with his plight with him as a convert. He felt deeply betrayed.[2]

For Christians there is a special challenge here. Some Christians, in following Christ's teachings, have adopted the idea of servant ministry to Muslims. But instead of serving people, they can end up serving Islam itself. When in March 2003, Archbishop Frank Griswold, leader of the American Episcopalian church, was interviewed for an Islamic website www.soundvision.com, he stated that the US should not be a

---

1 Interview of the Archbishop of Canterbury by Christopher Landau. BBC Interview – Radio 4 World at One, 7 February, 2008, viewed 8 June 2009, <http://www.archbishopofcanterbury. org/1573>. Williams and Phillips seemed ignorant of the fact that the Human Rights Court of Europe had ruled in 2003 that the *Sharia* is incompatible with its Human Rights Convention. The case was Refah Partisi (the Welfare Party) and others v. Turkey, reported in European Human Rights Reports 2003. Summary and discussion is found in Paul Taylor, *Freedom of Religion*, pp.314-15.

2 'Islam remains number one danger to the Christian church,' Interview by David W. Virtue, December 19, 2005. www.virtueonline.org.

superpower, but a 'superservant'.[1] The American Muslim community applauded this idea, and reproduced Griswold's speech on a number of its websites. According to the worldview of dhimmitude, of course Christians should be servants. They should serve Islam and the *Umma*.

Dhimmi dialogue

Interfaith dialogue can be another domain for the manifestation of dhimmitude.

The most characteristic sign of dhimmitude in interfaith dialogue is silence. Chawkat Moucarry's *Faith to Faith: Christianity and Islam in Dialogue* explores many key topics for Muslim-Christian dialogue. While Moucarry criticizes Israel's establishment as an 'immense injustice', he maintains a studied silence about *jihad* conquest, Islamic occupation and continuing impact of *dhimmitude*.[2] Moucarry also keeps his silence about the life of Muhammad.

Those involved in building relationships with Muslims must face the thorny question of when and whether to bring the ethical issues of Muhammad's life onto the agenda for discussion. This ought to be considered a legitimate subject for dialogue, because Muhammad's life impacts profoundly upon the lived circumstances of so many non-Muslims. However the principles of dhimmitude demand that this should not happen, so courage and sensitivity is required to determine when and how this issue is to be raised. The 'wisdom' which says that this subject should never be broached is not wisdom at all, but censorship, which inevitably reduces the dialogue to a manifestation of dhimmitude.

Another manifestation of dhimmitude in interfaith dialogue is Christian self-humbling and expressions of gratitude towards Muslims. In 2007 a letter entitled 'A Common Word between Us and You' was addressed by 138 Muslim scholars to the Christians of the world.[3] It received an appreciative response from a group of Yale theologians in a full-age advertisement taken out in the *New York Times*, which was endorsed

---

1 'An Interview With Bishop Frank Griswold,' viewed 8 June 2009, <http://www.soundvision. com/info/peace/bishop.asp>. The 'superservant' call was reissued by Griswold on the fifth anniversary of 9/11: 'Episcopal leader says US must become 'superservant'. *Ekklesia News Brief*, 9 December, 2006, viewed 8 June 2009, <http://www.ekklesia.co.uk/content/news_syndication/ article_060910griswold.shtml>.

2 Mark Durie, Review of *Faith to Faith: Christianity and Islam in Dialogue*, p.246.

3 The text of the Muslims' letter as well as many responses can be found on the common word site <http://www.acommonword.com>. My notes on the Common Word letter and the Yale response can be found at <http://www.acommonword.blogspot.com>.

by 300 Christian leaders, including such well-known figures as David Yonggi Cho, Robert Schuller, Bill Hybels, Rick Warren and John Stott.[1] Consistent with the worldview of dhimmitude, the Yale theologians adopted a tone of grateful self-humiliation and self-inculpation, using expressions such as:

- 'It is with humility and hope that we receive your generous letter';
- the Muslims' letter was 'extraordinary' and written in 'generosity';
- 'we ask forgiveness of the All-Merciful One and of the Muslim community around the world'.

No comparable expressions of humble gratitude or confession of guilt were offered from the Muslim side. No doubt the Christians believed they were relating from a position of strength, by invoking Christian virtues of humility and self-examination. However they appear not to have taken account of the dynamics of dhimmitude and the possibility that these statements could be understood by Muslim as a display of self-acknowledged inferiority.

Ironically, while this dialogue was being conducted in the pages of the *New York Times*, the Royal Aal al-Bayt Institute for Islamic thought, which had initiated and hosted the Common Word process on the Muslim side, was broadcasting *fatwas* on its website by its Chief Scholar which condemned converts from Islam to Christianity as apostates, characterizing them as deserving of death or else they should be stripped of all legal rights and treated legally as non-persons (because they ought to be dead).[2]

A call for reciprocity

For those who live in liberal democracies, the requirements of dhimmitude do not offer a healthy way to engage with the 'other' that is Islam. The doctrine of the superiority of the *Umma* means that Islam is deeply unfamiliar with the principle of reciprocity. In the Islamic worldview, Islam takes on the role of a dominator that expects to be treated as superior, to be praised, admired, and stroked. It takes this service for granted, feeling entitled to it. Moreover the dogmas of the perfection of the *Sharia* and the superiority of the *Umma* short-circuit necessary self-critique. The reaction to reasonable criticism, when it

---

1 Downloaded 8 June 2009, <http://www.yale.edu/divinity/news/071118_news_nytimes.pdf>.

2 'The Apostasy Fatwas,' viewed 8 June 2008, <http://acommonword.blogspot.com/2008/02/apostasy-fatwas-and-common-word-between.html>.

manages to find a voice, can be shock, denial and outrage. Even mild inquiry can cause a howl of rage to rise up.

In submitting to the requirement of grateful service to Islam, Christians may well interpret their own submissiveness in gospel categories of forgiveness and service, but from the Islamic side this can just look like the program of Islam as 'submission' is working. Muslims can often interpret such submissiveness as Islam's rightful due, not an expression of grace, and even allow themselves to feel generous in accepting this service. For this reason, Christians involved in partnering with Muslims should make every effort to understand the theological grid which dhimmitude would seek to impose upon the relationship, and while continuing to be gracious, back up the grace with a strong admonition to reciprocity.

The issue here is not so much whether Muslims will misinterpret the motives of Christians. It is rather the danger of a politico-theological framework being imposed upon the Christian-Muslim relationship, to conform it to the requirements of dhimmitude, while the potential exists for Christians to be blind to this development, because they are only evaluating the relationship in terms of Christian theological categories.

Dhimmitude is also bad for Muslims, for many reasons. It feeds a widespread pattern of Muslims claiming the role of victim, while blaming others for problems they themselves have responsibility for. Muslim communities are given permission to feel themselves aggrieved, and are discouraged from taking responsibility for their own circumstances. The resulting culture of victimhood damages the ongoing social and economic development of the whole Muslim world.

Christians living in free nations should not voluntarily submit themselves to the mentality of dhimmitude. They should not surrender their liberty. They should not use the language of appeasement as a tool of inter-faith relations. Today, with so many signs that the West is drifting steadily towards dhimmitude, how will the Christian world respond?

CHAPTER 9

A Way Forward

There are undoubtedly some Islamic states which treat non-Muslim
citizens in ways which can only be described as oppressive ...
It is of the utmost importance that Muslim jurists should consider
whether such treatment of non-Muslims is in accordance with the
Shari'ah *or contrary to it. More generally, does the* **Shari'ah** *allow*
Muslims to live peaceably with non-Muslims in the 'one world'
or must they regard it as **dar al-harb**? *To have an answer to these*
questions may be a matter of urgency in a few years time
William Montgomery Watt[1]

These prophetic words of W. M. Watt, written in the last decade of
the twentieth century, speak a warning message which urgently needs
to be attended to, and not only by Muslim jurists. The *dhimma* and
its conditions are returning as an integral part of the global Islamic
resurgence, which aims to revive the *Sharia*. How will the world respond?

Non-Muslims, and Muslims with compassionate hearts, cannot and
must not sit idly by while this ancient system of discrimination is
renewed, for a great toll is being exacted from non-Muslims who live
under revived *Sharia* conditions. Islamic religious authorities too should
be challenged, as Watt suggests, to reconsider this aspect of *Sharia* law.
The *dhimma* must be opposed and rejected for everyone's sake, because
this ancient code degrades and dehumanizes Muslims and non-Muslim
alike.

The profound changes in thinking which are needed to bring healing
and reconciliation to a world overshadowed by the legacy of the *dhimma*
must include acknowledgement of the truth. This cannot happen as long
as incompatible worldviews simply pass each other like ships in the night.
It will certainly not do to just overlook our differences. The differences
between us and their impact on people's lives must be permitted to be

---

1 Review of Bat Ye'or, *Les Chrétientés d'Orient entre Jihâd et Dhimmitude. Journal of Semitic Studies*,
1993.

revealed, acknowledged and given thorough consideration, for without a truth encounter, genuine reconciliation cannot be achieved.

A Boston interfaith event

A window onto the staggering potential for interfaith miscomprehension, and the impotence of ignorance to bring genuine reconciliation, was provided by a service held in Trinity Episcopalian Church, Copley Square, Boston, just three days after the World Trade Center atrocity.

The morning after this event, the Reverend Samuel T. Lloyd spoke warmly in his Sunday sermon about the participation of Dr Walid Fitaihi of Harvard Medical School, representing the Islamic Society of Boston:

> Many of us experienced a remarkable moment of hope at the service yesterday, when Dr. Wadid Fataihi (sic), a doctor at Harvard Medical School and member of the Islamic Society of Boston, spoke words of healing and support. His gentle, holy manner touched everyone in that church. And it seemed an enormously hopeful sign of a divided world looking for ways to draw closer together.[1]

For the Revd Lloyd, this interfaith event was an affirmation of common humanity and solidarity. It was a sign of reconciliation and hope. But what of Dr Fitaihi? What was his perspective? Four days later, on September 22, Dr Fitaihi sent a letter to the Egyptian weekly *Al-Ahram Al-Arabi* (Egypt), which was published on October 20, 2001. In it he describes the unfolding of events in the previous week and a half:

> On Saturday, September 15, I went with my wife and children to the biggest church in Boston, Copley Square, by official invitation of the Islamic Society of Boston, to represent Islam by special invitation of the senators of Boston. ... I sat with my wife and children in the front row, next to the mayor's wife. In his sermon, the priest defended Islam as a monotheistic religion, telling the audience that I represented the Islamic Society of Boston.
>
> After the sermon was over, he stood at my side as I read an official statement issued by the leading Muslim clerics condemning the incident [i.e. the attacks]. The statement explained Islam's stance and principles, and its sublime precepts. Afterwards, I read Koran verses ... These were moments that I will never forget, because the entire church burst into tears upon hearing the passages of the words of Allah!!

---

1 Samuel T. Lloyd, 'Where was God?', viewed September 14, 2001, <http://www.trinitychurch boston.org/2001_09_16_sermon.html>.

Emotion swept over us. One said to me: 'I do not understand the Arabic language, but there is no doubt that the things you said are the words of Allah.' As she left the church weeping, a woman put a piece of paper in my hand; on the paper was written: 'Forgive us for our past and for our present. Keep proselytizing to us.' Another man stood at the entrance of the church, his eyes teary, and said, 'You are just like us; no, you are better than us.' ...

[Fitaihi then tells of other similar events in the following days.]

These are only some of the examples of what happened and is happening in the city of Boston, and in many other American cities, during these days. ... I write to you today with the absolute confidence that over the next few years, Islam will spread in America and in the entire world, Allah willing, much more quickly than it has spread in the past, because the entire world is asking, 'What is Islam!'[1]

Fitaihi's report of American Christians crying on hearing the Koran evokes for Muslim readers the story of the conversion of the first group of Christians to Islam. On hearing recitation from the Quran, 'their eyes flowed with tears' and they entered Islam.[2]

Dr Fitaihi's letter shows that he evaluated the interfaith service at Trinity Church through the grid of Islamic theology, in terms of its value for *da'wah*, that is, for winning America to Islam. By this criterion, he judged the event a success, because the specific responses he reported showed the Christians' acceptance of key points of Islamic theology, including that the Quran is the word of Allah, infidels are guilty, and the *Umma* is superior ('no, you are better than us').

Dr Fitaihi revealed further dimensions of his understanding of interfaith relations in another letter sent to the Arabic language London daily *Al-Hayat*, published on November 11. This letter characterizes the aftermath of September 11 as a positive advance in the struggle against Zionism, and particularly for driving a wedge between Jews and Christians:

Despite the attacks of distortion coordinated by the Zionist lobby, to which it has recruited many of the influential media, there are initial signs that the intensive campaign of education about Islam has begun to bear fruit. For example, the rate of converts to Islam since September 11 has doubled ... There is solidarity with the Muslims on the part of many

---

1 MEMRI Special Dispatch Series 301: 'Terror in America (26) – Muslim American Leaders: A Wave of Conversion to Islam in the U.S. Following September 11,' viewed 19 November, 2009, <http://memri.org/news.html#1006182078>.

2 Guillaume, *The Life of Muhammad*, p.179.

non-Muslims in American universities. ... For this reason, the Jewish institutions have begun to contact Muslim institutions and have called on us to hold dialogues with them and cooperate [with them]. They are afraid of the outcome of the Islamic-Christian dialogue through the churches, the mosques, and the universities ...

There are many examples of the signs of change [for the worse] in Christian-Jewish relations, as a result of the openness towards Islam and the beginning of an Islamic-Christian dialogue. ...

Thus, the Muslim community in the U.S. in general, and in Boston in particular, has begun to trouble the Zionist lobby. The words of the Koran on this matter are true:

> They [the People of the Book] will be humiliated wherever they are found, **unless they are protected under a covenant with Allah, or a covenant with another people.** They have incurred Allah's wrath and they have been afflicted with misery. That is because they continuously rejected the Signs of Allah and were after slaying the Prophets without just cause, and this resulted from their disobedience and their habit of transgression. (Q3:112)

The great Allah spoke words of truth. Their covenant with America is the strongest possible in the U.S., but it is weaker than they think, and one day their covenant with the [American] people will be cut off.[1]

Fitaihi's citation from the Quran refers to the status of *dhimmis*, 'protected under a covenant', the *dhimma* pact. The great Quranic commentator Ibn Kathir explains Q3:112 as follows, in a section headed:

The Good News that Muslims will Dominate the People of the Book

... This is what occurred, for at the battle of Khaybar, Allah brought humiliation and disgrace to the Jews. ... Such was the case with the Christians in the area of Ash-Sham [Syria] later on, when the Companions defeated them in many battles and took over the leadership of Ash-Sham forever ... 'indignity is put over them wherever they may be, except when under a covenant (of protection) from Allah, and a covenant from men' meaning, Allah has placed humiliation and disgrace on them wherever they may be, and they will never be safe, 'except when under a covenant from Allah', under the *Dhimmah* (covenant of protection) from Allah that requires them to pay the *Jizyah* (tax, to Muslims) and makes them subservient to Islamic Law.[2]

---

1 MEMRI Special Dispatch Series 301: 'Terror in America (26) – Muslim American Leaders: A Wave of Conversion to Islam in the U.S. Following September 11,' viewed 19 November, 2009, <http://memri.org/news.html#1006182078>.

2 *Tafsir Ibn Kathir.* Commentary on Q3:112. Vol. 2, p.243.

By punctuating his reflections with this key verse, Dr Fitaihi is implying that when the protection extended by America to the Jews is withdrawn, they will be 'humiliated' – utterly defeated – and forced to submit once again to the 'protection' of a *dhimma* pact.

It is a truly remarkable thing that an interfaith event, which a Boston Episcopalian experienced as a moving affirmation of our common humanity, was regarded by a Boston Muslim as a successful act of *da'wah*, and, so it seems, a step towards the Islamization of America, the defeat of Israel, and the day when Muslims will dominate the People of the Book under a *dhimma* pact. In the cold hard light of Fitaihi's stated theological worldview, his participation in Trinity Church's service can hardly be regarded as 'an enormously hopeful sign of a divided world looking for ways to draw closer together', as the Revd Lloyd had naïvely supposed.

The challenge of engagement

The Western, post-Christian world has offered hospitality and the gift of inclusion to significant Muslim populations through immigration. It now faces the challenge of understanding Islam better.

Within the context of world history, in which we find ourselves today, the deep theological and psychological forces at work in interactions with Islam urgently need to be engaged with. In these explorations, non-Muslims must grasp what is at stake for them in relation to militant Islam and its claims over them. They need to be equipped to understand how to conduct themselves in the face of these claims. This requires an education about topics never before considered, as individuals and communities permit their worldviews to be reviewed and transformed, through deep reflection upon Islam's teachings, as well as upon their own Judeo-Christian spiritual inheritance. Through this process, the oppressive veil of silence which has been cast over the *dhimma* and its manifestations can be set aside, and the forces which had been empowering it exposed and disarmed.

This book is a contribution to this task. The main instrument of freedom offered here is a truth encounter with the theology, origins and impact of the *dhimma*, including the life of Muhammad. This is offered as a resource for understanding the times in which we live. In exposing the reader to these topics I have not only sought to lay out fundamental features without camouflage (including the contributions of the Quran and the *Sunna* of Muhammad), but also to acknowledge Islam's potency to shape the worldview of its adherents, as well as impose an Islamicized dhimmitude worldview upon non-Muslims.

Inevitable conflict?

According to Usama Bin Ladin, the 'three choices' are the whole reason for conflict between Muslims and the West:

> Thus our talks with the infidel West and our conflict with them ultimately revolve around one issue – one that demands our total support, with power and determination, with one voice – and it is: 'Does Islam, or does it not, force people by the power of the sword to submit to its authority corporeally if not spiritually?' [The answer is:] Yes. There are only three choices in Islam: either willing submission; or payment of the *jizya*, through physical though not spiritual, submission to the authority of Islam; or the sword – for it is not right to let him [an infidel] live. The matter is summed up for every person alive: Either submit, or live under the suzerainty of Islam, or die.[1]

This, Bin Ladin alleges, is the crux of the West's hostility to Islam: 'the West avenges itself against Islam for giving infidels but three options.'[2]

As Raymond Ibrahim has pointed out, this position has 'nothing to do with reciprocity'. Ibrahim's conclusion is stark:

> Thus even if Muslims are being oppressed, as long as these grievances are being articulated through an Islamic paradigm that perceives justice solely through *Shari'a* and not through anything universal or innate to the human condition, the West – in the interest of self-preservation as well as the preservation of freedoms – has no choice but to reject all accusations, offers, and threats from Islamists, and fight.[3]

One can only agree that as long as there are Muslims who, like Bin Ladin, accept and act upon Sura 9:29's call to fight against non-believers until they convert or surrender, conflict is unavoidable.

Of course Bin Ladin concedes too great a degree of intentionality to his foes, for it is quite possible for non-Muslims to fight wars caused by the ideology of *jihad* and the *dhimma* without consciously comprehending what the battle is about. Witness the many cries of 'Why do they hate us?' which Americans uttered after the 9/11 atrocity.

---

1 Raymond Ibrahim, *The Al Qaeda Reader*, pp.41-42.

2 Ibid, p.42

3 Raymond Ibrahim, 'An analysis of al-Qa'ida's worldview: reciprocal treatment or religious obligation,' p.10.

It is a simple matter for people to lose their lives in a *jihad* terror attack without ever realizing that, if they and their community had only consented to convert or surrender to Islamic rule, their lives might have been deemed to be 'protected'. Many times down through history non-Muslims have resisted the *dhimma* or surrendered to it, without ever having the chance to comprehend its logic, or the long-term transgenerational implications of the choice they were making.

However my concern here has not been with the right of Christians, Jews and others to defend themselves against those who, like Bin Ladin, would impose the three choices upon them. My focus has been very different. I have been concerned to inquire how non-Muslims, and Muslims with compassionate hearts, can resist the *dhimma*'s demands upon their thought patterns, and how a soul weighed down by the legacy of dhimmitude can find healing and freedom.

For many who already live under manifestations of *Sharia* law, this is a question about how humanity can live with dignity under conditions of humiliation and inferiority. For others, citizens of free nations, there is a pressing need to gain understanding, and in so doing to strengthen the will to be free, in the face of persistent and at times seductive pressures to condition one's thinking to the worldview of dhimmitude.

A better way

It is tragic that the doctrines of Islam have been relied upon by some Muslims to impose intimidation and self-rejection upon non-Muslims. Under threat of death or enslavement, many have found themselves cowed into self-defeating responses such as fear, denial, hatred, capitulation, self-rejection and silence. There is a better way.

Love for the other and truth are two attributes to be held together, the one complementing the other. Truth without love can be harsh and even cruel, but love without truth can be equally as dangerous, as, lacking discernment, it steers the soul into shipwreck after shipwreck. Neither of these alternatives is acceptable.

In this book I have striven to hold together truth and love for one's fellow human being, and have sought to clarify the nature of the *dhimma* and expose its inner workings out of a conviction that denial is a bitter prison for victims and oppressors alike. Archbishop Desmond Tutu rightly lamented the plight of oppressors who cling to denial after their power has ended. They suffer, he said, from a 'crippling self-inflicted blow to their capacity to enjoy and appropriate the fruits of change'.[1]

It might be objected that the bitter past is best left forgotten. However old scars often conceal festering wounds, which need to be opened and cleansed before genuine healing can take place. Of course it can be all too easy to find reasons to avoid this unpleasant therapy. We may avoid the truth because it is too painful to face up to, or its consequences can seem all too overwhelming. Yet truth, applied with love for the other, even in the face of the most appalling manifestations of inhumanity, can enable a healing of one's worldview, and cause a deep release of hope and compassion for one's victim or oppressor, offering realistic prospects for righting injustices and establishing reconciled relationships between people of good will.

It is in this spirit of hope that I have written this book.

---

1 Desmond Tutu, Chairperson's Foreword to Volume Six. *Truth and Reconciliation Commission of South Africa Report.*

Glossary of Arabic Terms

Allahu akbar   'Allah is greater'

Ansar   the helpers: people from Medina who helped Muhammad establish Islam there

asbab al-nuzul   'occasion of revelation': the context in which a particular verse or passage of the Quran was reported to be 'revealed' to Muhammad

ayah   verse of the Quran

dar al-Islam   the house of Islam, the region where Islam dominates other religion

da'wa   'to invite', 'summon' or 'command'; proselytization, spreading Islam by calling people to submit to Allah, an invitation which is understood to have the force of a command

dhimma   covenant or pact of surrender, by which a conquered non-Muslim community have agreed to live under Islamic rule, and by virtue of which this community is protected from *jihad*

dhimmi   a non-Muslim living under Islamic rule, who is considered to be subject to the conditions of a *dhimma* pact

falah   success in this life and the next, promised by Islam to its followers

fay   property which is won by Muslims from non-Muslims without having to be taken by force; including *jizya* payments

fatwa   a legal opinion or ruling

fitna   persecution or trials which could undermine a Muslim's faith; by extension, disbelief in Islam

ghazwa   a *jihad* raid

halal	something which Muslims are free to do, or to take for themselves without any lawful restriction, e.g. food which may be eaten, property which may be seized, or a life which may be killed
Hanafi	a school of Islamic law
Hanbali	a school of Islamic law
hadith	traditions, first spoken and later written, which record things which Muhammad is believed to have said or done, as well as things said and done by his companions
hijra	the migration of Muhammad and his followers from Mecca to Medina; marks the beginning of the Islamic calendar and the commencement of the Islamic state
huda	guidance, the solution to ignorance about Allah's requirements
hudud	laws which impose criminal penalties such as death and amputation (e.g. for adultery, theft and apostasy)
Islam	the word means 'submission' or 'surrender'
isnad	the attribution of a *hadith*: the introductory phrases which state who passed on the tradition
jahiliyyah	ignorance, lacking divine guidance
jihad	the word means 'to make war against non-Muslims, and is etymologically derived from the word *mujahada*, signifying warfare to establish the religion',[1] i.e. warfare to establish or maintain Islamic rule over non-believers; the root *j-h-d* has the meaning 'struggle'
jizya	tribute paid to Muslims to prevent *jihad* attack; for *dhimmis* this is payable as an annual 'head tax' by adult *dhimmi* males
kafir	infidel: an offensive term for someone who is not a Muslim

---

1 Sheikh 'Umar Bakarat, quoted in Nuh Ha Mim Keller, ed. and trans., *Reliance of the Traveller*, p.599.

kharaj	land-tax required to be paid by non-Muslims (and later by Muslims as well) to the *Umma*: this was distinct from and additional to *jizya* payments
khasirin	'losers': those who are not rightly guided
kufr	disbelief, a term implying concealment of the truth
Madinah	Medina
Makkah	Mecca
Maliki	a school of Islamic law
mushrik	'associater', someone who is guilty of *shirk*; pagans, but also People of the Book (Jews and Christians); usually translated 'idolater' or 'polytheist'
Muslim	the word means 'submitter'
najis	ritually unclean (see Q9:28); non-Muslims are regarded as unclean, especially in Shi'ite Islam
naskh	abrogation, referring to the doctrine that Allah can cancel earlier revelations by adding a newer revelation to override the earlier one, or by causing the earlier one to be forgotten
Quran	Allah's revelation to Muhammad, believed to be dictated to him by the angel Jibril (Gabriel); also spelled *Qur'an* or *Koran*
ridda	apostasy, abandoning Islam
sahih	'sound', referring to *hadiths* which are considered to be the most authentic
salat	the daily ritual acts of worship often referred to in English as 'prayers'
Shafi'i	a school of Islamic law
shahada	the creed of Islam: to recite this is to become a Muslim
Sharia	having a common meaning of 'way' or 'path'; as a religious term *sharia* refers to the whole system of principles and rules by which a Muslim is required to live

Shi'a	a denomination or branch of Islam, which separated from Sunni Islam in the first century over a dispute about the succession of the caliphate
Shi'ite	a follower of Shi'a Islam
shirk	'association': the unforgivable sin of associating anything with Allah, but especially idols and other gods
sira	biography (of Muhammad)
Sunna	the example and teaching of Muhammad, recorded in *hadith* and *sira* literature; the word *sunna* also means religiously recommended
Sunni	a denomination or branch of Islam, which separated from Shi'a Islam in the first century over a dispute about the succession of the caliphate; a follower of Sunni Islam
sura	a chapter of the Quran
tafsir	commentary (on the Quran)
taqiyya	lawful deception intended to protect a Muslim from persecution
'ulama	a religious leader (plural is *'ulema*)
Umma	the Muslim community, considered for theological reasons to be a unitary whole
zakat	one of the pillars of Islam, the *zakat* is a tax on wealth paid by Muslims which is used to help the Muslim poor, as well as other Islamic causes including *jihad*

A Note on Sources

References to the Quran use the abbreviation Q – e.g. Q9:29 refers to *sura* 9:29, and is a reference to chapter 9, verse 29 of the Quran.

Quranic citations are from the translation of Arthur J. Arberry, but the verse numbering follows the translation of Yusuf Ali. There are many different verse numbering systems for the Quran, so if readers are looking up a Quranic reference in a translation other than Yusuf Ali's, they may need to scan several verses either side of the referenced number to find it.

A few alterations to Arberry's translation of the Quran have been made to produce a more authentic Islamic style: the word *Allah* has been restored, where Arberry renders this as *God*; Islamic prophets are given their Arabic (rather than Biblical) names; and Arberry's *Gehenna* is rendered as the more familiar 'hell'.

Citations from the *hadith* collections of Muslim and al-Bukhari are referenced by physical volume, *kitab* ('book') number and title, and *hadith* number. For example, the reference:

> *Sahih al-Bukhari*. The Book of Manners (*Kitab al-Adab*).
> 8:78:6623

refers to *hadith* number 6623 in book 78, known as the 'Book of Manners' (in Arabic *Kitab al-Adab*), found in the 8th volume in the published set listed in the Bibliography.

Translations of *hadiths* into English often do not show quotation marks to distinguish reported speech (as the original Arabic does not use quotation marks). Where appropriate, these have been inserted for ease of reading.

Arabic transliteration is simplified throughout. No diacritical markings are used, although these are significant for vowel length and certain distinctions between consonants.

Translations of Arabic references derive from a variety of sources. In some cases they are translations into English via other languages. Wherever possible I have referenced all the sources relevant for translated material: the original Arabic text (if published), the intermediary language source (where applicable), and the published English translation (where applicable).

Muslims, when mentioning Muhammad and other Islamic prophets, will usually invoke a blessing after the name, saying or writing 'peace be upon him'. I have generally omitted this in citations from Muslim sources.

Biblical citations are from the New International Version, unless otherwise indicated.

Articles and books are referenced in abbreviated form in the notes: the full details may be found in the Bibliography.

References to newspaper articles, blogs, television and other media reports are detailed in the notes, but for the most part are not listed in the Bibliography.

Interpolations into citations are in square brackets [...]. This is to give explanations, summarize material, or to provide references to the Quran.

Unless otherwise noted, words in bold within citations are my emphasis.

Bibliography

'Abdullah bin Muhammad bin Hamid. 1999. 'The call to Jihad (holy fighting for Allah's cause) in the Holy Quran.' Appendix III, in Muhammad Taqi-ud-Din al-Hilali and Muhammad Muhsin Khan, *Interpretation of the meanings of the Noble Qur'an in the English Language*. Rev. ed. Riyadh: Darussalam.

al-Adawi – see Belin 1852.

Ahmad, M., ed. 1946. *al-Kashshaf...* [The Revealer, by al-Zamakhshari]. Cairo.

Aldeeb (Abu-Sahlieh), Sami Awad. 1993. *Mutiler au nom de Yahve ou d'Allah: Legitimation religieuse de la circoncision masculine et feminine*. Boulogne, Paris: Association contre la mutilation des enfants, viewed 8 June 2009 <http://ame.enfant.org.free.fr/mutiler.html>.

Ali, Yusuf, trans. 1999. *The Holy Qur'an*. Birmingham: IPCI – Islamic Vision.

Antes, Peter. 1990. 'Islam in the *Encyclopedia of Religion*.' Review of the Encyclopedia of Religion. *The Journal of Religion*, 70.3: 403-11.

Arberry, Arthur J. 1998. *The Koran Interpreted*. (Oxford World's Classics.) Oxford: Oxford University Press.

Ata, Abe. 2000. *Intermarriage between Christians and Muslims*. Ringwood, Victoria, Australia: David Lovell Publishing and the International Centre of Bethlehem.

Averroes. 2002. 'Bidayat al-Mudjtahid.' In Andrew Bostom, *The Legacy of Jihad*, pp.147-60. (Excerpted from Rudolph Peters. *Jihad in Mediaeval and Modern Times*, pp.9-25.)

al-Baladhuri. 1916. *The Origins of the Islamic State*. Trans. Philip Khuri Hitti. (Studies in History, Economics and Public Law, vol. 68.) New York: Columbia University.

Basic Principles of Islam. 1996. Abu Dhabi, UAE: The Zayed Bin Sultan Al Nahayan Charitable & Humanitarian Foundation, 1996.

Bat Ye'or. 1985. *The Dhimmi: Jews and Christians under Islam*. Madison: Fairleigh Dickinson University Press.

Bat Ye'or. 1987. 'Islam and the *Dhimmis*.' *The Jerusalem Quarterly* 42 (Spring): 84-88.

Bat Ye'or. 1995. 'The Tolerant Pluralistic Islamic Society.' An address presented on August 31, 1995.

Bat Ye'or. 1996. *The Decline of Eastern Christianity under Islam: from Jihad to Dhimmitude*. Madison: Fairleigh Dickinson University Press.

Bat Ye'or. 2002. *Islam and Dhimmitude: Where Civilizations Collide*. Madison: Fairleigh Dickinson University Press.

Bat Ye'or. 2005. *Eurabia: the Euro-Arab Axis*. Madison: Fairleigh Dickinson University Press.

Belin, François-Alphonse, trans. 1852. Ahmad ad-Dardi el-Adaoui. *Fetoua* [1772]: 'Réponse à une question.' *Journal Asiatique*, 4th ser., 19: 103-12.

Ben-Shammai, Haggai. 1988. 'Jew-hatred in the Islamic tradition and Qur'anic exegesis.' In Shmuel Almog, *Antisemitism through the Ages*. Oxford: Pergamon, pp.161-69.

Bostom, Andrew, ed. 2005. *The Legacy of Jihad: Islamic Holy War and the Fate of Non-Muslims*. Amherst: Prometheus Books.

Bostom, Andrew. 2005. '"Democrats" for Jihad and Jizya,' *American Thinker*, December 12.

Bostom, Andrew. 2007. 'Congress must recognize the Armenian genocide.' *American Thinker*, August 2007, viewed 8 June 2009, <http://www.americanthinker.com/2007/08/congress_must_recognize_the_ar.html>.

Bostom, Andrew, ed. 2008. *The Legacy of Islamic Antisemitism: from Sacred Text to Solemn History*. Amherst: Prometheus Books.

Bostom, Andrew, 2008. 'Islamic antisemtism – Jew hatred in Islam: a survey of its theological-juridical origins, and historical manifestations.' In Andrew Bostom, *The Legacy of Islamic Antisemitism*, pp.31-205.

Bravmann, Meïr. 2002. 'The ancient background of the Qur'anic concept *al-gizyatu 'an yadin*.' In Ibn Warraq, *What the Koran Really Says*, pp.350-63. Reprinted from *Arabica* 13 (1966): 307-14; 14 (1967): 90-91.

Bravmann, Meïr and Claude Cahen. 2002. 'A propos de Qur'an IX.29: hatta yu'tu l-Gizyata wa-hum sagiruna.' In Ibn Warraq, *What the Koran Really Says*, pp.348-49. Reprinted from Arabica 10 (1963): 94-95.

Browne, Laurence E. 1933. *The Eclipse of Christianity in Asia: From the Time of Muhammad till the Fourteenth Century*. Cambridge: Cambridge University Press.

Bukay, David. 2007. 'Peace or Jihad? Abrogation in Islam.' *Middle East Quarterly* 24.4: 3-11, viewed 11 April 2009, <http://www.meforum. org/1754/peace-or-jihad-abrogation-in-islam>.

al-Bukhari. *Sahih al-Bukhari.* See Muhammad Muhsin Khan.

Chalom, Jacques. 1908. *Les Israelites de la Tunisie: Leur condition civil et politique.* Paris: A. Rousseau.

Chapman, Colin. 1995. *Cross and Crescent: Responding to the Challenge of Islam.* Leicester: Inter-Varsity Press.

Cohen, Marc. 1986. 'Islam and the Jews: myth, counter-myth, history.' *The Jerusalem Quarterly* 38: 125-37.

Cohen, Marc. 1995. *Under Crescent and Cross: The Jews in the Middle Ages.* Princeton: Princeton University Press.

Crombie, A.C. 1953. *Augustine to Galileo: the History of Science AD 400-1650.* Cambridge, Massachusetts: Harvard University Press.

Cvijic, Jovan. 1918. *La Péninsule Balkanique: Geographie humaine.* Paris: Librairie Armand Colin.

Dashti, Ali. 1994. *Twenty Three Years: A Study of the Prophetic Career of Mohammad.* Trans. F.R.C. Bagley. Costa Mesa: Mazda Publishers.

Dennett, Daniel. 1950. *Conversion and the Poll Tax in Early Islam.* Cambridge, MA: Harvard University Press.

Denton, William. 1876. *The Christians of Turkey: Their Condition under Mussulman Rule.* London: Daldy, Isbister.

Doron, Aviva, ed. 1994. *The Culture of Spanish Jewry: Proceedings of the First International Congress (Tel Aviv, 1-4 July 1991).* Tel Aviv: Levinsky College of Education Publishing House.

Durie, Mark. 2002 'Amina Lawal and the Islamic Shari'a.' *Quadrant* 46.12: 37-39.

Durie, Mark. 2002. 'The dhimmitude of the West.' *Newsletter for the Centre for Islamic Studies*, Vol. 11, Summer. London School of Theology.

Durie, Mark. 2003. 'Remembering Khaibar.' *Quadrant* 47.11: 29.

Durie, Mark. 2005. Review of Chawkat Moucarry, *Faith to Faith: Christianity and Islam in Dialogue. Journal of Anglican Studies* 2005.3: 245-46.

Durie, Mark. 2006. *Revelation: Do we Worship the Same God?* Upper Mt Gravatt, Queensland: CityHarvest.

Durie, Mark. 2009. 'The Creed of the Sword.' In David Claydon, ed., *Islam, Human Rights and Public Policy*. Melbourne: Acorn Press, pp.115-24.

Emerick, Yahiya. 2002. *The Complete Idiot's Guide to Understanding Islam*. Indianapolis: Alpha Books.

Eton, William. 1799. *A Survey of the Turkish Empire: in which are considered* ..., 2nd ed. London: Cadell and Davies.

Fadl, Abu. 1999. 'Greater and "Lesser" Jihad.' Trans. Khalid Saifullah. *Nida'ul Islam* [The Call of Islam] 26 (April-May), viewed 8 June 2003, <http://www.islam.org.au/articles/26/jihad.htm>.

Fagnan, Edmond, trans. 1915. *Al-Ahkam as-Sultaniyya (Les statuts gouvernementaux)* [by al-Mawardi]. Algiers.

Fagnan, Edmond, trans. 1921. *Le Livre de l'impôt foncier (Kitâb el-Kharâdj)* [by Abu Yusuf Ya'qub]. Paris: Paul Geuthner.

al-Faruqi, Isma'il R. 1976. 'On the nature of Islamic Da'wah.' *International Review of Missions* 65: 391-409.

Fattal, Antoine. 1958. *Le statut légal des non-musulmans en pays d'Islam*. Beirut: Imprimerie Catholique.

Firestone, Reuven. 1999. *Jihad: The Origin of Holy War in Islam*. New York: Oxford University Press.

Friedman, Saul S. 1989. 'The myth of Islamic toleration.' In *Without Future: the Plight of Syrian Jewry*. New York: Praeger, pp.2-3.

Gabriel, Mark A. 2003. *Islam and the Jews*. Lake Mary, Florida: Charisma House.

Gad al-Haq, Gad-al-Haq 'Ali. 1983. 'Khitan al-banat.' In *Al-Fatawi al-Islamiyyah min dar al-Ifta' al-Masriyyah*. Vol.9. Cairo: Wazarat al-Awqaf, pp. 3119-25.

Gätje, Helmut. 1996. *The Qur'an and its Exegesis: Selected Texts with Classical and Modern Muslim Interpretations*. Oxford: Oneworld.

Gerber, Jane. 1994. 'Towards an understanding of the term "The Golden Age" as an historical reality.' In Aviva Doron, ed., *The Culture of Spanish Jewry*, pp.15-22.

al-Ghazali. 1979. *Kitab al-wagiz fi fiqh adhab al-imam al-Safi'i*. Beirut.

Glenny, Misha. 2000. *The Balkans: Nationalism, War and the Great Powers, 1804-1999*. New York: Viking.

Glubb, John. 1971. *The Life and Times of Muhammad*. New York: Stein and Day.

Goitein, Shlomo Dov. 1963. 'Evidence on the Muslim poll tax from non-Muslim sources: a *geniza* study.' *Journal of the Economic and Social History of the Orient* 6.3: 278-95.

Griffith, Sidney H. 2008. *The Church in the Shadow of the Mosque: Christians and Muslims in the World of Islam*. Princeton: Princeton University Press.

Guillaume, A. 1967. *The Life of Muhammad: A Translation of Ishaq's Sirat Rasil Allah*. Oxford: Oxford University Press.

Haq, S. Moinul and H. K. Ghazanfar. 1993. *Ibn Sa'd's Kitab al-tabaqat al-kabir*. 2 vols. New Delhi: Kitab Bhavan.

Hasan, Ahmad. 2000. *Sunan Abu Dawud*. New Delhi: Kitab Bhavan.

Hirschberg, Haim Z. 1974. *A History of the Jews of North Africa*. Vol. 1. Leiden: E.J. Brill.

Human Rights Monitor – 2001. 2001. National (Catholic) Commission for Justice & Peace, Pakistan.

Human Rights Monitor – 2002. 2002. National (Catholic) Commission for Justice & Peace, Pakistan.

Ibn Ishaq – see Guillaume 1967.

Ibn Kathir. 2000. *The Life of the Prophet Muhammad*. Vol. 1. Trans. Trevor le Gassick. Reading, UK: Garnet Publishing.

Ibn Kathir. 2003. *Tafsir Ibn Kathir (abridged)*. Abridged by a group of scholars under the supervision of Shaykh Safiur-Rahman al-Mubarakpuri. 2nd ed. 9 vols. Riyadh: Darussalam. (Also published at <tafsir.com>.)

Ibn Qayyim – see al-Salih.

Ibn Qudama. 1983. *al-Mughni*. Beirut: Dar al-Kitab al-Arabi.

Ibn Qudama. 2002. 'Legal War'. In Andrew Bostom, *The Legacy of Jihad*, pp.162-64. Trans. Michael J. Miller. (Excerpted from Henri Laoust, trans. *Le Précis de droit d'Ibn Qudama*, pp.273-76, 281.)

Ibn Rushd – see Nyazee; and Averroes.

Ibn Warraq. 2000. *The Quest for the Historical Muhammad*. Amherst, New York: Prometheus Books.

Ibn Warraq. 2002. *What the Koran Really Says: Language, Text and Commentary*. Amherst, New York: Prometheus Books.

Ibn Warraq. 2005. 'Edward Said and the Saidists.' In Robert Spencer, ed., *The Myth of Islamic Tolerance*, pp.474-516.

Ibn Warraq. 2007. *Defending the West: A Critique of Edward Said's 'Orientalism'*. Amherst, New York: Prometheus Books.

Ibn Warraq. 2008. Forward to Andrew Bostom, *The Legacy of Islamic Antisemitism*, pp.21-27.

Ibrahim, Raymond. 2007. *The Al Qaeda Reader.* New York: Broadway.

Ibrahim, Raymond. 2008. 'An analysis of al-Qa'ida's worldview: reciprocal treatment or religious obligation.' *Middle East Review of International Affairs* 10.4: 1-14.

Idris, Hady Roger. 1977. 'Les Tributaires en Occident Musulman Médiéval d'après le *'Mi'yar' d'al-Wansarisi.'* In Pierre Salman, ed., *Mélanges d'Islamologie. Volume dédié à la mémoire de Armand Abel.* Leiden: Brill, pp.172-96.

Johannes J.G. Jansen. Undated. 'Dhimmitude.' Trans. Rogier van Bakel, viewed 11 April 2009, <http://www.jihadwatch.org/dhimmiwatch/archives/005573.php>. (Orig. publ. in *Trouw* as a 'Letter en Geest,' November 27, 2004, p.33.)

Johns, Jeremy. 2002. *Arabic Administration in Normal Sicily.* (Cambridge Studies in Islamic Civilization.) Cambridge: CUP.

Kampeas, Ron. 'Jews in the middle as Turks, Armenians fight over history.' *JTA.* 23 July, 2007, viewed 11 April 2009, <http://www.jta.org/cgi-bin/iowa/news/article/20070423turkscommission.html>.

Keller, Nuh Ha Mim, ed. and trans. 1994. *Reliance of the Traveller.* Rev. ed. Beltsville, Maryland: Amana.

Khan, Muhammad Muhsin. 1997. *The Translation of the Meanings of Sahih al-Bukhari. Arabic-English.* 9 vols. Riyadh: Darussalam.

Kippenberg, Hans G. 2005. '"Consider that it is a Raid on the Path of God": The Spiritual Manual of the Attackers of 9/11.' *Numen* 52: 29-58.

Kister, M.J. 2002. '*An Yadin* (Qur'an, IX.29): an attempt at interpretation.' In Ibn Warraq, ed., *What the Koran Really Says*, pp.364-71. Reprinted from *Arabica* 11 (1964): 272-78.

Klein, Aaron. 2007. *Schmoozing with Terrorists.* Los Angeles: WND Books.

Kohlman, Evan F. 2006. *Protest rally outside the Danish Embassy in London, February 3, 2006.* (Video). The NEFA Foundation.

Landshut, S. 1950. *Jewish Communities in the Muslim Countries of the Middle East.* London: The Jewish Chronicle.

Lane, E.W. 1863. *An Arabic-English Lexicon.* London: Williams and Norgate.

Lane, E.W. 1860. *An Account of the Manners and Customs of the Modern Egyptians.* 5th Ed. London: John Murray.

Laoust, Henri, trans. 1948. *Le traité de droit public d'Ibn Taymiya. Traduction annotée de la siyasa shar'iya*. Beirut: Institut Français de Damas.

Laoust, Henri, trans. 1950. *Le Précis de droit d'Ibn Qudama, jurisconsulte musulman d'école hanbalite né à Jérusalem en 541/1146, mort à Damas en 620/1223*. Beirut: Institut Français de Damas.

Lewis, Bernard. 1974. *Islam from the Prophet Muhammad to the Capture of Constantinople*. 2 vols. New York: Harper and Row.

Lewis, Bernard. 1984. *The Jews of Islam*. Princeton: Princeton University Press.

Lewis, Bernard. 2002. *What Went Wrong? Western Impact and Middle Eastern Response*. New York: Oxford University Press.

Lewis, Bernard. 2005. 'Freedom and Justice in the Modern Middle East.' *Foreign Affairs* 84.3: 36-51.

Lindsay, James E. 2005. *Daily Life in the Medieval Islamic World*. Westport, CT: Greenwood Press.

Lings, Martin. 1983. *Muhammad: His Life Based on the Earliest Sources*. Rochester, VT: Inner Traditions International.

Littman, David G. 1979. 'Jews under Muslim rule: the case of Persia.' *Wiener Library Bulletin* 32: 2-15.

Littman, David G. 2005. ed. 'Human Rights and Human Wrongs at the United Nations'. In Robert Spencer, ed., *The Myth of Islamic Tolerance*, pp.305-472.

Littman, David G. 2008. 'Jews under Muslim Rule – II: Morocco 1903-1912.' In Andrew Bostom, *The Legacy of Islamic Antisemitism*, pp.535-47.

Loeb, Laurence D. 1977. *Outcaste: Jewish life in Southern Iran*. New York: Gordon and Breach.

Loeb, Laurence D. 2008. '"Outcaste": Shi'a Intolerance.' In Andrew Bostom, *The Legacy of Islamic Antisemitism*, pp.564-72. Chapter 2 and appendices I-III from Laurence D. Loeb, *Outcaste: Jewish Life in Southern Iran*.

Malachi, E.R. 2008. 'Palestine under the Rule of Ibrahim Pasha.' Trans. Rivkah Fishman. In Andrew Bostom, *The Legacy of Islamic Antisemitism*, pp.593-600. (Orig. publ. in *Ha-Doar* 14: 28-31 (1935), trans. from A. [sic] E.R. Malachi. 1962. *Studies in the History of the Old Yishuv*. Tel Aviv, pp.65-78.)

Matthews, Zachariah. 2001. 'The Hijrah: a necessary phase in the Dawah.' Lecture presented on 30 March 2001 organized by the University of Western Sydney (Milperra) Muslim Society, downloaded June 2005, from the website of *FAMSY*, <hppt://www.famsy.com/salam/>.

al-Mawardi – see Fagnan 1915 and Yate 1996.

Mawdudi, Sayyid Abul A'la. 1994. *The punishment of the apostate according to Islamic law*. Trans. and annotated Syed Silas Husain and Ernest Hahn. (From the 4th (1963) edition, Lahore: Islamic Publications Limited.) Viewed 25 August 2009, <http://answering-islam.org/Hahn/Mawdudi/>.

Mawdudi, Sayyid Abul A'la. 2006. *Towards Understanding the Qur'an: English version of Tafhim al Qur'an*. Trans. Zafar Ishaq Ansari. Leicester: Islamic Foundation.

Mehmedovic, Muzafer Ferro. 2009. *The Islamisation of the Albanians: An historical study of the Islamic influence on the Albanian people during the Ottoman Empire 15th – 19th Century*. (MA Thesis.) London: Brunel University.

Mingana, A., trans. 1922. *The Book of Religion and Empire: A semi-official defence and exposition of Islam written by order at the court and with the assistance of the Caliph Muta-Wakkil (A.D. 847-861) by 'Ali Tabari*. Manchester: Manchester University Press.

Moreen, Vera Basch, trans. 1992. *Risala-yi sawa'iq al-yahud* [The treatise lighting bolts against the Jews]. *Die Welt des Islams* 32: 187-93. (Reproduced in Andrew Bostom, *The Legacy of Jihad*, p.219.)

Moucarry, Chawkat. 2001. *Faith to Faith: Christianity and Islam in Dialogue*. Leicester: Intervarsity Press.

Muir, William. 1861. *The Life of Mahomet*. London: Smith, Elder and Co.

Murata, Sachiko. 1987. *Temporary Marriage in Islamic law. Al-Serat* 13.1, viewed 11 April 2009, <http://www.al-islam.org/al-serat/muta/>.

Muslim. *Sahih Muslim*. See Abdul Hamid Siddiqi.

Nardin, Terry, ed. *The Ethics of War and Peace: Religious and Secular Perspectives*. Princeton, NJ: Princeton University Press.

Nyazee, Imran Ahsan Khan, trans. 2002. *The Distinguished Jurist's Primer (Bidayat al-Mujtahid wa Nihayat al-Muqtsid)* by Abu al-Walid Muhammad ibn Ahmad ibn Rushd. 2 vols. Reading, UK: Garnet Pubootnoe.

Ohlig, Karl-Heinz and Gerd-R. Puin. 2008. *The Hidden Origins of Islam: New Research into Its Early History.* Amherst: Prometheus Books.

O'Neill, John J. 2009. *Holy Warriors: Islam and the Demise of Classical Civilization.* Felibri Publications.

Parfitt, Tudor. 1996. *The Road to Redemption: The Jews of Yemen 1900-1950.* Leiden: E.J. Brill.

Parfitt, Tudor. 2000, 'Dhimma versus Protection in Nineteenth Century Morocco.' In Tudor Parfitt, ed., *Israel and Ishmael: Studies in Muslim-Jewish relations.* New York: St Martin's Press.

Perlmann, Moshe. 1948-49. 'Eleventh-century Andalusian authors on the Jews of Granada.' *Proceedings of the American Academy of Jewish Research.* 18: 843-61.

Peters, Rudolph. 1977. *Jihad in Mediaeval and Modern Times.* Leiden: Brill.

Phares, Walid. 2005. The oppression of Middle East Christians: a forgotten tragedy. In Robert Spencer, *The Myth of Islamic Tolerance,* pp.227-31.

Pirenne, Henri. 1939. *Mohammed and Charlemagne.* Bernard Miall, trans. London: Allen and Unwin.

Pipes, Daniel. 2005. 'Jihad and the professors.' In Robert Spencer, *The Myth of Islamic Tolerance,* pp.517-25.

Pipes, Daniel and Lars Hedegaard. 2005. 'Something rotten in Denmark?' In Robert Spencer, *The Myth of Islamic Tolerance,* pp.300-04.

Qutb, Sayyid. 2003. *In the Shade of the Qur'an.* Leicester: The Islamic Foundation.

Raab, David. 2003. 'The beleaguered Christians of the Palestinian-Controlled Areas.' *Jerusalem Viewpoints,* No. 490, January.

Rahbar, Daud. 1961. 'Relation of Muslim Theology to the Qur'an'. *The Muslim World* 51: 44-49.

Riley, James. 1817. *An Authentic Narrative of the Loss of the American Brig Commerce.* Hartford.

Robinson, Chase F. 2005. 'Neck-sealing in early Islam.' *Journal of the Economic and Social History of the Orient,* 48.3: 401-41.

Ruqaiyah, Abu. 1996. 'The Islamic Legitimacy of Martyrdom Operations.' Trans. Hussein El-Chamy. *Nida'ul Islam* 16, viewed 20 February 2003, <http://islam.org.au/articles/16/martyrdom.htm>.

Sahih al-Bukhari. See Muhammad Muhsin Khan.

Sahih Muslim. See Abdul Hamid Siddiqi.

al-Salih, Subhi. Ed. 1981. *Ahkam Ahl al-Dhimmah* by Shams-al-Din Abi 'Abdallah Muhammad bin Abi Bakr ibn Qayyim al-Jawziyya. 2 vols. 2nd rev. ed. Beirut: Dar El Ilm Lilmalayin.

Schirrmacher, Christine. 2001. *The Islamic View of Major Christian Teachings.* Hamburg: RVB International.

Schmidt, Alvin J. 2004. *The Great Divide: The Failure of Islam and the Triumph of the West.* Boston, MA: Regina Orthodox Press.

Seed, Patricia. 1995. *Ceremonies of Possession in Europe's Conquest of the New World, 1492-1640.* New York: Cambridge University Press.

Serjeant, Robert Bertram. 1953. 'A Judeo-Arab House-Deed from Habban (with notes on the former Jewish communities of the Wahidi Sultanate).' *Journal of the Royal Asiatic Society,* Pts 3-4: 117-31.

Sewall, Gilbert T. 2003. *Islam and the Textbooks.* A report of the American Textbook Council.

Shakaryan, Artak. 2006. *Devshirme: the Blood-Tax in the Ottoman Empire.* (In Armenian). Yerevan: National Academy of Sciences of the Republic of Armenia, Institute of Oriental Studies

al-Shawkani, Muhammad b. 'Ali. 1985. *Kitab al-sayl al-jarrar al-mutadafiq 'ala hada'iq al-azhar.* 4 vols.

Short, Walter. 2005. 'The jizya tax: equality and dignity under Islamic law?' In Robert Spencer, *The Myth of Islamic Tolerance,* pp.73-89.

Siddiqi, Abdul Hamid, trans. 2000. *Sahih Muslim.* Rev. ed. 4 vols. New Delhi: Kitab Bhavan.

Siddiqi, Muhammad Zubayr. 1993. *Hadith Literature: Its Origin, Development and Special Features.* Cambridge, UK: The Islamic Texts Society.

Solzhenitsyn, Aleksandr Isaevich. 1975. *The Gulag Archipelago, 1918-1956: An Experiment in Literary Investigation.* Trans. Thomas P. Whitney. New York: Harper & Row.

Sookhdeo, Patrick. 2002. *A People Betrayed: the Impact of Islamisation on the Christian Community in Pakistan.* Fearn, Ross-shire: Christian Focus Publications and Pewsey, Wiltshire: Isaac Publishing.

Soage, Ana Belén. 2007. 'Faraj Fawda, or the cost of freedom of expression.' *Meria Journal* 11.2: 26-33.

Spencer, Robert, ed. 2005. *The Myth of Islamic Tolerance: How Islamic Law Treats Non-Muslims.* Amherst, New York: Prometheus.

Spencer, Robert. 2006. *The Truth about Muhammad: Founder of the World's Most Intolerant Religion.* Washington DC: Regnery.

Stalinsky, Steven. 2005. 'The next Pope and Islamic Prophecy.' FrontPagemagazine.com, April 14, viewed 15 September 2009, <http://www.frontpagemag.com/Printable.aspx?ArtId=8931>.

Stillman, Norman. 1979. *The Jews of Arab Lands: a History and Source Book.* PA: The Jewish Publication Society of America.

Sunan Abu Dawud. See Ahmad Hasan.

al-Tabari. 1992. *The Battle of al-Qadisiyyah and the Conquest of Syria and Palestine. The History of al-Tabari*, vol. 12. Trans. Yohanan Friedmann. (Bibliotheca Persica Series.) Albany: State University of New York Press.

al-Tabari. 1993. *The Challenge to the Empires. The History of al-Tabari*, vol. 11. Trans. Khalid Yahya Blankinship. (Bibliotheca Persica Series.) Albany: State University of New York Press.

Tachjian, Vahé. 2009. 'The expulsion of non-Turkish ethnic and religious groups from Turkey to Syria during the 1920s and early 1930s.' Online Encyclopedia of Mass Violence, viewed 11 April 2009, <http://www.massviolence.org/The-expulsion-of-non-Turkish-ethnic-and-religious-groups?artpage=6-7>.

Taylor, Paul. 2005. *Freedom of Religion: UN and European Human Rights Law and Practice.* Cambridge: Cambridge University Press.

Tibi, Bassam. 1996. 'War and peace in Islam.' In Terry Nardin, ed. *The Ethics of War and Peace*, pp.129-45.

Tobi, Yosef. 2008. 'Conversions to Islam among Yemenite Jews under Zaydi Rule: the positions of Zaydi law, the Imam and Muslim society.' Trans. Rivkah Fishman. In Andrew Bostom, *The Legacy of Islamic Anti-Semitism*, pp.577-88. (Orig. publ. in *Pe'amim* 42 (1990): 105-26.)

Tritton, Arthur Stanley. 1930. *The Caliphs and their Non-Muslim Subjects: A Critical Study of the Covenant of 'Umar.* The Royal Asiatic Society of Great Britain and Ireland. London: Oxford University Press.

Tutu, Desmond et al. 2003. *Truth and Reconciliation Commission of South Africa Report.* Vol. 6. Cape Town: Juta and Co.

Usmani, M. Taqi. 2008. *Islam and Modernism.* Trans. Mohammed Swaleh Siddiqui. Rev. and ed. Mohammad Wali Raazi. New Delhi: Adam Publishers and Distributors.

Vajda, George. 2008. "'Adversos Judaeos": a treatise from Maghrib – "Ahkam ahl al-Dhimma" by Sayh Muhammad b. 'Abd al-Karim al-Magili.' Trans. Michael J. Miller. In Andrew Bostom, *The Legacy of Islamic Antisemitism,* pp.346-51. (Orig. publ. in *Études d'Orientalisme dédiées à la mémoire de Lévi-Provençal.* Paris: G.-P. Maison-neuve et Larose, 1962, vol. 2, pp.805-13.)

Vambery, Arminius. 1864. *Travels in Central Asia.* London: John Murray.

Wehr, Hans. 1976. *A Dictionary of Modern Written Arabic.* 3rd ed. Trans. J. Milton Cowan. Ithaca, NY: Spoken Language Services.

Weiner, Justus Reid. 2005. *Human Rights of Christians in Palestinian Society.* Jerusalem: Jerusalem Center for Public Affairs.

Watt, William Montgomery. 1993. Review of Bat Ye'or, *Les Chrétientés d'Orient entre Jihâd et Dhimmitude* (Les Éditions du Cerf, Paris, 1991). *Journal of Semitic Studies,* 38.1: 166-67.

Woodberry, Dudley. 1996. 'Contextualization among Muslims: reusing common pillars.' *International Journal of Frontier Missions* 13.4: 171-86.

Yate, Asadulah, trans. 1996. *The Laws of Islamic Governance* [*Al-Akham as-sultaniyyah* by al-Mawardi]. London: Ta-Ha.

Ye'or – see Bat Ye'or.

Yusuf Ali, Abdullah. 1999. *The Holy Qur'an.* Birmingham: IPCI – Islamic Vision.

al-Zamakhshari – see Ahmad 1946.

Zametica, John. 1992. *The Yugoslav Conflict: An analysis of the causes of the Yugoslav war, the policies of the republics and the regional and international implications of the conflict.* Adelphi Paper 270. London: International Institute for Strategic Studies, Brasseys.

Zand, Michael. 2000. 'The inner structure of the Jewish community of the city of Bukhar in the mid-19th century.' In *The Bukharian Jews: History, Cultures, Perspectives.* (Abstracts of III Conference's Reports.) New York: Roshnoi-Light, pp.21-26.

Index

Arabic names may be found listed under the first or final part.

Averroes. *See* Ibn Rushd
Awqaf • 192
Al-Azhar University • 63, 70–1, 74
Azzam Tamimi • 62

B

Bachtiar, Da'i • 1
Badr • 97, 101, 110
al-Baghawi • 58, 131, 136–7, 141
Baghdad • 139, 193
Baha'is • 188
Bahrain • 13
Baker, Barbara G. • 55
al-Baladhuri • 167
Balkans • 168
Bandow, Doug • 3
Bangladesh • 13
al-Baqarah • 182
Basilan • 193
Bassam Zawadi • 141
Bat Ye'or • 72, 118, 121–2, 128–9,
     133–4, 138–9, 141, 143,
     146–9, 151, 158–60, 163, 167,
     179, 180, 184–6, 201–2, 206,
     207–10, 225
Bauchi State • 198–9
al-Baydawi • 130, 133, 138
bazr • 64
Bedouins • 150
beheading. *See* decapitation
Beirut • 163
Belin, François-Alphonse • 133, 138
belittlement • 131, 133, 135–6, 141–2,
     145, 193
bells
   silenced • 143, 209
   worn by *dhimmis* • 146, 173, 176
Benedict XVI, Pope • 81, 120
Ben-Shammai, Haggai • 105
Beslan • 214
Bethlehem • 166, 192, 202
Bhutan • 187
Bible • 12, 14–6, 18–20, 32–3, 35, 64,
     85, 107

Bible references
   Exodus 23:9 • 117
   Leviticus 19:33-34 • 117
   Deuteronomy 24:19 • 117
   Deuteronomy 31:15-21 • 18
   1 Samuel 25:31 • x
   Ezekiel 2:6-7 • 118
   Zechariah 8:19 • 1
   Malachi 3:5 • 118
   Matthew 5:30 • 14
   Matthew 5:43 • x
   Matthew 24:44 • 11
   Luke 10:25ff • 118
   Romans 1:18-20 • 19
   Romans 7:10 • 19
   1 Corinthians 1:18ff • 18
   1 Corinthians 7:20-24 • 15
   Ephesians 6:5-9 • 15
   1 Timothy 1:9-11 • 15
   Titus 2:9-10 • 15
   Hebrews 12:15 • ix
   1 Peter 2:18-21 • 15
Biblical faiths • 44, 49
Bilal ibn al-Harith • 54, 87
Bimha • 198, 199
Birmingham • 219
Blair, Tony • 213
blasphemy • 32, 54–5, 195, 196
blessings • x, 23, 27, 46, 88, 98, 105,
     117, 130, 142, 152–3
blood
   debt • 31, 71, 114, 121, 127–8, 144,
      147, 172
   oath • 140
   protected • 112
booty • 65, 100, 112, 125, 153, 160
   compensated by *jizya* • 126, 172
   division of • 66, 100, 120
   looting • 128, 150, 152, 156–8, 162
      as liberation • 111
      threat of • 166–7
   prophet's permission to take • 31,
      32, 115
   women and children as • 112, 153,
      160, 164

horses, restrictions on riding • 145, 176, 184
houses, restrictions on height • 145, 176, 184
huda. See guidance
al-Hudaybiyyah treaty • 34, 61, 103–5
hudud • 176
humanism • 16
human rights • 164, 188, 193, 195, 203, 212, 215
  as a concession • 159, 162, 166–7, 178
  Cairo Declaration on Human Rights in Islam • 214
  Human Rights Court of Europe • 220
  right to life • 178
  United Nations Commission on Human Rights • 63
  United Nations Human Rights Council • 216
  Universal Declaration of Human Rights • 215
  Universal Islamic Declaration of Human Rights • 214
humiliation • v, ix, 19, 90, 103, 114–6, 120, 131–6, 139–46, 148, 151, 169, 176, 179–81, 183, 185, 192–3, 222, 228–9, 231
humor • 32
Hungarians • 186
Hybels, Bill • 222
hypocrites • 44

I

Ibn 'Abbas, 'Abdullah • 31, 39, 108, 133, 137
Ibn 'Adil al-Dimashqi • 138
Ibn 'Ajibah • 130, 138, 140–1
Ibn al-Arabi • 137
Ibn al-Fuwati • 138
Ibn al-Qayyim al-Jawziyya • 132, 143, 173
Ibn 'Askar • 160
Ibn Athir, Majd al-Din • 127

Ibn Hisham • 30
Ibn Ishaq • 30, 54, 82, 84, 86, 94, 95, 103, 132, 183
Ibn Kathir • 35–40, 46–7, 53, 58, 83–4, 88, 94–7, 99, 103, 108, 132, 137, 142, 155, 228
Ibn Khaldoun Research Center • 200
Ibn Khaldun • 179
Ibn Naqib • 79
Ibn Qudama • 128–9, 132, 146
Ibn Rushd • 125, 128
Ibn Taymiyya • 125–7
Ibn Umar • 29
Ibn Warraq • 16, 202, 205–6
Ibrahim • 104, 109
  religion of • 109, 183
Ibrahim Pasha • 150
Ibrahim, Raymond • 230
'idda • 52
idolaters • 37–9, 44–5, 47, 95, 97, 100, 104–6, 110, 115, 120, 149, 152, 176, 190. *See also* association
Idris, Hady Roger • 179
ignorance • vi, 16, 18–9, 40, 45, 54, 56, 72–3, 76, 78, 182–3, 206, 208, 220, 226
Ijaz-ul-Haq • 114
Imam Ahmad • 47
immigration • 56, 189, 210, 229
immunity • 102
Imran Ahsan Khan Nyazee • 125
incitement • 56
India • 124, 186
Indians • 13
Indians, American • 7
Indonesia • 1, 4, 12–3, 77, 189, 200
inferiority • 51, 64, 81, 99, 116, 141–2, 149, 171, 179–82, 200, 212, 222, 231
infidels. *See* disbelief
inheritance • 143
Institute of Islamic Political Thought (London) • 62
interfaith. *See* multifaith
interfaith dialogue • 43, 44, 228

International Association of Muslim
Scholars • 178
intifada • 152
intolerance • 5, 206, 215
Iran • 6, 12, 13, 50, 66, 139, 164, 182,
186, 191, 197, 199, 200, 215
Iranians • 81, 180–1
Iraq • 13, 49, 151, 188
Isa • 39, 48, 109. *See also* Jesus
Isaac ben Samuel of Acre • 138
Isfahan • 164
Ishaq, Ibn • 107
Islam, passim • 10, 21, 28–9, 49, 118
the religion of Abraham • 109
Islamic Assembly of North America
• 66
Islamic Council of Victoria • 55, 72
Islamic revival • 188
Islamic Society of Boston • 226
Islamists • 191, 205, 230
Islamization • 49–2, 124, 168-9, 191,
195, 201, 213, 229
of history • 216–7
Islam Online • 27
Islamophobia • 68, 212, 215–6
Islam Studios • 75
Isma'il R. al-Faruqi • 20
isnad • 27
Israel • 18, 72, 109, 117–8, 122, 140,
163, 166, 183, 186, 201, 204,
221,
Israelis • 61, 152, 200, 204, 211
Izetbegovic, Alija • 208

J

jahiliyyah. *See* ignorance
Jakarta • 188
James, Williams • 9
janissary • 158, 163
Jansen, Johannes G. • 43, 218
Japan • 214
Jarir • 132
jaza • 172
Al-Jazeera • 3, 114
Jericho • 56

Jerusalem • 61, 106, 150–1
Jesus • x, 10, 11–2, 14, 28, 52, 118. *See
also* Isa
Jews • vii, 6, 8, 35, 38, 44–9, 55–6, 68,
72, 79, 81–2, 89, 100, 105–13,
115, 117, 121–25, 129, 134,
136–42, 146–7, 150, 152–3,
156–60, 164, 166–8, 172–3,
175–7, 179, 182–6, 188, 190–4,
206–9, 218–9, 227–9
and Muhammad • 81, 105
changed into pigs • 108
coexistence with Muslims • 72
covenant breakers • 108
cursed • 107, 153
by David and Jesus • 109
deceivers • 107
falsified scriptures • 107
hostility to • 48–9, 72, 207
idolaters • 38, 45
in the Quran • 113
killed prophets • 108
losers • 108
studying Islam • 79
transgressors • 47
under *Sharia* • 82, 121, 186
Jibril • 85, 87, 112
jihad • v–vii, ix, 1, 14, 26, 36, 40, 50,
61, 65–6, 72–3, 79, 81, 95, 97–
100, 111, 115, 118–9, 121–5,
128–31, 136–8, 147–8, 150–2,
155–67, 170–2, 175, 206, 208,
211, 216, 218, 220–1, 231
communal obligation • 156
future war • 122, 128, 155, 162
in the Quran • 119, 155
meaning of • 65–6
personal obligation • 156
jinn • 8
jizya, passim • v–vi, 48, 119–20,
123–31, 133–41, 147–9, 160,
164, 166–76, 181, 185–6,
189–94
as protection money • 174
being revived • 191

M

Macedonia • 180
MacKenzie, Major-General Lewis
        W. • 208
al-Maghili • 133, 138, 157, 160
Magians. *See* Zoroastrians
Mahmoud Ashur • 74, 76
Maimonides • 179, 182–3, 206
Majians. *See* Zoroastrians
al-Majlisi • 138
Makiya, Kanan • 205
Malachi, E.R. • 150
Malaysia • 3, 5, 13, 197, 198
Maliki jurisprudence • 70
Al-Manar Al-Jadid Magazine • 66
Manat • 87
Mandeans • 188
Manne, Robert • 150
Mansoura • 191
al-Marghinani • 128
Mariam. *See* Maryam
Maronites • 186
Marrakesh • 134, 139
marriage • 26, 59, 68, 84, 203
    domestic violence • 62
    polygamy • 11–2, 60, 70
    remarriage • 52
    temporary • 12–3
    to a prepubescent girl • 52–3
    wife's status • 84
    with a non-Muslim • 5–6, 38–9,
        143, 165, 197–8
martyr • 66
Marxism • 16
Maryam • 48, 109
Masih, Pervaiz • 55
massacres • 113–4, 132, 156–61, 165,
        179, 184, 201, 209, 214
    of the Serbian Knights • 158
Matthews, Zachariah • 56–7, 66, 73
al-Mawardi • 129, 141
Mawdudi, Sayyid Abul A'la • 51, 55,
        58, 177
Mazreku, Gregor • 169
MBC TV • 76

McLeod, Penny • 6
Mecca • 34, 36–8, 40, 61, 81, 83, 86,
        89–91, 93–6, 100, 102–4
Meccan suras • 37, 105
Medina • 34–8, 54, 81, 88–90, 93–8,
        100, 105–6, 156
    Medinan suras • 37, 109
Mediterranean • 217
Mehmedovic, Muzafer Ferro • 168
MEMRI • 74
MI6 • 187
migration • 40, 57, 73, 87
    of Christians • 167, 204
    of Jews • 166
    to Medina • 56, 90, 94, 96, 98
militancy. *See* warfare
Miller, Michael J. • 158, 180
mimetic tendency • 179, 181, 201
misinformation • 55
misleading impression • 59–60
Mogahed, Dalia • 50
Mogodore • 134–5
Moinul Haq, S. • 30
monotheism • 45, 47, 87, 89, 226
Montesquieu • 206
Moore, Niven C.B. • 163
Moreen, Vera Basch • 138
Mormonism • 12
Morocco • 133, 138–40, 146, 152, 186
Moses • 18, 95
mosques • 61, 68–9, 158, 184, 196,
        209, 228
Mudar • 88
Mughals • 186
muhajirun • 160
Muhammad, passim • 10, 17, 22,
        81–116
    and the *Sharia* • 50, 121
    biography • 29–30, 52–7
    character • 30–2
    example • 22–9
    mission • 119
Muhammad 'Abduh • 66–7
Muhammad Ali Jinnah • 195
Muhammad al-Mussayar • 74, 77

Y

Yale University • 221
Yate, Asadulah • 129
yawning • 27
Yemen • 139, 140, 163, 167, 171, 183,
    186
Yemenis • 139, 155, 160
yeniçeri. See janissary
Yonggi Cho, David • 222
Younas, Anila • 165
Younas, Saba • 165
Younus Abdullah Muhammad • 194
Yudhoyono, Susilo Bambang • 1
Yussef Salamah • 192
Yusuf Ali • 57, 63
Yusuf al-Qaradawi • 178

Z

al-Zabir • 132
zakat • 29, 106, 168, 170
al-Zamakhshari • 58, 130, 137
Zametica, John • 208
Zand, Berhard • 201
Zawadi, Bassam • 170
Zawahiri • 164
Zionism • 227
Zionists • 204, 227, 228
Zoroastrians • 121, 124, 128, 136,
    175, 191

Index of Quranic Verses

9:30 • 38, 45, 109

10 • 96
10:95 • 96

13:39 • 35

14:29 • 63

16:43 • 70
16:101 • 35

17:86 • 35

20:69 • 95

22:39-40 • 95
22:52 • 87

24:46-47 • 23
24:52 • 23
24:54 • 23

26:40-44 • 95

29:39 • 95

30:38 • 95

33:21 • 23
33:36 • 23

36:76 • 107

39:65 • 18

47:4 • 131

48:19-20 • 156
48:28 • 48, 98
48:48 • 99

52:9-16 • 92

53 • 87
53:1-3 • 24, 88

54:2 • 92
54:42 • 92
54:46-48 • 92

57:28 • 45

58:14 • 110

59:7 • 24

60 • 34
60:1 • 110
60:4 • 104
60:8 • 33–4
60:10 • 34, 104

65:4 • 52–3

67:6-11 • 92

68:1-4 • 23, 88
68:2-16 • 93

72:23 • 24

83:13-17 • 92
83:29-36 • 93

87:6 • 37
87:6-7 • 35

88:2-7 • 93

92:8-18 • 91

93:3-6 • 85

98 • 106
98:1 • 45
98:1-8 • 106
98:6 • 47

104 • 91

109:6 • 87

111 • 83

LaVergne, TN USA
10 September 2010
196615LV00003B/4/P